W9-ADE-059

Muskingum College Library
New Concord, Ohio

ASIA IN THE MODERN WORLD, No. 6

DS777.5
L53

THE SINISTER FACE OF THE MUKDEN INCIDENT

by

CHIN-TUNG LIANG

Research Professor

Center of Asian Studies

ST. JOHN'S UNIVERSITY

169232

JUN 15 1972

St. John's University Press, New York

1969

Published by the St. John's University Press under the auspices of the Center of Asian Studies

Copyright 1969 © by St. John's University

Library of Congress Catalog Card Number 68-59220

Foreword

The Mukden Incident was a turning point in Japanese and world history. It signified the beginning of Japan's fateful march toward World War II. On the basis of three principal sources—(1) the reports of the League of Nations at Geneva, (2) the records and the evidence of the Tokyo trial, and (3) the archives of the Japanese Foreign Ministry covering a period of seventy-seven years, Professor C. T. Liang has developed the thesis that "the Mukden Incident was an extension of Japanese internal revolt rather than an act purely of external aggression." (p. 24).

An eminent scholar and jurist, Professor Liang has excellent qualifications for this work—familiarity with the situation he describes, first-class linguistic equipment, good training as an historian, and most important of all, an approach to his subject which is neither prejudiced nor sentimental. He narrates the leading facts of Chinese-Japanese relations in the 1930's with just and impartial comment. Confined to essentials that are well-documented, he presents a meaningful account and analysis of this vastly complex story which will contribi substantially to the bulwark of truth, we are sure.

In publishing this book, we feel most grateful to the author for his cooperation in making this study available and also to Dr. Joseph W. Ballantine for writing the Introduction. Dr. Ballantine, Director of the Office of Far Eastern Affairs, U. S. Department of State 1944-45, and Special Assistant to the Secretary of State 1945-47, played a very important part in the situation to which this study is related.

As Editor of this series, I also wish to acknowledge the helpful assistance of Professors Kuang-huan Lu and Corita Kong.

PAUL K. T. SIH, *Director*
Center of Asian Studies
St. John's University

Introduction

The record of Chinese-Japanese relations during the two decades preceding the outbreak of the Pacific War, following Pearl Harbor, constitutes a pivotal chapter in the modern history of East Asia. The story centers in Japan's efforts, spearheaded by its Kwantung Army stationed in Manchuria, to establish its overlordship in East Asia. The activating element in the Kwantung Army was a reckless group determined to impose its will by the abuse of power, intrigue, duplicity, terrorism, and assassination. Their embarkation upon their designs set in motion a chain of events that led in 1937 to an all-out Japanese attack on China, to Pearl Harbor and the Pacific War in 1941, and ultimately, after the war to the arraignment, trial, and punishment of the offenders by the International Military Tribunal for the Far East (IMTFE) at Tokyo.

When in 1949, the records of the IMTFE and the archives of the Japanese Foreign Office going back for 77 years became available to scholars, the subject of Sino-Japanese relations in the prewar years became one of renewed and intensive study by historians, principally Chinese, Japanese, and American. The reports of the Lytton Commission of the League of Nations had, of course, been available before the war. In research made in China, Chinese scholars generally had an advantage over other nationals in consulting Chinese records and in interviewing individuals who had useful information to impart.

Among the Chinese scholars who have engaged in these studies is the author of this book, Dr. Chin-tung Liang, who since 1963 has been Research Professor at St. John's University at Jamaica, New York. He has already achieved distinction as author of other historical studies including *History of the First World War* (1925), *Extraterritoriality in China* (1928), *China and the Cairo Conference* (1963) and *The Crisis of September 18, 1931* (1965) and, in English, *The Revolution of 1911* (1962).

Dr. Liang has brought to his task a wealth of experience as a jurist, high executive officer in the Chinese government, and as a banker. For example, in 1926, when the Japanese forces occupied Tsinan, capital of Shantung Province, and massacred peaceful Chinese nationals and committed other outrages, he was manager in that city of the Chinese-American Bank of Commerce, and thus, an eye-witness to what had occurred.

The author's narrative begins with the Mukden Incident of September 18, 1931, when an explosion on the South Manchuria Railway tracks just north of Mukden caused the tearing of 31 inches of rail, but it failed to derail an oncoming train. Yet within six hours the Kwantung Army took over the city and launched their movement to overrun Manchuria.

The book comprises six chapters: the first deals with the historic background of the Mukden Incident; the second, with the responsibility for it and the military strength of the contestants; the third, with the identity of the main participants and their respective roles; the fourth, with Tokyo's reaction to the events in Manchuria; the fifth, with Nanking's reaction; and the sixth, with the causes underlying the Mukden Incident.

The influence of his legal training is apparent in Professor Liang's treatment of his subject, especially in the organization of his material. For example, some writers in dealing with this subject might have started with the assassination of Chang Tso-lin in 1928, three years before the Mukden Incident. The assassination in itself was at least as grave a crime as setting off an explosion on the railway track, but it was not, as was the Mukden Incident, the signal for launching a full-fledged military action which resulted, within an incredibly short time, in Japan's establishing its control over a territory twice as extensive as Texas and with a population of 30,000,000.

In his opening chapter, the author points out that the year 1931 was one of global economic depression. The absorption of the powers with their own troubles at home militated against a willingness on their part to intervene. The time was thus opportune for Japan to act. Japan, of course, was suffering parallel difficulties. Late in 1929, the New York silk market collapsed. Acute distress came to prevail through the Japanese countryside, since one-third of all Japanese agricultural households, crowded as they were in scant acres, were dependent upon cocoon raising as a secondary occupation to make ends meet. Japan began converting its economy to meet the new situation by expanding its industries to supply Asian markets. There was a marked drop in the ratio of Japan's American trade to its total trade and a corresponding decline in the importance attached by Japan to keeping American good will.

The Japanese Army had its roots in the physically vigorous agrarian class. The leaders saw no way out of the plight of their people except by force of arms, and in their desperation they moved boldly with no holds barred.

In Chapter VI the author lists a number of earlier attempts by Japanese agents to expand in Manchuria. In addition to those he mentioned was one cloaked under participation in 1918 in an inter-allied expedition to support anti-Bolshevik Russian elements in their efforts to set up in Siberia a regime capable of stemming the Bolshevik tide. Earlier, toward the end of World War I the Japanese militarists saw in the fall of the Tsarist Empire a "golden opportunity" to detach Siberia east of Lake Baikal from Muscovite control and to take over the Russian sphere of influence in North Manchuria. The Army launched a nation-wide publicity campaign to gain support for a military intervention to achieve this objective. Japanese business and agrarian interests, concerned over their country's vital dependence upon its trade with the United States, prevailed upon the government to consult the United States before undertaking such a step. The outcome of the consultation was an American counter-proposal for the inter-allied expedition already mentioned. It had been agreed upon that the quota of troops to be contributed by any one ally should not exceed 8,000, yet the Japanese High Command disregarded this commitment subscribed to by the Foreign Office and dispatched a force ten times as large. One of the principal activities was to disrupt the operation of the Russian-owned Chinese Eastern Railway, a function which under the inter-allied agreement was the responsibility of a Technical Board of which Colonel John Stevens, of Panama Canal, was chairman. It was clear from the activities of the Japanese Army that they still hoped to carry out their original objectives. I say this from first-hand knowledge, as I accompanied Ambassador Morris on a several week's tour to Manchuria and Siberia to learn what was going on.

In Chapter II of special interest is the translation of a testament by General Honjo, Commander in Chief of the Kwantung Army, at the time of the Mukden Incident. He had been summoned to appear in Court at the IMTFE trials, but rather than attempting to defend himself there he committed suicide.

According to the testimony of his secretary, the testament was indited by Honjo forty days before his suicide. Professor Liang assures us that today we have enough evidence to prove that Honjo did not tell the truth in his statements, in which he attempted to justify his wrongdoings, and then the author adds: "Though Honjo had the strength to commit suicide he did not have the courage to confess his wrongdoings."

Here is a good example of the complete discarding of moral principles into which the Japanese Army had degenerated from the days of Bushido ("the Way of the Warrior"), a moral code which was appropriate at least to a feudal society.

In Chapter IV of special interest is the listing of various plans by would-be reformers for the remolding of Japan's social and political system along socialistic and fascist lines. Many of the promoters of these plans were fanatical junior army officers. One of these plans called for forcing the Emperor at gun point to give way to their demands. Fears were raised in court circles that the Emperor Institution might be in trouble.

The emergence of reform and revolutionary philosophy in a time of national stress had had its counterpart in China more than a millennium before, when disturbed conditions produced Confucius and other philosophers, and in ancient Greece when the passing away of the "Golden Age" brought forth Socrates, Plato and Aristotle.

The depth to which Professor Liang has gone, in the course of his research, is evidenced by the extent of his documentation which consists of no less than some 400 references, and, where appropriate, a summary.

I am sure that Professor Liang's work will be widely read with interest and profit by the general public as well as by scholars and other specialists. Because of my lifetime association with East Asian affairs, I have a special claim to welcome and applaud his achievement.

JOSEPH W. BALLANTINE

Table of Contents

Chapter 1

Historical Background of the Mukden Incident

On September 18, 1931, at 10:30 P.M. there was an explosion on the South Manchuria Railway line north of Liutiaokou station in Mukden. Thirty-one inches of rail was torn by the blast. In six hours the Japanese Kwantung Army took quick action and occupied the entire city of Mukden, the arsenal, the North Barracks, and the Chinese local government office buildings. Thus occurred the Mukden Incident, which shocked the world.

Six years later, this Incident and its consequences led to the Lukouchiao (Marco Polo Bridge) Incident, which started the Sino-Japanese War. Four years afterwards the sequence of events led to Japan's attack on Pearl Harbor, which ignited the Japanese-American Pacific War. Four years after Pearl Harbor, the Soviet Army moved into Manchuria. Thus, within a period of four decades, as Japan signed the Instrument of Surrender on the U.S.S. Missouri in Tokyo Bay, Japan and Russia once more reversed their positions in Manchuria.

Contemporary Japanese historians, as they review the halcyon days of the Meiji Restoration cannot but lament the fact that Manchuria has been the symbol of the rise as well as the fall of the Japanese Empire. Chinese historians, for their part, recalling the loss and recovery of Manchuria and its influence on the fall of the Chinese Mainland to Communists, cannot fail to note the relationship of Manchuria to the fate of China.

Historical documents show that while the Mukden Incident was the handiwork of the Japanese Kwantung Army, the surprise attack on Pearl Harbor was planned by the Japanese Navy. To understand why Japan had to seize Manchuria in this devious way, it is pertinent to recall the joint intervention in 1895 of Russia, Germany, and France in the Far East to demand of Japan its return of the Liaotung peninsula to China. From that time, Manchuria became a center of interest in world politics. A nation that wished to extend its influence there would have had to assess the situation carefully before committing itself to resolute action. In the course of a generation, Japan had made at least three separate attempts to take over Manchuria and Mongolia. The first was in relation to the incident of Mongolian Prince Pa-lin in 1912;[1] the second was the Bapuchapu incident of Chao-yang-po in 1916;[2] and the third, the attempt to disarm the Fengtien Army under Chang Tso-lin in 1928.[3] All these attempts failed because of the lack of determined and co-ordinated plan and action. The plot engineered by the staff of the Kwantung Army in 1931 was, on the contrary, a thoroughly planned and meticulously executed coup through which Japan succeeded within three months in occupying 1,430,000 square miles of territory, subjugating 35,000,000 Chinese nationals, and disrupting China's unification and reconstruction.[4]

From evidence now available in archives and official documents, we may conclude that the Mukden Incident might have been an inevitable tragic turn in Sino-Japanese relations. September 18 might not have been the date set for enacting it. The Japanese General Staff had not planned to invade Manchuria until 1932.[5] The Kwantung Army Staff itself had originally set September 28 to carry out the plan.[6] Furthermore, arrangements had been made by T. V. Soong, Vice President of the Executive Yuan and Shigemitsu Mamoru,* then Japanese Minister to China to proceed on September 20 from Shanghai to Mukden to review the Manchurian problem and seek a solution.[7] If the Mukden Incident plan had been deferred to a later date it might have been forestalled altogether.

Although the instigators of the Mukden Incident paid for their crime in the sentences imposed on them by the International Military Tribunal for the Far-East (IMTFE),[8] the evil effects of their crimes are still felt not only in China

---

* Japanese names are given in the Japanese order with surname first.

and Japan but also more generally throughout the world. Even though the incident happened a generation ago, its historical significance has not yet been fully appraised. Because many documents relating to the background of this incident became available only after the Second World War and some even as late as 1963, this writer feels that although he started his study late, he is nonetheless fortunate in having more materials to draw upon than had earlier research students.

Usually the most difficult problem in historical research is to get first-hand documentation. However, first-hand materials on the Mukden Incident are unusually abundant because of Japan's surrender. There are at least three principal sources: (1) the reports of the League of Nations at Geneva; (2) the records and the evidence of the Tokyo trial,[9] and (3) the archives of the Japanese Foreign Ministry covering a period of seventy-seven years.[10] Of these three sources, the third is especially valuable. Although there are many contradictions and omissions, these documents, on the whole, should be considered as reliable primary data. Furthermore, because of the release of the micro-filmed archives of the Japanese Foreign Office, it has become increasingly clear to former Japanese government officials and others associated with the Incident that it is futile for them to keep on maintaining secrecy. Consequently, in their post-war studies of the Incident, they have generally been frank and truthful, thus filling some of the gaps found in the documents. This is most helpful to historians who wish to clarify points of doubt and establish historical authenticity.

In his *Far Eastern Crises* (pp. 5-6), Henry L. Stimson, Secretary of State of the United States, 1929-1933,* said, "If anyone had planned the Manchurian outbreak with a view to freedom from interference from the rest of the world, his time was well chosen." This statement reflects accurately the international situation at the time of the crisis. But when Stimson said that the timing of the crisis was excellent he referred only to the economic depression in Europe and the United States.

---

* He was also U.S. Secretary of War, 1911-1913, 1940-1945.

Now, more than a generation after the crisis, equipped as we are with historical documents and records, we are able, as we study the global situation at that time, to gain a more complete and accurate understanding of the background.

The year, 1931, was one of global economic depression. A month or so after the collapse on May 14 of the internationally renowned Credit Austalt, the German financial situaction began to show signs of instability.[11] President von Hindenburg appealed to the United States for help. Within 24 hours, President Hoover proposed that all nations defer payments, for a year, on their inter-government debts. This was the famous Hoover Moratorium[12] which was to cost the United States the sum of $53 million. Although the United States was very generous in this measure, France opposed it. After eighteen days of negotiations, the psychological effect upon stabilizing the situation as intended by the proposal was almost entirely lost. The Bank of Geneva closed down on July 12; so did Darmstader, one of the four largest German banks, on July 13. The run on the banks soon spread to Britain;[13] within ten days, £21 million were withdrawn from the Bank of England. North America was also affected. By the middle of September, within 35 days, $329,000,000 had been withdrawn in the United States. On the day that the news of the Mukden Incident reached Europe and America, Britain was just about to announce the abandonment of her gold standard. On the day of Britain's announcement, September 21, 1931, almost all the stock exchanges in Europe were suspended.

There was no doubt about the extent or the severity of the economic depression.[14] It not only affected the gold standard and the world financial market, but it also produced wide-ranging political repercussions. Austria had a change of cabinet; the political power of the National Socialist Party rose in Germany; and Britain's Labor Cabinet was re-organized into a coalition government including some Conservatives. At that time, the financial policies of Europe and America still followed the orthodox economic theory advocating the reduction of national expenditures as a means of balancing the budget. The livelihood of the people, therefore, became extremely difficult. Complaints were widespread. The British Navy, which had been noted for more than two hundred years for its iron discipline, became disaffected.[15] Its squadron in Chile mutinied to protest against a pay reduction.[16] Under such circumstances, Europe and America could not be expected to pay serious attention to the crisis in remote Liutiaokou. Even if a few Europeans or Americans understood the significance of the Incident, it was unrealistic to expect the Western powers to impose economic sanctions upon Japan in the midst of the depression. This is what Stimson meant when he said that the time of the crisis was excellent for Japan.

If the depression was the economic factor which diverted the world's attention away from the Mukden Incident, Nationalistic rivalry between China and Japan supplied the political factor. When the Chinese demanded that all foreign countries abolish their unequal treaties with China, the Japanese residents in Manchuria also formed the powerful "League for Manchurian Youth" in Dairen and adopted as their counterclaim the slogan "Manchuria is Japan's Life Line." [17]

Prior to the Mukden Incident, relations between China and Japan varied at different levels. Between the two governments, there was a common desire for conciliation. Between the two peoples, antagonism prevailed. Although Generalissimo Chiang Kai-shek was the first leader who led in urging the Chinese people to resist Japanese aggression, he was also the first to sense that Japan was determined to seize Manchuria by military force. This realization came after the Chinese secret emissaries, Chiang Pai-li and Liu Hou-sheng, interviewed Premier Tanaka on May 12, 1927, and Chiang Kai-shek's conversation with Tanaka in November of the same year in the latter's residence in Tokyo.[18] Chiang therefore had to remold China's policy on several occasions to avoid a Sino-Japanese clash. This was evidenced not only by his own addresses at a press conference in Shanghai (December 13, 1927)[19] and at the Fourth Plenary Session of the Kuomintang Central Executive Committee (January 1928),[20] but also in the way he restrained himself to the utmost by moving his Northern Expedition forces across the Yellow River to avoid a clash with the Japanese during the Tsinan Incident (May 8, 1928). On the Japanese side, it was Minister Shidehara who twice saved the situation in 1927. In January he declined the British request for sending troops to Shanghai, and in March he refused to join the naval bombardment in Nanking.[21] In 1928, we saw that as soon as Japan recognized the Nanking Government (July 3, 1929) the latter immediately issued orders to suspend the nation-wide anti-Japanese movement (July 18, 1929).[22] In response to this, the Japanese Cabinet also adopted a resolution not to use any insulting epithet for China (October 19, 1930).[23] Although the assassination of Minister Saburi in 1930[24] and the episode of Obata's being declared *persona non grata*[25] did produce some tension in Sino-Japanese diplomacy, yet thanks to the untiring efforts of Shigemitsu, the attitude of the two governments up to the first half of 1931 remained cordial.

But the antagonism between the peoples of China and Japan was a different story. Long before the establishment of Kuomintang Headquarters in Manchuria (March 1931), the "League for Japanese Manchurian Youth" at Dairen and the local committee of the Chinese Communist Party in Manchuria had already instigated trouble which led to antagonism between the Chinese and Japanese in Dairen and Chientao. "The League for Manchurian Youth" (sponsored by the various Japanese organizations at Dairen)[26] was organized in response to the Japanese Universal Manhood Suffrage System at home. From May 4-6, 1928, the ninety members elected from among the representatives of the twenty precincts of the South Manchuria Railway zone met at the Dairen Press Agency. At that time, Tanaka was Premier of Japan and the left-wing elements in Japan were against his positive policy towards China. They advocated that Japan abandon its designs on Manchuria and Mongolia. However, the Japanese youth in Manchuria insisted that "Manchuria and Mongolia be preserved at all costs." They also wished to make Manchuria and Mongolia "independent states" as a gift to Emperor Hirohito on the occasion of his coronation in November of that year. During the convention, a message of greeting from Premier Tanaka was read; the resolution to organize the League was passed; and the plan to establish branch associations along the Manchuria Railway was also decided upon. The purpose of the League was to unify the Japanese in Manchuria, consolidate their aspirations, and promote Japanese interests in Manchuria.

"The League for Manchurian Youth" sponsored three conventions: the first was held at the South Manchuria Railway's Joint Association at Dairen (June 1-2, 1928); the Second at Mukden (November 23-24, 1929); and the third at Changchun (September 21-22, 1930). The League prepared various propaganda pamphlets,[27] such as "The Plan for An Independent Manchurian State," "The Five Principles for the Administration of Manchuria," "The Three Questions on Manchuria and Mongolia," etc. The propaganda emphasized the importance of Manchuria as Japan's life-line and as the bulwark of Japanese national defense. Hence the necessity for annexing Manchuria by force. After the conventions, propaganda committees were formed to make strongly emotional speeches throughout Japan. They decided to affiliate with the "young officers' group" in the Japanese Army, and to persuade the labor and industrial unions in Kansai to support their cause.[28] This was used by the Seiyukai Party to attack the "weak" foreign policy of Foreign Minister Shidehara.[29]

Although the activities of the Chinese Communist Party in Manchuria started in 1925, they were by no means effective until Japan attempted to prevent Chang Hsueh-liang from joining the Central Government for a national unification. On November 5, 1928, Tang Hung-ching, Wang Li-kung, and others from the Manchurian Committee of the Chinese Communist Party issued the Proclamation for Manchurian Independence. They aroused the industrialists, laborers, farmers, soldiers, and students in Manchuria to boycott Japanese goods and to demand the return of the South Manchuria Railway (the line leading to Port Arthur and Dairen), mining rights and the other privileges which had been granted to the Japanese. The Committee also advocated that the Japanese Army be expelled from Manchuria, that the Chinese local Fengtien Army be dispersed, and that the weak foreign policy of the Kuomintang Government be denounced.[30] In 1928, the committee penetrated into military circles aiming at guerrilla warfare, and instigated acts of sabotage along the Peking-Mukden Railway and the South Manchuria Railway and throughout Anshan, Fushun, Pen-chi-hu and Antung. Simultaneously, the committee urged the Communist Party in Korea to boycott the Japanese. Although the plan of action fell into the hands of the police force of the Japanese Consulate,[31] the riots in Chientao broke out, nevertheless, in 1930.

Situated on the border between China and Korea, Chientao was then the center of activities for both the Korean independence movement and the Korean Communist Party. Some 400,000 of the inhabitants were Koreans, 200,000 were Chinese, 2,000 were Japanese, and a few hundred were White Russians (Caucasians). Naturally, their political, eonomic, and nationalistic aspirations did not coincide, so that here was an ideal spot for revolutionary agitation by the Communist Third International. The first Communist-inspired riot occurred on October 1, 1930, and the second one twelve days later. The rioters, though Chinese and Koreans, were under the direction of twenty-four Russian-trained experts behind the scenes. Since Japan did not enjoy any treaty rights to establish consular police forces in China, the Chientao clash between the Japanese police force and Chinese nationals naturally aroused anti-Japanese sentiment in Manchuria. Seeking every opportunity to fish in troubled waters, the Third International adopted new tactics. On the one hand it stirred Chinese feeling against Japan, and on the other hand adopted a conciliatory attitude toward Japan. Stalin hoped that by this means the Soviet Union would gain the necessary time to complete its first Five-Year Plan. But since Russia was hypothetically Japan's "Number-one Enemy", and since a strong Russia would menace Japan's security, the Kwantung Army was tempted to annex Manchuria and Mongolia at once.

The temptation of the Kwantung Army to act was not confined to this consideration alone. In 1921, Mao Tse-tung and Chu Te emerged as Communist leaders in Kiangsi; there was a major flood caused by an overflow of the Yangtze River in an area covering more than sixteen provinces. In March of the same year, after the Hu Han-min incident in Tangshan, Nanking, there was a split in the Kuomintang. The Cantonese faction in the Central Committee of the Kuomintang left Nanking en bloc and established a separate government in Canton. The Japanese Army was elated to see such internal conflicts in China and at the same time alarmed by the gradual recovery and growth of the Soviet Union. Perceiving also that Europe was in deep trouble on account of the economic depression and that the United States' naval strength in the Western Pacific was limited by the Washington Treaty of 1922, the Kwantung Army decided to take advantage of the prerogatives of the so-called "Supreme Command" to blackmail the Cabinet by demanding the use of force for the solution of the Manchurian and Mongolian problem.[32]

Chapter 2

The Incident at a Glance

1. *The Responsibility for the Incident*

The Mukden Incident lasted only a few hours. At 10:30 o'clock on the night of September 18, 1931, two explosions occurred outside the city of Mukden. One explosion was caused by two 24 cm. caliber heavy howitzers and the other by a pack of 42 sticks of TNT. Immediately after the explosions, the Japanese Kwantung Army and the Railway Guards began to attack the North Barracks with rifles, grenades, and other weapons while another company attacked the city walls of Mukden. The North Barracks were seized at 12:30 A.M., and Mukden was occupied at dawn.[1] At 6 A.M., September 19, copies of the proclamation of Honjo Shigeru, Commander-in-Chief of the Kwantung Army, were posted in and out of the city of Mukden. The translation of this proclamation read, in part, as follows:[2]

> At 10:30 P.M., on September 18, 1931, a unit of the Northeastern Frontier Defense Army of the Republic of China dynamited part of the South Manchuria Railway and attacked the Japanese Railway Guards near the North Barracks northwest of Mukden. It was the Chinese Army which began hostilities and was therefore responsible for what happened. Since the South Manchuria Railway was formally acquired by Japan in a treaty with China, the Railway legally belonged to Japan and no other nation had the right to interfere with its operation. The attack of the Chinese Northeastern Army on Japanese Imperial forces was clearly an act of provocation. Recently, there have been frequent acts of aggression infringing upon our rights and interests in Manchuria. These outrageous acts to affront Japan were by no means the outburst of emotions. They constituted deliberate acts to defy international principles

and justice. Therefore, we cannot but punish those responsible for these violences. It is patent that the acts of violence were not committed by the people of China, but by the ambitious military elements. Since I have been entrusted with the important responsibility of protecting the Railway and its established rights, in order to uphold the prestige of the Empire, I have no choice but to punish resolutely those who have violated our rights. Our Army is interested solely in punishing the Chinese military elements. I am very much concerned with the welfare of the common people. Because of this, I have ordered the Japanese Army to protect their lives and well-being. I urge the people of Manchuria to take good care of themselves, and carry out their daily life without any panic. In the meantime, I wish to warn those who harbor evil designs against the Japanese Army that drastic measures will be unrelentedly meted out to them.

Fourteen years later, in 1945, Japan surrendered, and the Far Eastern International Military Tribunal was established in Tokyo.[3] Honjo was summoned to appear in Court, but he committed suicide in the Allied Forces' Bureau of Occupation Guidance, at Tokyo, on November 20. On April 2 of the following year, his secretary testified in Court that Honjo had written a testament forty days before he committed suicide. The following is this writer's translation of an excerpt from this testament.[4]

My diary and documents on the Mukden Incident were lost during the air raids. I can only rely now on my memory to recall the circumstances of that event. In August, 1931, I was appointed Commanding General of the Kwantung Army. At that time, there were strong anti-Japanese movements in China despite the efforts of Foreign Minister Shidehara to bring about Sino-Japanese co-operation. Our position in Manchuria deteriorated steadily. Despite the fact that both Nakamura and Isugi were carrying legal passports, they were murdered. Korean residents in Wanpaoshan were also maltreated. . . . The Chinese frequently threw stones at our school children, and they restricted our military drills within the railway zone. At times, the Chinese

> Army deliberately scheduled their drills to coincide with ours so as to create tension. . . . On September 18, the Chinese Army from the North Barracks dynamited a section of the South Manchuria Railway. Our Army which happened to be conducting a drill, immediately attacked the Chinese. When I received the report, it was too late for me to seek instructions from Tokyo. I issued the necessary order on my own initiative. But before my order was issued, our Army had already started the attack, and soon the entire Kwantung Army was mobilized.
>
> Apart from protecting the Railway, it was the duty of the Kwantung Army to uphold the rights of Japan, and maintain the safety of the Japanese soldiers and the civilians residing in China. . . . At that time, the forces of the Kwantung Army numbered around 10,000 men while the Chinese Army was 200,000 strong. Had we not retaliated immediately, our Army might have been totally annihilated. I issued the emergency order purely for self-defense purposes. Later on, the conflict spread to Harbin and Tsitsihar. Even though we were criticized for our action, I felt that we were justified in using force, because our enemy was much superior numerically. For our own safety, we could not have done otherwise.

Today, we have enough evidence to prove that Honjo did not tell the truth in this testament. Though Honjo had the strength to commit suicide, he did not have the courage to confess his wrong-doings. In his proclamation and in his testament he accused the Chinese Army of dynamiting the railway tracks. However, on the question as to whether it was the Chinese Army that had fired the first shot, Honjo's testament seemed to contradict his proclamation. In the proclamation he pointed out that because the Chinese Army attacked the Railway Guards, they were the culprits. However, in his testament, he stated that the Railway Guards attacked the Chinese Army. Who fired the first shot is a very important question, for the fact would determine the responsibility for the incident. Honjo was not the only one who had made contradictory statements on the question. Ambassador Yoshizawa and Lieutenant Colonel Shimamoto also contradicted each other in their statements. At Geneva, Yoshizawa reported to the Council of the League of Nations that because the Japanese Army could not stop the Chinese Army from dynamiting the railway, the Japanese were forced to open fire on the Chinese. Thus, it proved that it was the Japanese Army which fired the first shot. However, in a press conference at Mukden, Shimamoto Masaichi told the reporters that the Chinese Army opened fire first. During the Tokyo trial, Colonel Hirata Yukihiro who led the attack on Mukden, was summoned to the court and asked to explain the source of the statement that the Chinese Army opened fire first. Hirata replied that the rumor had been spread by Shimamoto.[5] However, during the trial, Shimamoto did not mention this particular point in his confession.

Not only is the Japanese allegation that the Chinese Army fired the first shot incredible but it is also debatable whether there had been explosions on the railway at all.

Dr. V. K. Wellington Koo, the Chinese delegate to the League Commission of Enquiry (Lytton Commission), pointed out in a memorandum that on the night of the incident, at 10:40 (ten minutes after the explosions on the railway tracks), the train from Changchun passed Liutiaokou and arrived in Mukden on time. Therefore, if the tracks of the South Manchuria Railway at Liutiaokou had really been blasted, the train could not have arrived on time.[6] The Report did not deny the explosions on the tracks, but in an informal speech, Lytton pointed out that the explosions were not a mere accident.[7] Some Japanese scholars, such as Yoshino, Nakano, and others, held that the entire charge was fabricated by Japan.[8]

In the course of thirty years, numerous historical material on the crisis came to light, and we have the following evidences to prove where responsibility for it lay.

A. The testimony of Tanaka Ryukichi at the Tokyo trial: "To tell the truth, I cannot say that the Manchurian crisis was provoked by the Chinese Army's dynamiting of the railway tracks." [9]

B. The testimony of Miyake Mitsuharu, Chief of Staff of the Kwantung Army (1931-32), at the court in Moscow: "I only learned about the explosions in the reports submitted to me, and I did not investigate the matter further. I surmised that it was done by Japanese disguised in Chinese Army uniform, and Commander Honjo agreed with me." [10]

C. In his book, Morishima (Japanese Consul in Mukden in 1931) wrote: "Imada Shintaro was the one responsible for damaging the South Manchuria Railway. He ordered a Chinese laborer to dynamite the tracks, but the laborer refused. He threatened the laborer, who then reluctantly blasted a small section. After the explosion, Imada killed the laborer and fabricated a report that it was the work of a Chinese soldier." [11]

D. The secret telegram of Hayashi Hisajiro: In 1931, Hayashi was Japanese Consul General in Mukden. His secret telegram to Foreign Minister Shidehara was listed as No. 181 in *The Collection of Evidences of the International Military Tribunal for the Far East* (IMTFE). It also appeared in *The Japanese Foreign Ministry's Annual Report and Important Documents,* Vol. II, p. 180. The telegram reads in translation as follows: "According to the report of Kimura, a Director of the South Manchuria Railway, as soon as the maintenance crew of the South Manchuria Railway Company heard the news that the tracks at Liutiaokou had been damaged, they immediately set out to repair them, but were stopped by the Kwantung Army. From the various evidences that we have gathered, it would seem that the incident was planned by the Japanese Army." [12]

E. *The History of the Rise and Fall of Militarism* by Ito Masanori: Ito says: "On September 17, Imada paid a visit to Hanaya Todashi to offer the plan of blasting the tracks of the South Manchuria Railway and the latter agreed to it." [13]

F. *The Road to the Pacific War* (1963): A book compiled by the Asahi Shimbun says, *inter alia*: "Imada undertook the task of preparing the 42 square-shaped sticks of TNT. On the morning of September 18, 1931, he told

Lieutenants Kawamoto and Noda about the plan of action for that night. Ono Masao took a unit of 105 soldiers and proceeded to the south of Wen-kuan-tun while Kawamoto led Sergeant Matsuoka and seven or eight soldiers to ignite the explosives which had been placed on both sides of the railway tracks." [14]

By examining the foregoing six testimonies, we can establish the truth concerning the bombing of the railway tracks in the Mukden Incident. It seems that originally the Kwantung Army had planned to derail by iron bars the 10:45 P.M. train from Changchun and then take advantage of the confusion to launch an attack. However, the Army was afraid that the plot might be discovered by the Japanese Railway Guards, and so it was decided to blast the railway tracks at Liutiaokou. It was originally intended to blame China for the derailment. However, the damage on the tracks was so slight that the southbound train from Changchun was able to bump over the damaged rails. Thus the Kwantung Army aroused public skepticism in the way it created this incident.[15] Although the moves made by the Japanese Army on the evening of September 18th were well-coordinated, their technique of dynamiting the tracks seemed to be rather clumsy.

An answer has also been found to the mystery concerning the explosion of two 24 cm caliber howitzers. This is because the explosion formed part of the secret plan of 1930. These two howitzers had been mounted secretly in September, 1931 and were aimed at the airfield and the North Barracks. A separate chapter will be devoted to the details of this plot but what this writer wishes to point out here is why the Kwantung Army had to dynamite the South Manchuria Railway track.

According to article II of the organic law of the Kwantung Army, the authority of the commander was restricted to the protection of the South Manchuria Railway. Although he could freely exercise his powers within the railway zone, he had to ask permission of the Japanese Consul General if he wanted to send troops to areas outside the zone. This was so because the protection of the Japanese residents in China was not the duty of the Kwantung Army but of the Foreign

Ministry. In Manchuria, the authority of the Japanese Army and that of the civil government were rather ill-defined. There had been friction between the Kwantung Army and the Japanese Consulate General at the time when Yoshida was Consul General (1927-1928). Therefore, when Hayashi was appointed Consul General in Mukden he did not take up his post until Foreign Minister Tanaka had obtained a written statement from War Minister Shirakawa clarifying the Consul General's diplomatic powers.[16] Four days before the Mukden Incident, Miyake Mitsuharu, chief of staff of the Kwantung Army, had sent a confidential letter (No. 293) to Hayashi to ascertain the latter's views on the Kwantung Army's use of force outside the railway zone to attack the Chinese Army (which was described in the letter as bandits). Hayashi immediately replied that before taking any such action, the Kwantung Army must first consult the Consulate.[17] Because of this restriction, the Kwantung Army realized that since it could not take any military action outside the railway zone, it would be necessary to create some incident within the zone to be used as an excuse to extend its sphere of action. This was why the Army found it necessary to dynamite the South Manchuria Railway track in order to create an incident. In the spring of 1932, Kayano Chochi, a great friend of Dr. Sun Yat-sen, was sent to China by Premier Inukai. He secretly told Chu Cheng and Tsou Lu that the success of the Japanese Army in the Mukden Incident was not only unfortunate for China, but also undermined the government system of Japan.[18] What Kayano said proved to be true even before Japan's adventure and humiliation in the Second World War. But why then would not Honjo recant before his death?

2. *The Military Strength of the Contestants*

On September 18, 1931, the Japanese deployed two units of armed forces. One was the Third Company of the Railway Guards, around 500 men, commanded by Lieut. Colonel Shimamoto who led the attack on the North Barracks.[19] In this action, two were killed and twenty-two wounded.[20] The second was the 29th Regiment of the Second Division under the command of Hirata, who led the attack on Mukden and on the arsenal. Seven of this unit were killed in action.[21] That the Japanese could gain such phenomenal success by such small forces was probably due entirely to the non-resistance of the Northeastern Frontier Defense Army and the Public Security Forces. There were more than 10,000 men stationed at the North Barracks, but they had orders from Marshal Chang Hsueh-liang to offer no resistance. At the time of the Japanese attack, the order was confirmed by a long distance telephone call from Brigadier Wang I-che. Therefore, there was only a small skirmish between the Japanese and the 621st regiment of the Chinese Army, which was fighting to gain a way out. The rest of the Chinese Army had all retreated from the South Gate to Erh-tai-tzu through the North Barracks.[22] In November, 1931, Chang Hsueh-liang went to Nanking to attend the Fourth Plenum of the Third Central Executive Committee of the Kuomintang. Thereafter, he lingered in Peiping to seek medical treatment. In the autumn of 1931, after the murder of Captain Nakamura, he decided to return to Mukden on September 9. However, he postponed his departure because of the secret report that Doihara was plotting to assassinate him.[23] On the same day he issued the secret order of non-resistance. This order was one of the most important documents relating to the Mukden Incident. It reads in full as follows:

> At the present, in view of the mounting tension in our foreign relations with the Japanese, we have to be especially careful in our dealings with them. No matter how provocatively the Japanese act, it is imperative that we be extremely patient and tolerant. We must try not to resist them so as not to cause any incidents. Please immediately instruct your subordinates to observe this order meticulously. Signed, Chang Hsueh-liang.[24]

The order was issued to the Chief of Staff of the Frontier Defense Army and the Political Affairs Committee of the Northeastern Provinces. It was dated September 6, twelve days before the outbreak of the Mukden Incident. On August 25, the Mukden Bureau of Public Security had issued a secret order stating that "the Japanese were doing everything to provoke us, and therefore, we should try not to shoot first; in the event that the Japanese open fire, the Chinese should withdraw into the precinct stations to avoid conflicts."[25] A copy of this secret order has been found in the archives of the Japanese Foreign Ministry. This proves that this secret order was known to the Japanese at the time of the crisis. It explains also why the Kwantung Army was bold enough to attack the Chinese Army with such a small force. During the Tokyo trial, Morishima testified that the Chinese secret code could be broken easily. Furthermore, at the time when the Kwantung Army was planning the Incident, it had also decided that whether the Chinese would fight or not, the Japanese must occupy the city of Mukden.[26] This further proves that the Japanese had already known that the Chinese army and police would not offer any resistance.

On the night of September 18, 1931, the entire Japanese Army in Manchuria was unleashed.[27] Japan declared later that she only had some 10,400 soldiers, 500 military police, and 16 field artillery pieces in China. According to the Chinese source, Japan had more forces than that. Here was the full report:

A. Second Division (under the command of Tamon), 14,750 soldiers and 52 air force personnel.
B. Independent Railway Guards (under the command of Amano), 5,400 soldiers in 6 companies.
C. Artillery brigade at Port Arthur, 3,400 soldiers.
D. Military police in Manchuria, 2,561 men.
E. Marines, 960.
F. Special Police Force, 720.

Thus, Japan had at least a force of 27,700. If we were to include the Japanese reserves, the total number would be no fewer than 40,000.[28] But of course the Chinese Frontier Defense Army numbered at least six times as many. The following was a listing of the Chinese Frontier Defense Army presented in China's memoranda to the Lytton Commission.[29] (See Koo's Memoranda, Vol. 1, p. 122.)

A. In Liaoning:
Men—78,666
Horses—16,064
Rifles—34,523
Artillery—24
Airplanes—262

B. In Kirin:
Men—80,944
Horses—10,477
Rifles—40,900
Artillery—36
Airplanes—none

C. In Heilungkiang:
Men—19,895
Horses—6,340
Rifles—21,464
Artillery—36
Airplanes—none

Therefore, in the above-mentioned three Northeastern provinces, there were altogether 179,505 men, 32,881 horses, 96,897 rifles, 916 artillery pieces, and 262 airplanes.

There is no simple answer to the question of how Japan could have stationed such a large number of Railway Guards in Manchuria. Since Czarist Russia began military occupation of the Chinese Eastern railway zone in 1900, and despite Russia's having agreed in 1902 to return it to China, at the outset of the Russo-Japanese War in 1905, there were still Russian troops in Manchuria. In the Treaty of Portmouth, Russia, with the consent of the Chinese Government, agreed to transfer the Russian leased territory of Port Arthur and her rights on the South Manchuria Railway to Japan. However, the first article of the Annex to the Treaty of Portsmouth specified that Japan and Russia could station no more than fifteen guards per square kilometer of territory. Consequently, because of this provision, Japan had stated that her understanding of her right to station railway guards in Manchuria was acquired by treaty. However, in point of fact, China played no part in drawing up the Annex to the Treaty of Portsmouth, and therefore, the provisions of that instrument had no binding power on China. Towards the end of 1905, when China and Japan were negotiating a treaty on Manchuria, China persistently requested Japan to withdraw her Railway Guards. As a result, in the second article of the Annex, Japan reluctantly stated that since the Chinese Government desired that Russia and Japan withdraw their regular troops as well as their Railway Guards from Manchuria, Japan would be glad to comply with China's wish. Thus, if Russia agreed to withdraw her Railway Guards . . . the Japanese Government would be glad to follow suit. Additionally, if there were no disturbances in Manchuria, and if the Chinese Government could guarantee the safety of all foreigners and their property in China, Japan and Russia would withdraw their Railway Guards simultaneously.

At that time, Japan thought that Russia would never withdraw her Railway Guards, and therefore she made the foregoing statement just to pay lip service to China. Unexpectedly, since 1917, as a result of the Bolshevik Revolution, there was a great change in the situation relating to the Chinese Eastern Railway. The Chinese Government assumed the duty of protecting that Railway. In 1924, China and Russia reached an agreement whereby Russia recognized China's right to protect the Railway. Russia withdrew her Railway Guards. Because of this situation, Japan should have withdrawn her Railway Guards from the South Manchuria Railway in accordance with the statement that she had made in the Annex. However, Japan not only refused to do so, but also protested to the Chinese Government that the Sino-Russian Agreement had jeopardized Japan's privileges under the Treaty of Portsmouth.[30] This dispute was still unresolved at the time of the Mukden Incident.[31] It clearly shows that Japan had no right to station Railway Guards in Manchuria, and the Japanese knew it.

Chapter 3

Conspiracy Relating to the Incident

1. *Main Participants in the Conspiracy and Their Roles*

It is well known that the Mukden Incident was a conspiracy of the young officers of the Japanese Army. This is indisputable. But who were the young officers? How did the conspiracy come about? Few have studied these questions. Although the Incident was examined twice by international investigations (the Commission of Enquiry of the League of Nations in 1932 and the Tokyo Trial in 1946-1948), Japan, in the first investigation conceded the truth, and in the second investigation, only a general outline of the events was revealed. At present, we have abundant historical materials on the Incident to identify the main participants:

1. *From the Kwantung Army*:
   Lieutenant General Honjo Shigeru, Commanding General;
   Major General Miyake Mitsuharu, Chief of Staff;
   Colonel Itagaki Seishiro, Senior Staff Officer;
   Lieutenant Colonel Ishihara Kanji, Staff officer (Chief, Military operations);
   Colonel Doihara Kenji, Chief, Army Special Agency at Mukden;
   Lieutenant Colonel Mitani Kiyoshi, Chief, Police garrison;
   Major Hanaya Tadashi, Assistant, Army Special Service Agency at Mukden;
   Lieutenant Colonel Shimamoto Masaichi, Battalion Commander, Railway Guard;
   Captain Kawashima Tadashi, Commanding Officer, Third Company;
   Captain Kawakami Seiichi, Commanding Officer, Second Company;

Captain Imada Shintaro, Assistant, Army Special Service Agency at Mukden;
Captain Ono Masao, Commanding Officer, First Company;
Colonel Hirata Yukihiro, Commanding Officer, 29th Regiment;
First Lieutenant Kawamoto Suemori, Patrol Officer.

2. *From War Ministry, Tokyo*:

Major General Koiso Kuniaki, Chief, Military Affairs Bureau;
Colonel Nagata Tetsuzan, Chief, General Affairs Section.

3. *From General Staff, Tokyo*:

Major General Tatekawa Yoshitsugu, Section Chief, Military Affairs Division;
Colonel Hashimoto Kingoro, Chief, Intelligence Section;
Lieutenant Colonel Nemoto Hiroshi, Chief, China Section;
Colonel Shigeta Chiaki, Chief, Chinese Intelligence Section;
Captain Cho Isamu, Member, China Section;
Major Wachi Takaji, Member, Intelligence Section.

4. *From Korea Army*:

Lieutenant General Hayashi Senjuro, Commanding General;
Lieutenant Colonel Kanda Masatane, Chief Staff.

In the foregoing, only a few of the participants were generals, and the majority were of colonel rank. Their age range was 35 to 45. Thus, they could appropriately be described as "young officers." Although both Koiso and Negata had opposed the Kwantung Army's plan for direct aggression, they were definitely associated with the planning of the Incident. Ishihara was the person responsible for the actual planning and Itagaki, for its execution.[1] Doihara was known as "The Lawrence of Manchuria" and had been in China for a long time. A month before the Incident, he secured the consent of Miyake Mitsuharu to order Mugita Hirao to take Yen Hsi-shan from Dairen back to Shansi under cover in a Japanese military plane. He also instigated Shih Yu-san to attack Chang Hsueh-liang, but the plot incurred Saionji's [2] displeasure. In the Mukden Incident, however, Doihara's role was to persuade the Tokyo Government to accept the accomplished fact, and it was his assistant, Hayana, who actually participated in the conspiracy. As a result, Ishihara, Itagaki, and Hayana became known as the three pillars of the Kwantung Army at that time.[3]

The conspiracy had originated in a study made by the Intelligence Department of the General Staff of the Kwantung Army of the possibility of war with Russia. This study prompted the three well-known trips of the staff officer of the Kwantung Army.[4] The first trip to North Manchuria was made in July 1929 (when Soviet Russia severed diplomatic relations with China on account of disputes concerning the Chinese Eastern Railway). Its purpose was to study military operations in the vicinity of Harbin. On July 4, 1929, Ishihara gave a lecture on "military history" at Changchun and this was the prelude to the Mukden Incident.[5] The second trip was made in November of the same year to South Manchuria and the western part of Liaoning to examine the strategic position of Chinchow. As a result of the study, the plans for an attack on Mukden and a night skirmish on Kung-chu-ling were drafted.[6] The third trip, in July 1931, was made to complete plans for a possible war with Russia. It was at this time that Itagaki's plan to solve the Manchurian-Mongolian problem and the Liutiaokou plan was first discussed. The young officers of the Japanese Army had realized that under the restrictions imposed by the Japanese Cabinet, the League of Nations and the Kellogg-Briand Pact (for the renunciation of war as an instrument of national policy), any attempt openly to annex Manchuria would arouse international opposition and be deterred by internal politics. Although they cared little about international reaction, they were concerned with obstruction by their own Cabinet. For this reason, they devised a plan to cope with the possible reaction of the Japanese Cabinet. Besides planning a mliitary conquest of Manchuria and Mongolia, they also decided on a revolutionary plan to seize political power by eliminating all undesirable persons in the Emperor's entourage.

To achieve their ambitions, the young officers planned three incidents during 1931: (1) the March incident in which they attempted to overthrow the party Cabinet and to install the War Minister, General Ugaki, as Premier; (2) the Mukden Incident of September 18, which was an attempt to destroy Chang Hsueh-liang's regime; (3) an October incident intended to assassinate all the elder statesmen and Cabinet members to supporting General Araki as Premier. On the surface, these three plans seemed to be unrelated, but in reality they were all part of a power play to destroy the Constitutional system of Japan and to establish Fascism with power in their own hands to achieve Japanese hegemony in East Asia. Before the March incident, the young officers and the Kwantung Army were undecided as to whether they should first carry out their schemes against the Japanese Government before executing their plan against China.[7] After the failure of the March incident, it was decided to give priority to the plan of external aggression. Accordingly, the September 18th plot was staged. At first, there were some setbacks in the development of the Mukden Incident plan. It became necessary to speed up the planned October incident.[8] Thus, it may be said that the Mukden Incident was an extension of Japanese internal revolt rather than an act purely of external aggression. A few days after the incident, Harada, who was then Saionji's political secretary, made a rather revealing speech in the Upper House of the Diet. He said, *inter alia*: "Gentlemen, if you consider the Mukden Incident as merely an international affair, I am afraid your judgment is inaccurate. Actually, the Incident is only an echo of the March incident. If the Mukden Incident should succeed, the Japanese militarists would consider that if they could do what they want in external expansion, they could also do what they like in internal politics. This is the dangerous situation we are facing today." [9]

Harada's statement revealed also the inside story of the conspiracy. To understand the Incident fully, we must understand the planned March and October incidents. Let us begin first with an account of the March incident.

2. *Prelude to the Conspiracy and Its Fermentation*

The March incident was sponsored by the "Cherry Blossom Society," an association organized by the Japanese young officers in September, 1930, exactly a year before the Mukden Incident. According to the secret files of the Police Section of the Japanese Ministry of Interior,[10] the "Cherry Blossom Society" was the most influential organization behind the March and the projected October incidents. About early September of the 6th year of Showa (1930), it listed the names of Army officers, such as Hashimoto Kingoro, a colonel in the artillery section of the General Staff; Sakata Yoshio, a lieutenant colonel in the Ministry of War; Higuchi Kisaburo, a major at the Tokyo Garrison Headquarters, and many others. In view of the unrest in Japan, they met at the Army Officers' Club in Tokyo to discuss the forming of an organization to study national reforms. Major Tanaka Hiyoshi drafted the constitution for the Society which comprises the following points:

(1) The ultimate objective of the Society is national reforms in Japan and to achieve this objective force will be used, if necessary;

(2) Membership in the Society is open to officers in active service below the rank of colonel who seek the reform of their country without any ulterior selfish motivation;

(3) Preparatory work:

- (a) To persuade fellow army officers of the necessity for internal reforms;
- (b) To enlarge the membership of the Society (according to the archives of the police department, there were 105 members in May, 1931);
- (c) To draft a concrete plan for internal reforms.

In accordance with a decree of Emperor Meiji, Japanese military persons were prohibited from participating in political organizations. This was also specified in the penal codes of the Army and the Navy.[11] But about 1930, the General Staff and the Ministry of War vied with each other in political deliberations under the pretext of national defense. Moreover, as a result of the world economic depression, there was a decline in Japanese foreign trade, and rural unrest was acute.[12]

Hashimoto and Sakata as well as many others took the view that this was due to the corruption in political parties and the ineptitude of the administration which had concealed the realities from the Emperor and had deceived the people. They wanted to get rid of all the elder statesmen and high echelon officials, abolish the Constitution, and establish a military dictatorship after the current vogue of Fascism so as to avoid the fate which befell the ancient Greek and Roman Empires.[13] At that time, the international conference on disarmament was about to convene, and War Minister Ugaki instructed Nagata Tetsuzan to draw up a new formula which, in order to cope with the situation, would "reduce the number of divisions without affecting Japan's military strength." [14] The young officers, however, feared that even under such a formula, the disarmament conference would be harmful to Japan in much the same way as was the London Naval Conference. For this reason, they decided to intensify their revolutionary plot to destroy Japan's political system.

The Japanese young officers' attempt to meddle in political affairs did not begin with the establishment of the "Cherry Blossom Society." Even at the time of General Utsunomiya Taro, the young officers had clandestinely organized the partisans and followers of Saga into the "left-shoulder" clique to oppose the militarists of the Choshu faction.[15] In 1922, Utsunomiya Taro summoned to his death bed Colonel Araki and ordered his aide Dobashi to mark out on the map with a red pencil longitudes 60° E. to 170° E. as the area designated for Japanese conquest in the future.[16] According to this design, the future map of Japan would embrace all of Siberia in the North, and China, India, Southeast Asia, Australia, and New Zealand to the south. This plan of conquest differed little from the scheme of the so-called "Greater East Asia Co-prosperity Sphere" advocated by Hashimoto Kingoro at a later date.[17] In October, 1921, at Baden Baden Warm Springs in Germany, Majors Nagata, Kobatake, and Okamura, who had been classmates at the Japanese

Military Academy, made a secret agreement in which they planned to reorganize the Japanese Army and to purge the militarists of the Choshu faction.[18] Later on, they were joined by Komoto Daisaku (of the fifteenth class) and other important officers of the eighteenth class to form "the Double-leaf Society."[19] They later founded, with the participation of comrades of the 21-25th classes, the Thursday Society. On May 29, 1929, forty young officers, colonels, majors, captains, and lieutenants, all graduates of the 15th to 25th classes of the Japanese Military Academy, formed the "One Evening Society" at Fujimi-ken.[20] The Society aimed at reorganizing the personnel of the Japanese Army, finding a solution to the Manchurian-Mongolian problem and giving support to the proper leadership in Japan. The objectives of this Society were similar to those of the "Cherry Blossom Society." This shows that after 1929, it had become popular among many Japanese officers to find themselves in different societies in defiance of the Imperial decree.[21]

The "Cherry Blossom Society" was formally inaugurated in January, 1931. To draft a plan for action, the following persons were chosen: Sakata Yoshio, Nemoto Hiroshi, Hashimoto Kingoro, Cho Isamu, and Tanaka Hiyoshi. The important points of the plan were:[22]

(1) To coordinate with the various civic organizations and designate Okawa Shumei to lead a group of 10,000 in a rally at Hibiya Park, Tokyo, to attack the policies of the Cabinet, stage demonstrations, and create riots.

(2) To order the first Division of the Japanese Army to seize the Diet and cut off its communications with the outside world under the pretext of suppressing the riot.

(3) To ask the members of the Society who hold the rank of general to map out the routes and direct the next movement.

(4) To select an officer of lieutenant general rank to accompany Major Generals Koiso and Tatekawa to break into the Diet and announce their non-confidence in the Cabinet.

(5) To demand the resignation of the Cabinet en bloc.

(6) To select delegates to call on Prince Kanin and Saionji,

who would then recommend to the Emperor the appointment of War Minister Ugaki as Premier.

According to the diary of Tanaka Hiyoshi, meetings were held at the homes of Tatekawa and Shigeto. At first, opinions on the plan were divided into three groups: one approved the plan; another disapproved, and a neutral group.[23] Upon the insistence of Hashimoto and Shigeto the plan was finally adopted, and March 20, 1931 was designated as the date for action. Hashimoto and Tatekawa were told to borrow 300 bombs from the Chiba Military Training Camp and hide them in the home of Shimizu Konosuke. Count Tokugawa donated 300,000 yen to the cause, with the understanding that after the coup he was to be rewarded with the ministership of the Ministry of Imperial Household.[24] Finally, Okawa was instructed by Koiso to call on General Ugaki at his official residence and to request his endorsement of the enterprise.

Okawa was a graduate of the Tokyo Imperial University. He was employed for a while in the South Manchuria Railway Company and later earned a doctoral degree in colonial economics. He studied Buddhism and spoke six languages: English, French, German, Italian, Chinese, and Sanskrit. In 1916, he and Mitsukawa Kametaro organized the Rosokai, and he wrote a book, *The Spirit of Japanese Idealism,* in which he expressed his deep contempt for Western political theories. He also studied classical Chinese poetry. In 1919, he and Kita Ikki organized "The Survival Society" (Yozon-sha). The name of the Society is derived from a poem composed by Wei Cheng of the T'ang period of China, which reads, "Although the well-contemplated plan is not realized, my flamboyant spirit still survives." When the Society was disbanded, he became a university professor along with Yasuoka Masaatsu, a well-known sociologist. He became acquainted first with Koiso, Tatekawa, Shigeto, Hashimoto, and through them with Ugaki.[25] On February 10, 1931, he had an interview with General Ugaki. The results of this meeting were reported variously. According to Okawa himself, Ugaki approved the coup at the meeting, but changed his mind at a later date.[26] However, according to Ugaki, at no time did he approve the coup, and he even tried to stop it.[27] According to American and Japanese scholars who studied this episode, it seems that under the persuasion of the members of the "Cherry Blossom Society," General Ugaki at first got the impression that the coup was to be carried out peacefully, and therefore he did not oppose it. Later, when he learned that the coup was to utilize the Army to overthrow the Cabinet, he immediately ordered Koiso to stop the plan.[28] Of the above three versions, the last one seems to be most credible.[29] The plan for the coup was cancelled two days before the designated date only because Koiso had ordered Shimizu to return the bombs. Hashimoto was very much irritated by the turn of events. Since then, priority was given to the Mukden plot.

3. *Formation and Development of the Conspiracy*

It is a fact that the shaping of the conspiracy of the Mukden Incident had a unique history. Let us examine the evidence as it appeared in the Tokyo Trial. It was pretty comprehensive.

(1) The testimony of Tanaka Ryukichi.[30] Tanaka testified briefly that the Mukden Incident was not a chance occurrence, but a premeditated plan; the conspirators at Tokyo were Tatekawa Yoshitsugu, Hashimoto Kingoro, Okawa Shumei, and Lieutenant Colonel Cho Isamu; and the conspirators in the Kwantung Army were Itagaki Seishiro and Ishihara Kanji. After the Incident, Hashimoto and Cho Isamu spoke to Tanaka about it. Toward the end of 1934, Hashimoto told Tanaka that the Incident had two aims: (1) to overthrow the tyrannical rule in Manchuria and to promote security and prosperity, and (2) to use the Incident to force political reform in Japan. In October, 1934, Okawa also told him that in order to liberate the Asian people from the colonial domination of the white imperialists, it was necessary to liberate Manchuria from the Chinese National Government in Nanking. Okawa also said that in 1930 he had tried to persuade Chang Hsueh-liang to proclaim independence from the Chinese National Government, but Chang refused.

(2) The conversation between Tatekawa and Professor Ayuzawa.[31] In 1932, Tatekawa and Matsuoka were sent as dele-

gates to the special session of the League of Nations at Geneva. On their way, Tatekawa told Ayuzawa that the Mukden Incident had been carried out as planned.

(3) The remark made by Okawa when he was drunk.[32] A month before the Mukden Incident, Shimizu Konosuke was told by Okawa that he and Hashimoto, Nemoto, Itagaki, and other officers were about to do something great in Manchuria.

(4) The boastful prediction of Shimamoto Masaichi.[33] In August, at a farewell party before he was sent to Mukden, Shimamoto predicted that he was going to perform some great deeds in Manchuria.

(5) The diary of Kido Koichi.[34] On June 23, 1931, Kido wrote the following in his diary: "Because of my office as secretary-general to the Lord Privy Seal, I was able to learn from Baron Harada, the secretary of Saionji, that the young officers in Manchuria were about to create an incident. This is very regrettable."

(6) The conversation between Shigeto Chiaki and Fujita Isamu.[35] Before the occurrence of the September 18th incident, Shigeto told Fujita that something serious was about to occur in Manchuria. He also placed in Fujita's custody a large sum of money which he and Hashimoto had collected so that it could be drawn and spent freely. After the Incident, Fujita congratulated Shigeto on the success, and Shigeto gayly replied that he and his comrades were the officers in the General Staff responsible for Chinese affairs. If they should fail, they would have to commit harakiri in order to pay for their guilt.

(7) The diary of Tanaka Hiyoshi.[36] On August 9, 1930, Tanaka wrote in his diary: "Hashimoto told me that the Kwantung Army's secret plan would be carried out in the middle of September. This action will be a turning point in the Manchurian-Mongolian affair!"

The above-mentioned seven testimonies exposed somewhat the main outlines of the conspiracy. The staff officers of the Kwantung Army had some of the most brilliant personnel in the Japanese Army. They had meticulously planned and set the stage for the Incident. The entire plan, from its conception to its execution, was characterized by skillful planning in these three aspects: (1) personnel; (2) finance; (3) planning.

Before the establishment of the "One Evening Society," Nagata Tetsuzan, Yamazono Shigeatsu, Kobatake Toshihiro, Muto Akina, and others had already turned their attention to placing their comrades in key positions in Manchuria. In Japan, the duties of the colonels and lieutenant colonels were usually assigned by the Chief of Personnel Section of the Ministry of War. In August, 1929, Okamura became the Chief of Personnel. It was then (August 12) that Imamura Shintaro and Nemoto Hiroshi were appointed to their then current posts. In July, 1930, Hashimoto was transferred to be Chief of Russian Affairs in the General Staff of the Army; in August of the same year, Shigeto Chiuki was assigned to be Chief of Chinese Affairs, and Nagata Tetsuzan, Chief of the Military Affairs Section of the Ministry of War. Doihara Kenji, Hayana Tadashi, and Shimamoto were assigned to Mukden when Okamura was the Chief of Personnel. Because of these arrangements, the members of the "One Evening Society" and those who shared their views on the Manchurian-Mongolian problem occupied all the important positions having to do with Manchuria in the General Staff and the Ministry of War. With the help of Itagaki in the Kwantung Army and Tatekawa and Koiso in the General Staff in Tokyo, their preparation for conspiracy was greatly facilitated. Therefore, the appointment of Okamura as Chief of Personnel of the Ministry of War was instrumental in paving the way for Itagaki and Ishihara to upset, through insubordination, the policies of the Japanese Cabinet.[37]

In regard to the financing of the affair, the most important supporter was Fujita Isamu who contributed 100,000 yen.[38] Fujita was the nephew of Shigeto's sworn brother, and he was persuaded by Komoto and Hashimoto to contribute the money. In August, 1931, he gave Komoto and Nakajima Shinichi 30,000 yen each and Doihara 20,000 yen to finance the Incident.[39]

The planning was more complicated. In December, 1928, soon after Ishihara was assigned to the Kwantung Army, he drew up a secret plan for attacking Mukden.[40] Besides this plan, there were four others: (1) Ishihara's study "on the conquest of Mongolia and Manchuria" drawn up in December, 1930;[41] (2) Ishihara's war plan for solving the Mongolian-Manchurian problem drawn up in March, 1931;[42] (3) Itagaki's plan dealing with the problems of Manchuria and Mongolia made in May, 1931;[43] (4) an outline plan for solving the Manchurian problem drafted by the General Staff at Tokyo in July, 1931.[44] The first plan divided the occupation of Mongolia and Manchuria into three stages: (1) the period of pacification; (2) the period of consolidation; (3) the period of defense. Each stage would last a period from six months to two years. The second plan was nominally directed against Manchuria and Mongolia, but in reality it was a war plan against the United States. Only 30 copies of the plan were printed. They were numbered and classified as top secret. The third plan emphasized the methods of implementation, namely: (1) the plan for Mongolian independence; (2) the plan for the independence of Chientao; and (3) the plan for creating disturbances in North Manchuria. The main objective of these plans was to create "anti-Japanese riots" in Manchuria so as to give the Kwantung Army an excuse to use force. The Liutiaokou incident was part of the plan to create such disturbances in North Manchuria. The fourth plan was the one drawn up in consultation between the General Staff and the Ministry of War in Tokyo and approved by the authorities of these two departments. Although this plan also called for solution of the Manchurian problem by force, the time for action was set for one year later. This is the most important evidence to prove that by unleashing the Mukden crisis in 1931, the Kwantung Army had violated the orders of their superiors in Tokyo. Because of its importance, we must discuss this plan in detail.

Although both the young officers' faction of the Ministry of War in Tokyo and the young officers of the Kwantung Army advocated the occupation of Manchuria and Mongolia by armed force, they nevertheless held different views on the procedure and timing for the occupation. The young officers in Tokyo had misgivings about the reaction of the Soviet Government; they were also apprehensive lest the Japanese Cabinet deter their plan. Thus, to ensure the success of the Kwantung Army, they deemed it necessary to bring about internal political reforms and to foster favorable international opinion as preparatory steps. As a result, comrades of the "Cherry Blossom Society" wanted to give priority to political reforms, while the

General Staff and the Operations Section of the Ministry of War emphasized the cultivation of favorable international opinion. After the failure of the March incident, although Hashimoto and others in the "Cherry Blossom Society" had abandoned their stand for giving priority to domestic political reform,[45] Nagata and others in the Ministry of War still insisted on the cultivation of favorable international opinion. The fourth plan was made in accordance with the wishes of the Ministry of War. Imamura Hitoshi was the one who drafted the plan. In his memoirs, he said, "Although the plan was not completed until August, 1931, its main ideas were told to Mike Mitsuharu, the Chief of Staff of the Kwantung Army, in June when he was secretly summoned to Tokyo and ordered to transmit them to the Commander-in-Chief of the Kwantung Army." [46]

The fourth plan consisted of eight important points on the solution for the Manchurian problem:[47]

(1) The Japanese Foreign Office should undertake the responsibility for Chang Hsueh-liang's anti-Japanese movements.

(2) No military actions would be taken unless anti-Japanese activities became intensified.

(3) It was necessary to gain domestic and international understanding for the solution of the Manchurian problem; the Minister of War should explain the existing situation to members of the Cabinet.

(4) The Military Affairs Section of the Ministry of War should closely co-operate with the Intelligence Section of the General Staff in making the Japanese people understand the actual situation in Manchuria.

(5) The Intelligence Section of the Ministry of War should coordinate closely with pertinent Bureaus and Sections of the Foreign Office in making all the nations concerned with the Manchurian problem realize the gravity of the "anti-Japanese movements" in Manchuria. This is to insure that in the event of Japanese military action in Manchuria, they would be sympathetic towards Japan.

(6) The strength of the necessary forces for the military action should be determined by the Operations Section of the Ministry of War and the Kwantung Army.

(7) There should be at least a year's time to cultivate sympathetic national and international understanding (that is, until the Spring of 1932).

(8) Before the Spring of 1932, the Kwantung Army should exercise extreme patience and self-control, and avoid any accident by all means. If any should develop, it must be localized, and not be aggravated.

Points (7) and (8) were intended to hold back the Liutiaokou plot which was planned to be carried out on September 28, 1931 by the Kwantung Army.[48] Nagata, Tatekawa, and Koiso knew about the plan, and because of this knowledge Tatekawa ordered Imamura to complete the fourth plan in August so that it could be discussed in time. At the Tokyo Trial, when Okawa and Ishihara testified that the Mukden Incident had been carried out as planned, he was merely referring to the plan made by the Kwantung Army and not the original plan of the Ministry of War at Tokyo.[49]

Besides drawing up the plan, the General Staff of the Kwantung Army paid special attention also to political agitation. Particularly the "League for Manchurian Youth" was chosen for this purpose. In March 1931, the League organized the "Society for Japanese Self-Determination in Manchuria" to advocate Manchurian and Mongolian independence. It published the following pamphlets: "The Truth of the Manchurian-Mongolian Problem," "Dance on the Top of a Volcano," and "The Three Questions Concerning Manchuria and Mongolia."[50] The League attacked the Tokyo Government for unrealistic policies concerning Manchuria and Mongolia, sponsored Fascist movement in the Railway Zone of Manchuria and sent "lobbyist" groups to Tokyo and other cities to make speeches and to present petitions. As a result, on July 16, 1931, the "Japan Productive Party" called a conference of the sponsors of the "League of Korean and Manchurian Nationals"; on July 17, 140 lieutenants who were members of the "Small Cherry Blossom Society" submitted a memorandum to Saionji. (The "Small Cherry Blossom Society" was organized by officers who were graduates of the 28th to 42nd classes of the Military Academy and whose attitude was even more radical than that of the members of the "Cherry Blossom Society"). On August 5, a

National Assembly sponsored by 71 civic organizations was convened at Hibiya Park; on September 7, the 16th Division of the Army stationed in Tokyo used Army aircraft to drop 100,000 propaganda leaflets at Fukui and Kanazawa and the surrounding areas.[51] Thus, the advocacy for solving the Manchurian-Mongolian problem by force gained momentum. Okawa Shumei was also effective in making speeches to advance the cause.

In the spring of 1930, Okawa tried to persuade Chang Hsueh-liang to agree to the establishment of an "Autonomous State of Manchuria."[52] In May, 1931, Okawa and Hashimoto formed a plan to get rid of Chang.[53] In July, 1931, with the financial support of the General Staff, he travelled from one prefecture to another to give speeches on the following topics: (1) the status of the Manchurian problem; (2) the present situation of China and Chang Hsueh-liang; (3) the American policy towards Manchuria and Mongolia; (4) what do we mean by the Manchurian-Mongolian problem; (5) Japan's position in East Asia, and (6) China's International Relations.

In all his speeches, Okawa drew the conclusion that Manchuria and Mongolia formed Japan's lifeline.[54] Altogether he made 135 speeches, and his audience numbered at least 100,000. Because of the tremendous force of his proselytizing, even the Imperial Court became concerned about his speeches. Thus, by June or July, 1931, it was common knowledge that the Kwantung Army would sooner or later create incidents in Manchuria. This has been borne out by the testimonies of Premier Okada[55] and Ishihara[56] in the Tokyo Trial, and the Diaries of Saionji[57] and Kido.[58]

By the latter part of July, 1931, preparations for the Mukden Incident had been completed, and Itagaki, under the pretext of attending a meeting of the "Double Leaf Society" in Tokyo, paid a secret visit on July 26 to Nagata and Okamura to seek their understanding. Nagata considered that the Kwantung Army's action should have the approval of the entire Army and the wholehearted support of the Government and the people. During their discussions, Nemoto Hiroshi requested Itagaki to postpone the action. Koiso also told Hanaya that before Japan was militarily prepared, she should not provoke interference from the Soviet Union.[59] Early in August Finance Minister Inoue submitted a budget which called for the revamping of the military establishment. As a result of consultations between the General Staff and the Ministry of War, it was decided to reduce Japan's wartime military forces from 32 divisions to 28 divisions. On August 4, Minami Jiro, the Minister of War, delivered a political speech before the conference of divisional commanders convened in Tokyo. In the speech he attacked the policy of retrenchment and encouraged the militarists to be prepared for any eventuality.[60] Representative Ozaki initiated an interpellation against Minami on the grounds that his speech had violated the military penal code,[61] but General Suzuki Soroku, President of the Veterans' Association, defended Minami's action.[62] At that time, the Tokyo Government was greatly disturbed by Captain Nakamura's alleged murder. Ishihara immediately took advantage of the situation to agitate for a military investigation by sending infantry and artillery to occupy Supinchieh, a strategic railway junction in Manchuria. The Ministry of War referred Ishihara's proposal to the Foreign Ministry for approval, but Minister Shidehara thought that Japan should not use the alleged Nakamura case as an instrument to solve the Manchurian-Mongolian problem by force.[63] Accordingly, he refused to endorse the plan, which was dropped. On the eve of the Mukden incident, Nakano, Kataoka, and other Japanese ronin in Manchuria had conceived the plan of creating an incident by destroying the Liaoyang Bridge at Mukden. This plot was to be directed by Lieutenant Wada Tsuyoshi, but it failed to materialize.[64] This proves that the young officers of the Kwantung Army spared no effort to create a crisis in Manchuria and that their plans were by no means limited to the Liutiaokou plot.

The plan for the Mukden Incident had obtained the understanding of Hayashi Senjuro, the Commander-in-Chief of the Japanese Army in Korea, and Kanda Masatane, his Chief of Staff. In April, 1931, Hayashi, Watanabe Jotaro, then Governor of Taiwan, and Hishikari Takashi, the Commander-in-Chief of the Kwantung Army, met in Tokyo where Hashimoto invited them to dinner. During the dinner, Hashimoto consulted their opinions on the Kwantung Army's plan for solving the Manchurian-Mongolian problem. Watanabe voiced his opposition, while Hishikari remained silent. Hayashi alone expressed his approval. A few days later, Hashimoto interviewed Kanda in another restaurant where, under the influence of wine and geisha girls, Kanda promised to send troops across the Korean border into Manchuria to help the Kwantung Army. After the Incident occurred, Kanda fulfilled his promise. The presence of these troops in Manchuria caused Hayashi to bear the nickname of the "trespassing general" and Itagaki was helped to realize his scheme in Manchuria.[65]

Among the young officers who voiced opposition to the Kwantung Army's plan for the Mukden Incident, Nagata Tetsuzan's attitude was most vigorous. In November, 1930, Nagata was sent to China on official business. On his way back to Japan, he passed through Manchuria and discussed with Ishihara policies for Manchuria and Mongolia to be carried out after the Manchurian-Mongolian problem had been solved by force. Three alternative measures were then suggested: (1) China should retain her jurisdiction in Manchuria though pro-Japanese Chinese should be placed in charge of the government; (2) creation of a pro-Japanese puppet regime by detaching Manchuria from China proper; (3) Japan should annex Manchuria and Mongolia. In regard to these measures, the conspirators were unable to arrive at an agreement even after a long night's heated debate.[66] However, during their discussion, Nagata acceded to Ishihara's request for the delivery of two 24 cm. caliber howitzers to Mukden for possible use.[67] These two howitzers were heavy artillery with a range of fifteen miles, and it was apparent that they were not intended for the use of a railway garrison. This proves that Nagata had intimate knowledge of the Kwantung Army's conspiracy before it was carried out. On September 10, 1931, the howitzers were secretly mounted at the fort of Hirata Yokiniro's cavalry battalion under the cover of well-digging.[68] Even Consul Morishima was unable to find out the truth.[69] During the incident in the evening of September 18, these two howitzers shelled the North Barracks and the airfield.[70] Afterwards, Itagaki bragged about this to Tanaka Ryukichi.[71] At the time when the howitzers were being installed, Honjo was already the commander-in-chief of the Kwantung Army. The testimony of Honjo's secretary at the Tokyo Trial that Honjo did not know anything about the plan for Liutiaokou plot was, therefore, absolutely untrue.

4. *The Conspiracy's Setback and Realization*

After the staff officers of the Kwantung Army had completed their third trip to Manchuria in July, 1931, it was decided to carry out the Mukden plan in the latter part of September. Imada, Hanaya, and others immediately started to canvass comrades and make preparations. It was then that Mitani Kiyoshi, an officer of the Japanese military police at Mukden, and Kawashima Tadashi, Ono Masao, and Kawakami Seiichi, all officers of the Railway Guards, were taken into confidence. They met secretly at Hanaya's Special Service Agency. After several meetings, a solemn pledge was made [72] under which they agreed to occupy the North Barracks, attack the Chinese airfield, blast the railway, and use as pretext provocative action by the Chinese Army. Imada was assigned to prepare the 42 TNT sticks; Kawamoto Suemori, being familiar with military engineering, to dynamite the railroad; Shimamoto to occupy the North Barracks; Kawakami to attack the airfield; and Hirata to occupy Mukden. They were also to take orders from Colonel Itagaki. Although the plot was supposed to be kept top secret, it leaked out during August and September.

The leak came from the Chinese intelligence staff in Dairen and from the intelligence report of the Japanese leased territory administrator. The former stated briefly that "Japan, taking advantage of the retaliation of Korean peasants in connection with the Wanpaoshan incident, would instigate military actions in Manchuria." [73] On the basis of this, the police bureau in Mukden issued a secret order on August 15 instructing its personnel to be on the alert and to exercise extreme patience and self-control.[74] The latter secretly informed the Japanese Foreign Ministry that the young officers of the Kwantung Army were forcing the Chinese Army to a clash of arms.[75] Based on this report, Foreign Minister Shidehara sent a telegram on September 5 instructing Consul General Hayashi to exercise stringent control over the Japanese ronin. The telegram reads as follows: "I have heard recently that Colonel Itagaki of the Kwantung Army had collected a considerable sum of money at Mukden to finance the ronin of the "National Patriotic Society" to create a Sino-Japanese incident. I also understand that concrete actions were to be carried out in the middle of September irrespective of the outcome of the investigation of Captain Nakamura's case. I earnestly hope that you will effectively check the activities of the ronin." [76]

Shidehara's telegram was the first setback to the Liutiaokou plot. At that time, Honjo paid his first official visit to Hayashi. The latter wanted to make use of this opportunity to discuss the current situation in Manchuria, but he was deterred by Ishihara.[77] In view of the Consul General's vigilance, Ishihara also once wanted to postpone the Liutiaokou plot.[78]

In the meantime, increasing pressure was brought to bear on the military by the Japanese Emperor, the elder statesmen, and the Cabinet. On September 9, Prince Kanin expressed his desire to tighten the discipline of the army. On September 11, during the military exercise at Kumamoto, the Emperor summoned War Minister Minami and told him to pay special attention to the discipline of the Kwantung Army.[79] After listening to His Majesty's order, Minami called on Prince Saionji. Saionji then reminded him that as Manchuria was Chinese territory, and as diplomacy was outside the sphere of the War Ministry, it was necessary for the Army to exercise prudence.[80] Minami listened to Saionji with deference and decided to send an emissary to Mukden to convey the Imperial order. In the Upper House of the Diet and among the military councillors, those who at first favored a tough policy towards Manchuria and Mongolia retracted their views in deference to the Imperial order. Thus, the Liutiaokou plot encountered its second setback.[81]

From September 10 to 14, the War Ministry received two different versions on the settlement of the Nakamura case. On September 10, Doihara returned to Tokyo where he reported that the attitude of Chang Hsueh-liang had not been softened. However, when Shibayama Kenshiro arrived in

Japan from Peiping a few days later he stated that Chang Hsueh-liang desired a quick and peaceful settlement of this case.[82] Actually, after the news of Nakamura's murder was revealed, the Headquarters of the commander-in-chief of the Northeastern Frontier Force made two prompt investigations into the matter. As a result of the September 9 report by Wu Ken-hsiang, head of the investigation team, a military-political conference was held in Peiping on September 10. After the conference, Counselor Yano of the Japanese Embassy at Peiping was informed that Chang Hsueh-liang desired a quick and peaceful settlement and would do everything within his power to facilitate that settlement. This was in keeping with Shibayama's report. In the meantime, Chang Hsueh-liang's advisor, Tang Ehr-ho and Consul General Hayashi were meeting in Mukden while T. V. Soong and Shigemitsu also held a conference in Shanghai to make a general review of the pending problems between Japan and China. Thus, there was some hope that Sino-Japanese relations would change for the better.

Nevertheless on September 14, the War Ministry suddenly received a secret telegram from Miyake, Chief of Staff of the Kwantung Army. The telegram stated, in part, "In view of the critical situation, it is desirable that the Kwantung Army should maintain closer contact with the Ministry of War. Please send either Koiso or Tatekawa to Mukden for guidance and consultations."[83] In the meantime, Tatekawa also received a telegram from Miyake complaining that Chang Hsueh-liang had become increasingly arrogant toward the Japanese Army and stating that it was almost impossible for the soldiers of the Kwantung Army to take the insult. He also asked Tatekawa to go to Mukden.[84] On the other hand, Foreign Minister Shidehara received a secret report from the consul general at Mukden that Captain Kawakami of Fushun had told the Reservists Association and the station master of the Railway there that he was ordered to attack the Chinese airfield on September 18[85] and it would be necessary to make preparations for local communications and security. Minami was questioned on this by Shidehara. Because of the Emperor's order and the pressure of his colleague, Minami decided to send Tatekawa as a special emissary to Mukden to convey the Imperial order.

He also asked Tatekawa to deliver a private letter to Honjo instructing him to pay special attention to the discipline of the Kwantung Army.[86] As Tatekawa and Itagaki had been classmates in the Military Academy and were senior in rank to Ishihara, the Japanese elder statesmen and the Ministry of War had every confidence that Tatekawa would be able to accomplish his mission without any difficulty.[87]

When the War Ministry decided to send Tatekawa to Mukden, a conference was held on September 14 among the chiefs of all the important sections. Hashimoto and Nagata participated.[88] After the conference, Hashimoto used the special code used between Tatekawa and Itagaki to send the latter three telegrams. The first stated that the plan had leaked; the second, that fortunately the special emissary to stop the plot was Tatekawa, and the third, that Hashimoto hoped that action would be taken before Tatekawa's arrival.[89]

Before leaving Tokyo, Tatekawa had consulted Okawa and said that he wished to see either Itagaki or Ishihara before visiting Honjo to convey the Imperial Order. Okawa then instructed his assistant, Nakajima Shinchi, to obtain a private plane to fly to Port Arthur via Dairen. Itagaki was asked to meet Tatekawa at Penchihu. On September 15, after everything had been arranged Tatekawa went incognito to Mukden by train.[90]

On the same day, after Itagaki had received Hashimoto's messages he invited Ishihara and several others to discuss the matter in a room of the Army Special Service Agency. When the telegrams were read, opinion was divided. Imada thought it would be too bad to cancel the plot; Hayana preferred postponement to await a better opportunity; Kawashima was noncommittal. Itagaki merely smiled when he was asked by Ishihara for his opinion. By two o'clock in the morning, they were still unable to make a decision. They therefore resorted to the fall of a pencil, much as Westerns would flip a coin to seek the answer. The answer was that it would be "more prudent to stop the plot." After the conference, Mitani, Imamura, Kawashima, and Ono appeared to be indignant, and expressed the hope that Itagaki would say something for the final decision.

On the morning of September 16, Mitani received a telephone call from Ishihara stating that the execution of the Liutiaokou plot depended entirely on whether or not the Railway Guards had the courage to carry it out. This was a hint that it had been decided to take action. Imada was overjoyed. He immediately reported the message to Kawashima in order to advance the date for the execution of the plot. Initially it was proposed to start action on September 17, but because there was insufficient time for preparation, they fixed on the eighteenth. The realization of the Mukden Incident was thus assured. They also discussed the possibility that the Chinese Army might not resist, but finally decided that irrespective of whether the Chinese Army offered resistance or not, the city of Mukden must be occupied. The troops under Hirata's command were assigned to occupy the city.[91]

The official telegram announcing Tatekawa's visit to Mukden was transmitted by Miyake on September 17 to Honjo, who was then inspecting troops in Liaoyang. On the same day, Nakajima Shinchi arrived secretly at Liaoyang to inform Itagaki of Tatekawa's desire to see him privately.[92] That evening, Itagaki and Ishihara held a meeting at the White Pagoda Hotel at Liaoyang. It was decided that Itagaki should go to meet Tatekawa and Ishihara to stay with Honjo to help him issue orders after the incident started.[93] Itagaki left Liaoyang for Mukden on the morning of September 18. After making the necessary arrangements for the incident scheduled for that evening, he went to Penchihu at 11:29 A.M. to meet Tatekawa.[94] Together Itagaki and Tatekawa took the 5:18 P.M. train to Mukden, arriving there at 7:05. Hanaya greeted them at the station and they all went to a Japanese hotel.[95] Morishima, the Japanese Consul at Mukden, received a report from the consular police informing him that Tatekawa had arrived at Mukden incognito. Morishima was very much surprised, being apprehensive lest an incident occur immediately. He went to confer with Consul General Hayashi, who wrote at once to Honjo urging him to watch out for any untoward actions by the Army. The letter was pocketed by Honjo's aide-de-camp, Katakura, and did not come to Honjo's attention until after the September 18 Incident.[96]

At ten P.M., Itagaki left Tatekawa and went to the Army Special Service Agency to direct the Liutiaokou plan. At his hotel, Tatekawa was cavorting with a geisha. When the guns boomed and fires broke out in Mukden, the geisha became panic-stricken. This then was the emissary charged with the task of conveying an Imperial order to stop the incident.[97] It was rumored that at that time Tatekawa was actually house-detained by the Kwantung Army. Whether there was any truth in this rumor, we may never know. Even if he had been detained, it was merely to exonerate him. From his testimony in the Tokyo trial, it is evident that from the very beginning Tatekawa did not intend to carry out his duty.[98]

At the time of Itagaki's arrival at the Agency, Hanaya, Shibayama, Yazaki, Suda, Wada and others were already there. Kawashima had led a special column of 105 soldiers to the south of Wen-kuan-tun; Kawamoto took Sergeant Matsuoka and seven or eight others to the railway tracks at Liutiaokou to prepare for the dynamiting. The designated time for the explosion was 10:30 P.M., it being intended to derail the 10:40 train from Changchun. This was meant to take advantage of the confusion to camouflage their part in the incident. After the tracks had been blasted the train managed to jump over the section without mishap. This was a surprise to the Japanese. The news was reported by Kawashima to Itagaki and Shimamoto. Nevertheless, the plot was executed as planned. Itagaki ordered the second independent corps to attack the North Barracks, and the 29th Infantry Regiment to attack the city of Mukden. Under the direction of the commander of the second corps, the independent fifth corps of the garrison forces went to attack the north of the North Barracks. Thus the Incident started.[99]

The distance between Mukden and Port Arthur is 250 miles. Among all the Japanese agencies in Mukden, only the Special Service Agency had a direct telegraph line to the headquarters of the Kwantung Army's commander-in-chief at Port Arthur. The news of the Mukden Incident did not reach Port Arthur until 11:40 P.M., an hour and 10 minutes after its occurrence. By that time the northeast salient of the North Barracks had fallen into Japanese hands and the city of Mukden was under the siege of the Japanese without any resistance. These facts show that the Mukden Incident was unleashed not only without the order of the Japanese General Staff at Tokyo but also that no orders had been issued by Honjo.[100] When the news of the Incident reached Katakura, he immediately reported it to Miyake, the Chief of Staff. Miyake called for a meeting of his staff officers at his residence. They decided unanimously to "penalize the brutal Chinese" and went en masse to the Commander-in-Chief's office to call on Honjo. Honjo received them at 12:20 A.M., September 19. Ishihara, in his capacity as the Chief of the Operations Section, appealed to Honjo for permission for the Japanese Army to resort to self-defense.[101] Honjo was silent, as he deliberated for a moment, before deciding to assume the responsibility himself.[102] He then assigned the Army division at Liaoyang to attack the suburbs of Mukden. Two independent garrison units were ordered to attack Liaoning; the 3rd column to halt any Chinese reinforcement from Yingkow; the 4th battalion of the independent brigade to attack Feng-huang-cheng; the 6th column, Anshan and the 3rd Cavalry Brigade, Changchun. He also ordered the artillery regiment at Port Arthur to proceed to Mukden. Simultaneously, he sent telegrams to Admiral Tsuda at Tsingtao and Commander-in-chief Hayashi Senjiro of the Japanese Army in Korea for assistance.[103] Actually at that time both the North Barracks and the city of Mukden had already fallen into Japanese hands. Fourteen years later, in consequence of this Incident, Honjo, Itagaki, Doihara, and others paid with their lives either by suicide or by execution.

Chapter 4

Tokyo's Reaction

When the Liutiaokou plot was launched the military leaders realized that the Kwantung Army, whose main force consisted of the Tamon Division, did not have sufficient strength to take over Manchuria. It was therefore necessary to have the collaboration of the Japanese Army in Korea. Reinforcements from there to Manchuria would have to cross the Yalu River in the south and/or the Tumen in the north. This would enable the Kwantung Army to attack Kirin, Harbin, and to occupy North Manchuria. The Army hoped that by such action it would be able to control Manchuria and Mongolia and stop Soviet Russia at the Hsing-an Mountains. Thus the ultimate goal of the Liutiaokou plot was to establish control of the area between the Yalu River and the Hsingan Mountains. In order that the creation of a Mukden incident might have some strategic value, the incident would have to be further expanded. This is why such expansion became an integral part of Itagaki's scheme to create disturbances in North Manchuria.

The War Ministry in Tokyo had a different view. Its experienced officers were well versed not only in military tactics but also in political strategy, although their respective appraisals of China's strength may not have been dissimilar. However, the War Ministry had greater misgivings as to the possible reactions of the Soviet Union, and of the Powers who supported the Covenant of the League of Nations, the Kellogg-Briand Pact and the Nine-Power Treaty of 1922. Consequently, a divergence developed between the War Ministry's caution and the Kwantung Army's rashness.

The Mukden Incident developed before the Kwantung Army and the War Ministry could reconcile their views. This situation led to criticisms of the War Minister and the Chief of the General Staff as being "incompetent" and to their making gestures of resigning. The Commander-in-Chief of the Kwantung Army also offered to resign on the ground that he had been unjustly accused of carrying out an independence movement. Although the Japanese forces from Korea had advanced into Kirin, the Kwantung Army's drive into Heilungkiang was called back. Concurrently, the planned October coup was abortive. Finally, an Imperial rescript stopped attacks against North Manchuria. Thus, during the life of the Wakatsuki Cabinet the ambitious designs of the Kwantung Army were frustrated.

I. *Unauthorized Dispatch of Troops from Korea*

Before dealing with the dispatch of troops from Korea into Kirin it is necessary to give an account of the chaos at the Japanese Consulate General at Mukden, in the evening of September 18, 1931. On that day a secret meeting was held to consider measures for resolving the Nakamura case. The meeting lasted until 8:00 P.M. Consul Morishima tried unsuccessfully to relay the information to Hanaya. At 10:30 gun shots were heard. Morishima had learned from Chao Hsin-po, an influential advisor of Chang Hsueh-liang, that the Chinese Army would not resist. At 10:45 he hastened to see Itagaki to ask that the attack be called off. Itagaki declined, insisting that the Army had made its own decision. When Morishima was about to repeat his request, Hanaya rose in anger, threatened Morishima with a dagger and told him to stop interfering.[1] Morishima then went to inform Consul General Hayashi of what had happened. Hayashi immediately telephoned Itagaki and advised him to stop the attack, but Itagaki refused. Hayashi then sent three telegrams in succession to Shidehara. The messages, in translation, read as follows:

First telegram: "Since the Chinese government has repeatedly expressed a desire for peaceful negotiations I immediately telephoned Itagaki that as China and Japan are not in a state of war and as they have adopted an non-resistance policy, he should stop the attack to avoid further damage. Itagaki has replied that because the prestige of the Imperial Army is involved it has decided to deal with the problem by force. Please note that my representation was wholly rejected."[2]

Second telegram: "Judging from the concurrent total mobilization of the Railway Guards the creation of the incident must have been premeditated by the Army. I have already asked the President of the South Manchuria Railway Company to request Commander-in-Chief Honjo to stop it. I hope our government can stop the Army." [3]

Third telegram: "The Army's arbitrary attitude and peremptory action have deprived me of any power of effective action." [4]

It is worth noting that in none of these telegrams was there any suggestion of provocation by the Chinese. Although the Kwantung Army tried to be very secretive about the conspiracy, it had become an open secret in Japanese diplomatic circles. The same is true of Shigemitsu's secret telegram to Shidehara.[5] The American Embassy in China also was well informed on this matter.[6]

Late in the evening of September 18, the War Ministry in Tokyo received three telegraphic reports from the Kwantung Army on the Mukden Incident, all sent under the name of Doihara's Special Service Agency, as Doihara was at that time en route from Tokyo to Mukden. Therefore, the messages were actually sent by Hanaya.

The first message from Mukden despatched at 11:18 P.M. reached Tokyo at 1:00 A.M. on the 19th. It stated: "At 10:30 tonight the Chinese Army west of the North Barracks blasted the South Manchuria Railway line and attacked our Railway Guards, forcing a clash with our units. The second corps of our patrol units is now heading for the scene."

The second telegram, dated Mukden, September 19, 1:10 A.M. was received in Tokyo at 2:00 A.M. In translation, this message read: "The strength of the Chinese troops of the North Barracks which dynamited the Manchuria Railway is about three or four companies. They gradually fled into their barracks. At 11 o'clock, a company of our troops was fighting with some 500 to 600 Chinese troops. We have now seized a corner of the North Barracks where the enemy artillery and infantry are now being reinforced. In the combat our Lieutenant Noda was seriously wounded."

The third telegram reached Tokyo an hour later. It reported: "Itagaki has ordered the second railway patrol unit to wipe out the North Barracks, the 29th Infantry Battalion to attack Mukden, and the 5th Railway Patrol Unit to attack the area north of the North Barracks. We have asked for reinforcements for the Second Division."

It is now clear from these allegations, that the Chinese had started the incident, were engaged in fighting, and that Noda was seriously wounded, were fabrications. These allegations, however, prompted the responsible officers of the General Staff and the War Ministry to declare at their joint meeting that "the action of the Kwantung Army was appropriate and should be supported." [7]

At 10 A.M. on the 19th Premier Wakatsuki called an emergency cabinet meeting where War Minister Minami reported the views of the staff officers at the earlier joint meeting mentioned above. Foreign Minister Shidehara then recited the various intelligence reports received by the ministry,[8] namely that (1) Captain Kawakami of Fushun possessed a secret communique that an incident would be staged on the 18th; (2) a report that the Chinese Army had not offered any resistance; (3) a report that Hanaya had intimidated Morishima with a dagger and refused to agree to a truce; (4) Consul General Hayashi had appealed in vain for a cease fire; (5) the reports made by Kimura, a Director of the South Manchuria Railway Company, Goto of the Fushun Coal & Mining Company, Tsukamoto, Director of the Kwantung Affairs Bureau, and Nakaya, Chief of the Police Force, had all testified that the Japanese Army had not been motivated by considerations of self-defense. This produced a turn unfavorable to the Kwantung Army. Thus Minami no longer had the courage to urge reinforcements for the Kwantung Army.[9] Accordingly, the Cabinet decided that: (1) the incident must not be expanded; (2) the Ministry of Colonial Affairs, the Kwantung Affairs Bureau should wash their hands of the affair; (3) the Consulate General was to supervise and report on the actions of the Kwantung Army; (4) the commanders of the Tamon Division and the Amano Brigade at Liaoyang and the patrol troops should deploy their forces in the vicinity of Mukden;

and, (5) the Changchun Brigade should assume a defensive posture in its garrisoning.[10]

After the Cabinet meeting, Wakatsuki reported to the Emperor the decisions reached. War Minister Minami telegraphed Honjo the decisions reached and added two instructions to his message: (1) no attempt should be made to occupy Manchuria and (2) no military government or similar organ was to be set up. Such was the first reaction of Tokyo to the Mukden Incident.

In addition to dealing with the Kwantung Army, the Tokyo government was faced with another equally serious matter: namely, how to deal with the unauthorized action of the Japanese Army in Korea. Commander-in-Chief Hayashi, of that unit, and his chief of staff, Kanda, had reached a clear understanding with the staff officers of the Kwantung Army and had promised to help. They had also made secret plans for attacks on Chientao and Hunchun. Immediately after the Mukden Incident, Hayashi sent two squadrons of his Air Force to Mukden to be placed at Honjo's disposal and ordered one mixed brigade of his 20th Division to cross the Yalu in the south and a section of the 19th Division to advance from the Tumen in the north for concerted action. At 10 A.M. on the 19th the War Ministry at Tokyo received two secret telegrams from Hayashi reporting these troop movements.[11] In the first, he reported that, in view of the situation at Mukden, he had sent two air squadrons to help the Kwantung Army and that one mixed Army brigade was being held in readiness to proceed there. In the second, he reported that the situations at Chientao and Hunchun were critical and that, in order to coordinate with the Kwantung Army and to prepare the ground for future occupation, it would be necessary to send one mixed brigade there. Chientao, in East Manchuria, borders on the Soviet Maritime Province on the east and is bounded on the south by the Tumen River. The Chientao district was the cradle of Korean independence movements and a scene of power plays between Japan and Russia. To send troops into that area was therefore a direct challenge to the Soviet Union. Hayashi's unauthorized action caused great concern to the General Staff and the War Minister and was interpreted as an usurpation of the prerogatives of the Throne. At first, the

General Staff thought that Hayashi was merely preparing for possible military action in the Yalu River area. While the matter was being discussed, Hayashi's third telegram arrived. He reported that he had already ordered the brigade to cross the Yalu and that this unit, together with the two air squadrons, would be placed under the command of the Kwantung Army.[12] Because of this development, the General Staff and the War Ministry promptly decided:

1. To telegraph instructions to Hayashi to await an Imperial order before sending any aid to the Kwantung Army;
2. To telegraph Brigadier Yoshimura directly not to cross the border;
3. To instruct the Patrol Unit to watch the movements of the Yoshimura Brigade and stop it from crossing the Yalu River.[13]

The three telegrams were sent at 12:30 P.M. on September 19 and at 3:50 P.M., Hayashi's reply reached Tokyo. He still pleaded for aid to the Kwantung Army and reported that the troops would cross the Yalu about midnight the same day.[14] It was then that Chief of Staff Kanaya again telegraphed Hayashi that the situation at Mukden had improved, that it had been decided not to expand the incident and that the troops in Korea must await an Imperial Order before crossing the border.[15] Hayashi made no reply. On the following two days Kanaya and Minami tried their best to obtain an Imperial Order for Hayashi in order to legalize his action.[16] At 3 P.M. on the 21st, a telegram from Yoshimura reported that the vanguards of his brigade had crossed the Yalu at 1 P.M. and that at 5 P.M. his troops would be under the command of the Kwantung Army.[17] A telegram was received also from Hayashi that he was worried not to have received the Imperial Order authorizing the dispatch of troops beyond the Korean border and that it was beyond his power to stop the military movements.[18] After World War II, Imamura, who was then Chief of Operations in the General Staff, wrote that at the time it was not Hayashi but Kanda Masatane, his Chief of Staff, who had ordered the troops to cross the Yalu.[19] Thus, what Kanda did to Hayashi was exactly what Itagaki had done to Honjo and what Tatekawa had done to the General Staff. It seems that the insubordination of the young officers was by then already deepseated and that the Wakatsuki Cabinet was unable to control it. But the control over the troop movements into Tumen, Chientao and Hunchun was much more firm and therefore effective. When the Yoshimura Brigade was crossing the Yalu border, the General Staff also had the report that the 19th Brigade, too, was preparing to cross the Tumen. The General Staff at once ordered the movement stopped. On the following day, the Chief of Staff of the Japanese Army in Korea forwarded petitions by Japanese and Korean residents in Chientao and Hunchun requesting the dispatch of troops. The petitions were referred to Premier Wakatsuki, who decided that no troops should be sent, even if he had to withdraw the Japanese and Koreans from that area. On the 23rd and 24th, Hayashi persisted in calling for troops. By that time, international pressure was mounting. Wakatsuki had received the Emperor's authorization to withdraw the residents. Accordingly, the General Staff was able to tell the Japanese Army in Korea that the Emperor would not sanction the dispatch of troops in Chientao.[20]

In dealing with the Kwantung Army, there had never been agreement between the General Staff and the War Ministry. The latter seemed to be more sympathetic with the Foreign Ministry and the General Staff with the Kwantung Army. At a conference between the General Staff and the War Ministry on September 19, the General Staff, though it did not oppose localizing the incident, refused to order a halting of the Kwantung Army's advance.[21] After the conference, Hashimoto, Nemoto, Muto, and others expressed the opinion that the incident had reached a point where the field commander should be entrusted to use his own discretion in deploying his troops and not await Cabinet authorization. Kanaya evidently had been influenced by that opinion. Consequently, the phrasing of the General Staff's telegrams to the Kwantung Army was more flexible than those of the War Ministry.[22]

In the late afternoon of the 19th, Honjo got around to sending two telegrams to the Army Headquarters in Tokyo. In the first, he reported the disarming of Chinese troops at Yingkou and Feng-huang-cheng. He pointed out that here was the best opportunity to maintain security throughout Manchuria, and he asked for a reinforcement of three divisions to complete the task.

He said that the funds required for the task could be raised locally. In the second, he urged the Central Army Headquarters not to adopt a policy of retreat, as it would postpone indefinitely the solution of the Manchurian-Mongolian problem.[23] The General Staff and the War Ministry apparently did not approve of that plan. They replied that "in local administration, nothing should be done beyond maintaining order." [24] On that night, before the replies from Tokyo reached Manchuria, Itagaki and Ishihara had consulted Tatekawa on how best to wind up the affair. At first they were dismayed by Tatekawa's insistence not to set up a pro-Japanese regime and by his opposition to the use of force in North Manchuria. However, after a long debate, Tatekawa suddenly softened. He agreed not only to use force in Kirin and Harbin, but to create a puppet regime with Henry Pu-yi at its head.[25] In reviewing this history, we are convinced that the lengthy talks of Tategawa, Itagaki, and Ishihara at Mukden on the night of September 19 were really the crucial point of the incident. The discussion ended in the victory of those who favored the subjugation of all Manchuria over those who advocated localizing the incident. This led at a later date to the creation of "Manchukuo."

After the Kwantung Army's plan of dispatching troops to Kirin and Harbin had been approved by Tategawa, Itagaki and Ishihara, they sought to persuade the Chiefs of Special Intelligence Agency in Kirin and Harbin to draw up petitions for Army protection in the name of the Japanese residents there. This would persuade Honjo to join their cause. In the meantime, disturbances were created to justify the petition. On September 20, Osako Michisada (Kirin Chief) presented the petition from Kirin to Honjo through Ishihara, Itagaki, and Miyake. Honjo rejected the petition on the ground that Ishide, the Consul General at Kirin, had not asked for help. The staff of the Kwantung Army then pleaded with him for the safety of the 900 Japanese residents in Kirin, but Honjo still refused to send troops. Katakura, Honjo's aide, then asked the staff to leave but kept Itagaki for further discussion. At 3 A.M., September 21, after he had learned that the Japanese Army in Korea would come to his aid, Honjo finally agreed to dispatch troops to Kirin. The Tamon Division took Kirin on September 22.[26] The decision to send troops there was a crucial one, the making of which involved much greater responsibility than the Mukden Incident. Since Liutiaokou was within the defense perimeter of the Kwantung Army, Honjo could always justify his decision to send troops there on the ground of "military necessity." However, Kirin was outside the area of the Kwantung Army and it had no right to go there without Imperial order. Besides, the Japanese Cabinet had already instructed the Kwantung Army not to aggravate the situation and both the General Staff and the War Ministry had advised the Kwantung Army also to use its troops only in the line of duty.

In Harbin, through the machinations of such Japanese militarists as Momotake Harukichi, Amakasu Masahiko, Yoshimura Sokichi, and others, incidents were created by throwing bombs at the Japanese Consulate, the Bank of Chosen, and other public places. On the ground of these incidents, they requested Ohashi (Chuichi), the Consul General at Harbin, to seek help from Honjo. Ohashi, who had had close associations with these militarists, complied immediately. On September 22, Honjo issued the order to send troops to Harbin.[27] But on the same day, Ando Rikichi, chief of the Section of the War Ministry, arrived at Mukden with Minister Minami's "3-no order" for Honjo. The "3-no order" read as follows:

1. The troops proceeding northward should not pursue north of Kuan-cheng-tzu.
2. The Army must not interfere with the operation of railways other than the South Manchuria Railway.
3. Unless authorized by the General Staff, new military action must not be taken.[28]

Even after Ando had arrived at Mukden with Minami's order, Ishihara and others still tried to disobey by invoking their own authority. On that very day, China's accusation of Japan had been placed on the agenda of the League of Nations. Also, Yoshizawa, Japan's delegate to the League had announced, at the League's Council that the Japanese troops were being withdrawn into the railroad zone in Manchuria.[29] United States Secretary of State Stimson had sent an aide memoire to the Japanese ambassador in Washington, that the "September 18 incident involves more than Sino-Japanese relations." [30] The president of the League Council had appealed to both China and Japan to "refrain from any new provocative actions." [31] In the meantime, the Soviet Union had asked Hirota (Koki), then Japanese ambassador to Moscow, for an explanation of the occupation of Kuan-cheng-tzu by Japanese troops.[32] Under such overwhelming international pressure, Japan was forced to restrain the actions of her militarists. On September 23, 1931, the General Staff issued a stringent order forbidding the Kwantung Army to advance north of Taonan.[33] On September 24, the Cabinet formally decided that the Kwantung Army should withdraw from outside areas into the South Manchuria Railway zone.[34] As a result of Ninomiya's persuasiveness and under the supervision of Major General Hashimoto Toranosuke,[35] the Kwantung Army reluctantly stopped its advance to Harbin and began to change its tactics, bribing various Chinese troops, to prepare for another showdown with the Tokyo Government.

2. *Planned October Incident*

It now becomes clear that the so-called "October Incident," planned by the Japanese young officers' Group, was merely a part of both the March incident and the Mukden Incident. The inter-relationships of these two incidents were long kept in the files of the Tokyo Police Bureau.[36] The following from the Police Bureau may serve to support this explanation.

1. According to Harada's diary: "A few days after the Mukden Incident, Itagaki and Ishihara declared at Mukden that they would return to Japan to stage a revolution. They have stated: 'We have already achieved our first step. Our second step is to return to Japan to stage a coup so as to abolish the parliamentary system, and to set up a socialist government'." [37]

2. Okawa testified at the Tokyo Court of Appeals: "The October incident was to be a sequence to the Mukden Incident. After the Mukden Incident, Shidehara and the War Ministry were found to be undecided. After two days of debate, they had still failed to reach an agreement on Honjo's action. Such procrastination was bound to nullify the efforts of the Kwantung Army . . . I was under Hashimoto's order to stage the incident. My duty was to hoist the flag of the revolutionary headquarters

on the roof of the General Staff's Bureau of Survey. It was a highly confidential plan known to only five persons: Hashimoto, Shigeta, Itagaki, Doihara and myself."[38]

The planned October incident was known in Japan as the Silk-banner Revolution. Its purpose was to enable General Araki to become the Premier of Japan. This incident was not unlike the March incident which supported War Minister Ugaki for the premiership, though it was made more important both in its complexity and its revolutionary tactics. The conspirators in the March incident, with the exception of Okawa and his friends, were all members of the "Cherry Blossom Society." Membership in that society was restricted to junior officers. Consequently, the sentiment for revolutionary conspiracy was not too prevalent in the Japanese Army. Although the October plot also was unleashed by such members of the "Cherry Blossom Society" as Hashimoto, Cho Isamu, and others, it was participated in by members of the Navy, Air Force, as well as the Army. Most of the participants were below the rank of Colonel, and these young officers were more radical in their thinking. Consequently, their revolutionary approach was more intense than the one adopted in the March incident. It is important to note that no member of the Imperial family participated in the March incident, but during the October one, the palace guards were involved and Prince Chichibu, the younger brother of Emperor Hirohito, also was implicated.[39] After the discovery of the October plot, the list of conspirators was burned by order of General Minami.[40] Although Japanese historians were reluctant to mention Chichibu's role in the incident; nevertheless, we are still able to learn something about it from available sources.

Beginning in the 1920's there was a steady boom in Japan's urban economy, but her rural economy declined. As a result of two successive retrenchments in military expenditures during the Taisho and early Showa periods, the social status of the military also deteriorated. Young officers who had come mostly from rural areas were very unhappy over the situation. At that time, there was much corruption in the political parties, graft and bribery were rampant. The Fascist movement was also on the rise. Kita's plan for the reform of Japan,[41] Gondo's project on rural self-government,[42] which is Okawa's Great Nippon doctrine,[43] and the doctrine of Tachibana and Inouye for I-chi-nin (one person to kill one person)[44] had all been most disturbing to the young officers. Kita's plan was especially popular among the young officers. Kita's original name was Kita Terujiro. During the Chinese Revolution of 1911, he travelled frequently between Hankow and Shanghai on errands for the Kokuryukai (Black Dragon Society) and thus he made the acquaintances of Huang Hsing and Dr. Sun Yat-sen. He wrote a book on the Chinese revolution and declared his conviction that the success of the 1911 Chinese revolution was due to the conspiratorial activities of the officers of the new army. He wanted the Japanese Army to rise in revolt against Japan's maladministration. Being steeped in socialistic thinking, his plan for reform in Japan was also highly socialistic.[45] Thus, although his recommendation was different from that of Hashimoto or Okawa, nevertheless, his advocacy of war with a redistribution of world resources, Japanese expansion in Siberia, Manchuria and Mongolia, Japanese hegemony over China, India, the Philippines and Australia, and a banishing of Anglo-American influences from the Pacific was not unlike that of Hashimoto or Okawa. His tactic of using the reserve soldiers' association as an organ to investigate, assess, and redistribute wealth was especially popular with the young servicemen.[46]

Long before the establishment of the "Cherry Blossom Society," Nishida Zei had already organized the "Heavenly Sword Society" to advocate military revolt.[47] As long as the purpose of revolution was for governmental reform, measures no matter how brutal even to the extent of assassination, would be considered justified. Nishida was a graduate of the Military Preparatory School and had served for a while in the cavalry regiment in Korea. He had been discharged because of illness and had joined the Reserves. Although he had little personal prestige, he was respected by his colleagues because of his friendship with Prince Chichibu.[48] Besides Nishida, Fujii Hitoshi of the Navy had organized the "Imperial Commander's Society," [49] the aim of which was to have the Navy take the responsibility for national reform. Inouye, a graduate of Maebashi High School, was an intelligence clerk in the General Staff, and also had served under Sakanishi Rihachiro, who had been Yuan Shih-kai's adviser in

1913. Returning to Japan, he pretended at a Buddhist temple to embrace the White Lotus sect, though he was actually interested in resorting to assassination to reform National politics. In 1931, a secret council took place at the Aoyama Youth Club, Tokyo, to plan for the October incident. It was participated in by the followers of Okawa, Kita and Nishida. Fujii brought the different factions together.[50] Among the participants at the Youth Club were seven lieutenants from the Army, six from the Navy, and a dozen or more civilians including Inouye, Nishida and Tachibana.

Inouye presided at the Council. While representatives from the Navy demanded immediate action, the Army faction was more moderate. While no decision was reached on the date for the incident, they nevertheless agreed on the list of persons to be assassinated, which comprised a dozen persons, the most prominent being Prince Saionji, Baron Makino and Premier Wakatsuki.

In his plan for revolution, Kita suggested it should entail as little violence as possible, but advocates of assassination dominated the young officers and civilians. As a result, friction arose, causing the subsequent exposure of the plan.

The plan for the October incident was first found in Tanaka Hiyoshi's diary. He wrote that after the Mukden Incident he called on Hashimoto to find out the details. Hashimoto, however, declined to reveal the truth. It was not until October 3 that he was invited to the restaurant for a meeting which was also attended by Cho Isamu and Tanaka. In September 1931, Cho was sent to the Japanese Embassy at Peiping where he served under the military attaché. He was therefore most eager to return to Tokyo to participate in the October incident. Tanaka Hiyoshi had thought that in the October plot there was only destruction but no construction and suspected that some persons were merely making use of the plan to establish socialism. Accordingly, he had a heated debate with Hashimoto.[51] The proposed plan embraced the following items: (1) date—October 24; (2) participating strength—120 officers who were key members of the "Cherry Blossom Society," ten infantry companies and two machine-gun companies of the garrison division, thirteen bombers and four reconnaissance planes of the air force, ten specially trained hand-to-hand combatants, and one regiment comprised of the followers of Kita and Nishida; (3) targets of attack—Major Cho Isamu was assigned to direct an attack on the Premier's residence to assassinate all the Cabinet Ministers in attendance and Lieutenant Ohara to direct the occupation of the Police Bureau, and a siege of the Ministry of War and the General Staff, in order to force their superiors to endorse the revolution. All those who opposed the revolution were to be arrested; (4) political action—Admiral Togo to be asked to report to the Emperor so that revolutionary generals might be invited to form the Cabinet as follows: Premier, Araki Chiaki; Minister of Interior, Hashimoto Kingoro; Minister of Finance, Okawa Shumei; Minister of Foreign Affairs; Tatekawa Yoshitsugu; (5) funds for the revolution—200,000 yen (author's note: a knowledge of the source of the funds is unavailable.)[52]

The leaders of the so-called Silk-banner Revolution were members of the "Cherry Blossom Society." Okawa and certain civilian leaders were merely accomplices. There are still differences regarding the date for the incident. Tanaka Hiyoshi said that it was set for October 21. According to Inouye, it was October 23, but according to Ito Masanori's book, *The History of the Rise and Fall of Militarism,* it was October 24. At the Tokyo War Crimes trial, Okawa testified that it was either October 22 or October 23. According to the records of the Labor Mass Party, the date was to be October 17, October 26, or November 3.[53] No great importance, probably, should be attached to the exact date for the incident. It is interesting that there was then a rumor of the possible overthrow of Emperor Hirohito. According to Nishida, most of the low-ranking officers were inclined toward Prince Chichibu as Hirohito's successor, while Hashimoto and his followers preferred Prince Higashikuni. Since Hirohito had no male heir, it would be proper for Chichibu to be the heir in accordance with the law of Japanese imperial succession.[54] During the October 15 conference, Hashimoto and Inouye suggested that the Palace guards should hold Emperor Hirohito at gun point.[55] Then Lieutenant Ida was to read a plea before the Emperor and to commit hara kiri on the spot.[56] Although there was no mention of this in the works of Japanese scholars, in both Harada's papers and Kido's diary it was stated that the Imperial throne seemed to be in trouble. Harada wrote that Prince Saionji had told him: "From the study of past history, I have learned that prior to the downfall of a dynasty, there would be usually some signs of revolution. The present situation seems to presage this. Some veterans have recently said that the Palace guards have seen that the Emperor's quarters were lighted deep into the night. Their first impression was that His Majesty was working very hard, but later they found out that the lights were on because the Emperor and Empress were playing Mahjong . . . In Japanese history, there is no lack of precedents for a younger brother murdering his elder brother, and this is most disturbing." [57]

In his diary, Kido recorded that since the Army had insisted upon perpetrating the Mukden Incident, it might have been difficult to carry out the orders of the central government. Although the policy of localizing the Incident had been approved by the Emperor, the militarists attributed this to the bad advice of his entourage. For this reason, members of the Upper House of the Diet suggested that the Emperor refrain from expressing his views.[58] Moreover, if the wish of the military is not observed, the Emperor's entourage might be imperiled and be replaced by more radical elements. This would increase the pressure on the Emperor.[59]

It seems that the anxiety of Saionji and Kido over the security of the Imperial throne was perhaps not unfounded. On October 18, the day after the blocking of the October plot, Commander Toyama of the gendarmerie, in the course of his interrogation of the plotters, learned that the Kwantung Army had intended to form an independent state in Manchuria and Inner Mongolia.[60] He immediately reported what he had heard to the Minister of War and the Chief of the General Staff, who were shocked and relayed the information to the Minister of the Imperial Household. The Emperor's military aide Kawagishi was hurriedly dispatched to Mukden with an Imperial message to soften the Commander and the Staff of the Kwantung Army. Concurrently General Shirakawa and Colonel Imamura were sent on an investigation tour.[61] At one juncture Honjo felt so frustrated that he wanted to resign. Later, he discovered that the rumor of secession had been spread by Cho Isamu alone.[62] This was an indication that after the Mukden Incident the Tokyo government had lost the courage to curb the ambitions of the Kwantung Army!

There are various versions of how the planned October incident was betrayed. According to Imamura, Tanaka Hiyoshi and Ikeda Samihisa were responsible for the exposure. The following two passages are taken from his Memoir, *The Imperial House and the Officers*: (Imamura Memoir No. II)

> "One night in early October, around 8 o'clock, Lieutenants Tanaka Hiyoshi and Ikeda came to visit me at my home. Ikeda has been an old subordinate of mine, but it was the first time that I met Tanaka. They told me about Hashimoto's plan for the coup and how they opposed it. They asked that the General Staff devise a way to handle the matter. After they left, I immediately went to see Major General Tatekawa and told him what I had heard. Tatekawa promised to question Hashimoto about the matter on the next day. Then at the office of the General Staff, I saw Hashimoto enter Tatekawa's room where they had a long talk. After Hashimoto left, Tatekawa summoned me to his room and told me that Hashimoto had cancelled his plan because it had not been adopted by the 'Cherry Blossom Society'.
>
> "On October 16, at 4 P.M., Majors Nemoto, Sato, and Kagesa came to visit me. They said that what Hashimoto had told Tatekawa about the change of the plan was untrue and that the coup would be carried out at 4 o'clock early the next morning. They also said that at this very moment, the conspirators were holding a meeting at the Golden Dragon Restaurant and that it would be advisable to send gendarmes there to arrest them. I consulted Negata and we decided to discuss the matter at a joint meeting of the General Staff and the Ministry of War. The meetings was held at 5:30 that afternoon in the reception room of the Minister of War. It was attended by Sugiyama, Koiso, Nakamura, Nagata, Okamura, Ninomiya, Tatekawa, Umezu, Tojo, Araki, Toyama, and myself. I reported to them what Nemoto, Sato, and Kagesa had told me. With the exception of Araki, they all agreed that it would be

advisable to send gendarmes to arrest Hashimoto and his collaborators. Because of Araki's dissent, it was decided that instead of making the arrest, Araki should dissuade Hashimoto from staging the coup. After obtaining the address of the Golden Dragon Restaurant from Nemoto, Araki left to see Hashimoto while we waited at the office of the General Staff for his return. By 8 o'clock P.M., Araki still had not returned. But while we were debating whether we should send Okamura also, Araki was back at 11 P.M. and reported that although Hashimoto had refused to cancel his plan for the coup, he had agreed to postpone it for four days. Sugiyama and others suggested that since there was little difference between arresting them on that day and four days later, it seemed advisable to make the arrest right away. Because Araki still dissented, it was decided that Sugiyama, Ninomiya and Araki should call on War Minister Minami to seek his decision. After they had left, a guard of the General Staff told me that someone had asked to see me and had left his card as well as a message. The card indicated that the caller was a Yokohama merchant whom I had never met before. The message said: 'Do not believe that Hashimoto has postponed the coup for four days. A crisis will occur at 4 A.M.' Because of this warning, we all decided to call together on Minami. After listening to our report, Minami ordered Sugiyama to instruct Toyama, the gendarmes commander, to arrest Hashimoto and his eleven collaborators. The arrest was made at 1 A.M., October 17, three hours before the time set for the coup." [63]

For their attempt to stage a revolution, Hashimoto and his collaborators were sentenced by the Military Court to twenty days detention. Chief of General Staff Kanaya at first wanted to impose the death sentence on Cho for his desertion of duty to attempt a coup, but later changed the sentence to ten days confinement. In his report to the Lord Privy Seal on the October plot, Minami emphasized the point that "the motivation for the coup was good, though the act was reprehensible." [64]

As a result of this episode, the young officers of junior rank became bolder. It was because of this that the May 15 coup of 1932 and the February 26 incident of 1936 eventuated later. And, because of his defense of and support for the conspirators of the October incident, Araki became the hero and leader of the young officers. He succeeded Minami as Minister of War. By then the Mukden crisis had become intensified.

3. *Maneuvres in Heilungkiang and Chinchow*

It may be recalled that between October and November 1931, the movements of the Kwantung Army seemed to be constantly fluctuating. In North Manchuria, the Kwantung army first collaborated with Chang Hai-peng against Ma Chan-shan, but then it made peace with Ma Chan-shan and began to secure Chang Ching-hui's service. In South Manchuria, although at first the Kwantung Army had bombed Chinchow, attacked Ta-ling-ho, and brought pressure on Ta-hu-shan, it then suddenly withdrew to the east of the Liao River, and some regiments even returned to Liaoning and Mukden. There was the impression then that the Kwantung Army was either adhering to the Tokyo Government's policy of localizing the Mukden Incident or paying due respect to the League of Nations' request for "not aggravating the situation." Now we learn from historical facts that these reversals were the results of a bitter struggle for power between the Tokyo military authorities and the Kwantung Army. During the struggle, both the Kwantung Army's staff officers and the Japanese envoys to four European countries had threatened to resign en bloc. The following is an analysis of the struggle:

(a.) *In Heilungkiang*

After the Kwantung Army had reluctantly cancelled its plan to send troops to Harbin, its new policy in North Manchuria was to win over some of the Chinese troops by bribery. The fund appropriation for this was about three million dollars. The existence of this scheme has been confirmed by confidential telegrams exchanged between the Kwantung Army and Minister Minami.[65] This new policy of bribery was first suggested during a secret meeting at Mukden on September 22 at 8 A.M.

attended by Miyake, Itagaki, Ishihara, Doihara, and Katakura.[66] At the meeting, Doihara advanced the plan for a Manchuria-Mongolian Republic under Japanese auspices. Henry Pu-Yi was to be made the Chief of State, and there would be five pacification commissioners, with Hsi Ch'ia at Kirin, Chang Hai-peng at Tao-so, Tang Yu-lin at Jehol, Yu Chih-shan at Tung-pien-tao, and Chang Ching-hui at Harbin.[67]

After Doihara's suggestion was approved by his colleagues, on the day following the meeting, Imada Shintaro and Kono Masanao were sent to make contact with Chang Hai-peng through Yoshimura Sokichi. They persuaded Chang to desert Chang Hsueh-liang and himself to take over the control of Heilungkiang. For this he was offered 3,000 guns and 200,000 silver dollars as well as the secret support of the Kwantung Army. On October 1, Chang Hai-peng proclaimed himself Frontier Defense Commander and led his troops toward Heilungkiang. In the meantime Ma Chan-shan, then Garrison Commander at Heibo, had been appointed by Chang Hsueh-liang and Wan Fu-lin as acting Chairman of Heilungkiang. When Ma learned that Chang Hai-peng had revolted against Chang Hsueh-liang, he ordered the destruction of the Nonni Bridge on October 7 in order to halt the latter's advance.[66] This bridge had formerly been known as the Taonan-Angangchi Railroad Bridge and was built by China with a Japanese loan. Because the loan repayments were still outstanding, the Kwantung Army, on the pretext of repairing the bridge sent troops to capture Heilungkiang.[67] On October 26, Major Hayashi, chief of Special Service Agency at Heilungkiang, demanded that the bridge be repaired within a week. This demand was later repeated by Consul Shimizu in the name of the Japanese Government. On October 29, Chinese and Japanese troops clashed in the vicinity of Ta-hsing.[68] Thus, on November 5, the Kwantung Army made the following harsh demands: (1) removal of Ma Chan-shan; (2) withdrawal of the Chinese forces from Heilungkiang; (3) transfer of administrative power of Heilungkiang to Chang Hai-peng; and (4) occupation of Lung-kou station by the Japanese Army.[69] The reason why the Kwantung Army dared to make such insolent demands was that it had been secretly informed by Consul General Ohashi of Harbin that the Soviet Union would not intervene.[70] However, the Japanese General Staff at Tokyo did not agree at all with this assessment. As soon as it learned about the Kwantung Army's designs on Heilungkiang, the General Staff telegraphed Honjo to admonish him. The first telegram was sent on October 13.[71] and the second one on November 2.[72] The Kwantung Army, undeterred by these admonitions, went ahead with its preparation. It was because of this circumstance that Kanaya, Chief of the General Staff, began to make use of the "Provisional Imperial Mandate" granted by Emperor Hirohito. From then on, the Chief of the General Staff was to exercise direct command over the Kwantung Army.

The "Provisional Imperial Mandate" of the Chief of General Staff was granted first by Emperor Meiji during the Russo-Japanese War (1904-1905). This meant that the Emperor delegated some of his own powers as the nation's Commander-in-Chief temporarily to the Chief of the General Staff. This "Provisional Imperial Mandate" was Kanaya's last "trump card" in his dealings with the Kwantung Army. As early as October, Kanaya seemed to have realized that it was not easy to control the Kwantung Army. Thus, about the time of the Kwantung Army's unauthorized bombing of Chinchow, he had secured the consent of the Emperor to the advisability of using the "Provisional Imperial Mandate" to check Honjo's recklessness.[73] Notice of Provisional Imperial Mandate arrived on November 5 when hostilities between Japanese and Chinese troops had already broken out at Ta-hsing station by the Nonni River Bridge. Ma Chan-shan was then putting up a stiff resistance. When Katakura, Honjo's aide, received this Provisional Imperial Mandate addressed to Honjo, he immediately conferred with Miyake and other staff officers on the matter. They all felt that this was a manifestation of non-confidence in the Commander-in-Chief of the Kwantung Army, and it would hamper the fulfillment of its tasks in Manchuria. Headed by Miyake, they sent a joint protest to the General Staff.[74] On the following day, the General Staff replied: "The duty of the Kwantung Army is to defend the Kwantung leased territory and the South Manchuria Railway. What you suggested to be done are new tasks which have great political implications. It is therefore more appropriate to adhere to the outlines of the instructions of the Provisional Imperial Mandate of the General Staff.[75]

Within a period of three weeks from November 5 to November 27, the General Staff invoked the Provisional Imperial Mandate as many as nine times. On five occasions, it was used to deal with the withdrawal of troops from Heilungkiang, and on the other four occasions, to stop the attack on Chinchow. This was indeed an important episode in the power struggle between the Tokyo Military Headquarters and the Kwantung Army.

The first Provisional Imperial Mandate of the General Staff was issued on November 5. It instructed the troops guarding and repairing the Nonni River Bridge not to proceed beyond Ta-hsing Station. The Kwantung Army protested on the ground of unfavorable local topographical conditions. On the following day, the second Provisional Imperial Mandate came. It reiterated what had been said the day before and specified that even in the vicinity of Ta-hsing, the troops would be allowed to maintain only a defense perimeter from Hsinmintun to Tang-chih and Ta-pa-tai. Some of the staff officers of the Kwantung Army suggested that the order be disregarded, but Honjo decided to comply. Thus, although the Kwantung Army succeeded in raising the Chinese Army's siege in Heilungkiang, it did not pursue the retreating forces.[76] The third Provisional Imperial Mandate was dated November 17. The General Staff permitted the Kwantung Army to take what military actions it deemed proper if Ma Chan-shan should refuse either to retreat or to accept the Japanese demands.[77] This was thought by Honjo and others as indicating a change in Tokyo's policy towards Manchuria. But when they were making preparations to occupy Heilungkiang, the fourth Provisional Imperial Mandate arrived on November 18. It not only forbade the Kwantang Army from taking North Manchuria, but also ordered that the main forces be withdrawn to the east of Cheng-chia-tun.[78] It is understood now that the abrupt change of policy was caused by the joint resignation of four Japanese envoys in Europe.

At the Cabinet meeting on November 16, Minami had proposed that the Kwantung Army be permitted to occupy Heilungkiang. There was the unanimous opposition by fellow Cabinet members who had affiliations with the various political parties. They threatened to resign en bloc. At the same time, four Japanese ambassadors in Europe, namely: Yoshizawa (France), Matsudaira (Great Britain), Yoshida (Italy), and Arita (Austria) also asked to resign jointly because the recklessness of militarists jeopardized Japan's international relations. In view of this grave situation, Minami went to visit Marshal Uehara that very night to ask his advice. On the next day, to placate his Cabinet colleagues and the Japanese ambassadors, Minami suggested to Premier Wakatsuki that the Kwantung Army be allowed to take Heilungkiang first. After Ma Chanshan was ousted, the Japanese troops would then be withdrawn. In point of fact, since the October incident, Premier Wakatsuki was no longer in position to check the militarists, and so he was glad to mediate for Minami in order to prolong the life of his Cabinet. This was then the origin of the fourth Provisional Imperial Mandate issued by the General Staff.[79]

The General Staff was aware that because of this abrupt change, it was necessary to send some high-ranking officials to explain the situation to the Kwantung Army. On November 20, two days after the fourth Provisional Imperial Mandate was issued, the General Staff sent its Deputy Chief Kinoninya, to Manchuria. His mission was partly to explain the inside story and partly to supervise the withdrawal of troops. However, by that time, the Kwantung Army had already entered Heilungkiang without any fighting.[80] Moreover, because of the absence of adverse reactions from the Soviet Union,[81] the Kwantung Army had no wish to withdraw its troops. As a result, Kinoninya not only failed to carry out his mission, but he also telegraphed Tokyo as a pleader on the Kwantung Army's behalf. Because of this development, the General Staff issued its fifth Provisional Imperial Mandate, November 25, ordering the Kwantung Army in two week's time to withdraw its troops from Heilungkiang to the east of Cheng-chia-tun. The telegram also stated that "although we have considered your difficulties, it is, nevertheless, necessary also to pay due regard to international faith and the situation. It is imperative that you follow the instructions in the previous telegram. Should there be any further wavering, it might gravely affect the status of the personnel from the commander downward." [82]

Because of the terse wording of that telegram there was general disaffection among the staff officers of the Kwantung Army, who contemplated resignation. Ishihara felt that they were being unjustly reprimanded, and Honjo that he had been accused of showing a bad example to his staff.[83] But, after an evening's consideration and upon the receipt of a secret report on the outbreak of a second incident at Tientsin, it was decided, on the one hand, to withdraw the main force and the fourth mixed brigade and send them southward along the Peiping-Liaoning Railway to invade Chinchow and Shanhaikwan and, on the other hand, to report to Tokyo that they had withdrawn the troops as instructed so that this might serve some diplomatic purpose. Thus while the occupation of North Manchuria had come to a halt, the spearhead of military aggression was turned westward to another sector.[84]

(b) *In Chinchow*

The Kwantung Army's maneuvers in Chinchow also had been checked by the Provisional Imperial Mandate of the General Staff. On September 27, nine days after the outbreak of the Mukden Incident, Chang Hsueh-liang established the temporary Headquarters of the Commander-in-Chief of Northeastern Frontier Defenses and appointed Chang Tso-hsiang as Commander. Although this action did not conflict with the Tokyo policy of not expanding the incident, it was, nevertheless, incompatible with the Kwantung Army's plan of seizing all of Manchuria. On October 7, Honjo issued a statement refusing to recognize Chang Hsueh-liang's authority in Manchuria. On the following day, the General Staff announced also that it would be impossible for the Kwantung Army to withdraw its troops into the South Manchuria Railway Zone.[85] These two pronouncements became the subject of protest by the U.S. Secretary of State Stimson and also brought a denial from Foreign Minister Shidehara.[86] Thus, the discord between the Tokyo Government and the Japanese military became a matter of serious international concern. On October 8, airplanes of the Kwantung Army bombed Chinchow. At the time of the bombing, Major General Hashimoto, Chief of the First Section of the General Staff, was conveying a sense of Japan's conciliatory attitude in his capacity of special envoy of the General Staff. It was evident that Hashimoto had not been informed of the bombing beforehand, and afterwards, he was even derided. In fact, he did not even have freedom of movement while he was in Mukden.[87] Thus there was a wide gap between the course of the Kwantung Army and the policy of the Tokyo Government.

Not only the Kwantung Army, but also the Japanese garrison at Tientsin wanted to eliminate Chang Hsueh-liang's influence. This garrison, with a total force of less than 1,000 was stationed at posts in Shanhaikwan, Chinhuangtao, Tangku, Peiping and Tientsin. Without outside aid, it would have been impossible for such an insignificant force to stage an incident. General Kashii, Commander of the Tientsin Garrison, first sought help from Tokyo, his plea was rejected by Kanaya.[88] He then decided to organize Chinese ronin and to supply them with arms and money to create incidents. He hoped that these incidents would provide an excuse for the Kwantung Army to drive westward into Chinchow and Shanhaikwan and to seize North China. He had reached an understanding with the Kwantung Army at the time when the latter was attacking Heilungkiang. In October, Doihara made a secret trip to Tientsin. In addition to kidnapping Henry Pu-yi, he had also the mission of stirring up troubles there. While at Tientsin, he was instrumental in manufacturing two incidents. The first occurred on November 8, but it failed, and the second on November 26, which though unsuccessful, gave the Kwantung Army the excuse to send a considerable force by way of the Peiping—Mukden Railway to invade Chinchow under the pretext of sending help to Tientsin. Prior to that, the Kwantung Army had also telegraphed Hayashi, Commander-in-Chief of the Japanese Army in Korea, to cross the border for a second time.[89] On November 27, when the matter was discussed by the Operations section of the General staff, it was revealed that Tatekawa had received a report that the Japanese residents were not being maltreated at all. It was decided that the Kwantung Army's westward advanced be stopped. As a result, for the sixth time, Kanaya had to invoke the Provisional Imperial Mandate by telegraphing Honjo to halt its advance. The telegram reads: "You are hereby instructed that your Army's arbitrary action to relieve Tientsin by moving south of Cheng-chia-tun, Tung-liao, and west of the Liao River must not be carried out."

The telegram was sent on the morning of November 27. In the afternoon, the General Staff received a telegram from Honjo reporting on the Kwantung Army's movements. The General Staff then immediately made use of its Provisional Imperial Mandate for the seventh time by ordering Honjo to withdraw part of his troops to the east of the Liao River. Under these two orders from the General Staff and with a reply from Hayashi stating that he had been instructed not to give aid to the Kwantung Army, Honjo had to discontinue his adventure. Nevertheless, he still wanted to keep the Kwantung Army on the west bank of the Liao River. On the same evening, another Provisional Imperial Mandate arrived. It enjoined emphatically: "Whatever may be the situation, the units west of the Liao River must be withdrawn to the east bank without delay." Before Honjo could make a reply, another Mandate on the morning of November 28 arrived requesting a detailed report on the withdrawal of the Kwantung Army. Under such circumstances, the Kwantung Army had no alternative to compliance. It was explained that failure to carry out the General Staff's previous orders more promptly was due to obstructions along the Pai-chi-pao line. Was it not then most unusual that the General Staff had to invoke its Provisional Imperial Mandate four times in one evening before it could exact compliance from troops in the field?[90]

In halting the Kwantung Army's advance to the west of Liao, the Wakatsuki Cabinet kept an eye on the development of a plan which had been discussed at the Council of the League of Nations in Geneva. The plan was to de-militarize Chinchow.[91] It was tantamount to asking China to withdraw her army from her own territory. China at first, compromised with a certain condition, but finally rejected this idea. On December 11th, the Wakatsuki Cabinet fell. Prince Saionji recommended Inukai to be the new premier, and the three army chiefs (i.e., the outgoing War Minister, the Chief of the General Staff and the Inspector General of Military Education) chose Araki to replace Minami. Araki favored Honjo's plan for taking over the four provinces of China.[92] With the strong man of the "Imperial Way" faction now in power, the Kwantung Army felt much freer in its action. So, the fourth and the eighth Divisions were dispatched to Manchuria and the 20th Division crossed the Yalu River with the full approval of the new Cabinet. Harbin was occupied and Chinchow taken. It was amazing that so vast a plan, drawn up only a few months prior to the conquest of the whole of Manchuria by a few conspirators, could so quickly materalize without much military sacrifice. Yet, in this lay also the source of Japan's future peril.

Chapter 5

Nanking's Reaction

I. The Dilemma between Peace and War

From the archives of the Japanese Foreign Office, as well as from the intelligence files of the Bureau of Kwantung Affairs, we have now found the telegrams to Chang Hsueh-liang sent in July by Generalissimo Chiang and Yu Yu-jen, (President of the Control Yuan) cautioning Chang to refrain from creating any incidents.[1] Also found were Chang Hsueh-liang's telegrams to the Northeastern Political Council regarding the avoidance of conflicts with Japan.[2] These telegrams show that before the outbreak of the Mukden Incident, the Chinese authorities had envisioned some trouble from the Kwantung army. It is therefore rather inexplicable that they failed to take any precautionary measure and eventually had to abandon Mukden without resistance. This ineptness was lamented not only by Chinese youths who were generally emotional but also bitterly attacked by many experienced people, including Wang Jung-pao,[3] then Chinese minister to Japan, Hu Shih, and Ting-fu Tsiang.[4]

By the time the news of the Mukden Incident reached Nanking, it was already the afternoon of September 19.[5] Generalissimo Chiang had left for Kiukiang by gunboat two days earlier to take charge of military affairs against Communists in Kiangsi and was still en route when the news arrived. An emergency meeting was convened by the Standing Committee of the Kuomintang Central Executive Committee in Nanking. After deliberating far into the night, the following three steps were decided upon and taken: (1) the Ministry of Foreign Affairs was instructed to lodge a strong protest with Japan, to submit a complaint before the League of Nations, and to notify the United States government; (2) a telegram was addressed to Generalissimo Chiang urging him to return at once to Nanking; (3) a telegram was sent to the Council of the Kuomintang in Canton to persuade the dissident leaders to give up their schismatic regime and to come to Nanking to face the national crisis.[6]

When he heard of the report,[7] Generalissimo Chiang immediately left Hu-kou (in Kiukiang) by airplane. On September 21, a conference was held at his official residence in Dr. Sun Yat-sen's Mausoleum to discuss measures to meet the crisis. It was decided that (1) diplomatically, a Special Foreign Affairs Committee be set up as the policy-making organ for dealing with Japan; (2) militarily, armed forces be rushed north to assist in the defense, plans for a campaign in Kwantung were abandoned, and plans for Communist suppression were suspended;[8] (3) politically, Ts'ai Yuan-p'ei, Chang Chi and Chen Ming-shu were to proceed to Canton to bring about national solidarity in the face of Japanese aggression;[9] (4) the National Government and the Central Party Headquarters of the Kuomintang were to issue written appeals to the people and armed forces urging them to be calm, ready, and determined to defend the nation, as well as to have faith in an expected settlement by the League of Nations.[10] On September 22, Generalissimo Chiang spoke again at the Nanking municipal headquarters of the Kuomintang urging an attitude of patience pending justice from the League.[11] On the following day, Chiang reiterated in his speech at the Sun Yat-sen memorial service the necessity for upholding justice and for resisting the brutal enemy.[12]

It would seem from these events that the attitude of the National Government toward the Incident was nothing more than "faith in the League of Nations" and "preparation for resistance." Nonetheless, it would be impossible to comprehend the limits of such faith and preparation unless one examined the most secret reports of the Special Foreign Affairs Committee for that period. That Committee was headed by Tai Ch'uan-hsien as chairman and T.V. Soong as vice chairman, while V.K. Wellington Koo served as secretary-general. Among its members were Chiang Kai-shek, Yu Yu-jen, H. H. Kung, Chen Li-fu and Ting Wei-fen, W. W. Yen, Chu Chao-hsin and others. The Committee had daily meetings starting at 7 A.M. It took the responsibility of making decisions on all diplomatic policies and measures. All public documents also were drafted and worked out at the meeting.[13] Although it has been said that Mr. Tai had personally kept three of the most secret documents, a check of his collected articles (published posthumously) reveals that there was only one.[14] This was the report submitted to the Central Political Council by that Committee in November, an excerpt of which follows: [15]

1. It is clear that the military policy of Japan is to achieve the goal of complete occupation of Manchuria. Initially, there had been some divergence of views between Japan's diplomatic and military authorities. However, after the decision of October 24 by the second meeting of the Council of the League of Nations which set the date for the withdrawal of Japanese armed forces on November 16, the Japanese Foreign Office gradually followed the footsteps of the War Ministry. Now, Japan's foreign policy is completely dominated by military strategy. Thus, all judgments should be based upon the military situation.

2. It is clear that Japan's aim is to eradicate China's administration in Manchuria. It is therefore inevitable that our political and military influence in Chinchow will be jeopardized. Any Japanese intrigues in the meantime in Peiping, Tientsin, Tsingtao, Tsinan, Shanghai, Nanking and Wuhan would merely be a means of achieving this goal. . .

Once the Chinese Central Government resorts to military action, it is conceivable that Japan would use her armed forces and nationals in China to create trouble in the Yangtze valley, to sabotage the economic foundations of China, and to place the national capital under military threat. . .

3. It is clear that the aim of the League of Nations is to do everything in its power to defeat the Japanese plan. Our attitude is shared by Britain and France. Various misgivings about France seem to be unfounded. . . Nevertheless, since the Powers have not yet consummated their own national plans, it would be impossible for them to go to war with Japan. Thus, the League is not in a position to adopt any effective sanctions.

4. It is clear that the United States, whenever necessary, might eventually invoke the Nine-Power Treaty against Japan. . . .

5. It is clear that China would eventually be victorious internationally. Thus, at this moment, the most important thing is to rally public support and keep up the people's confidence in their government.

In our foreign policy, firstly, under no circumstances must China, in her relations with Japan, be the first to declare war; second, we must do everything to maintain the goodwill of other nations; third, though it is necessary to have every regard for practical interests, whenever necessary we must undergo military sacrifices to maintain national unity. Thus, if Japan should attack Chinchow, we must resist in order to maintain public confidence in the government so that China shall not perish through disintegration. . . .

6. It is clear that the Chinese government must now express its complete confidence in the League of Nations. There are three advantages in this: (a) internally, this can reduce the blame the people attribute to their government; (b) externally such a step is conducive to international friendship; (c) it would make it more opportune to ask the United States to invoke the Nine-Power Treaty at some later time.

7. The current strength of the Japanese Army is inadequate to achieve its military policy. It is believed that when its current strength is exhausted, influences opposed to such a military policy are bound to rise to assume the reins of the Japanese government. By that time, Sino-Japanese relations will be normal again. . . . However, the coming of such a period is still remote. Although we should know that it would be appropriate to have diplomatic relations with Japan in the future, we cannot do so now.

All but the seventh of these conclusions seem to be sound. The estimate that the League of Nations would not be in a position to apply effective sanctions against Japan refuted the allegation that "the government has been passively relying on the League of Nations." Item Five points out that, if necessary, China would also be compelled to make military sacrifices. This shows that the National Government was then prepared for armed resistance. The decision that "if Chinchow is attacked, everything will be done to defend it" proves that the end of China's forebearance toward Japan, would be reached at Chinchow.

Besides China's appeal to the League of Nations, there were three other recourses in China's policy toward Japan: declaration of war, severance of diplomatic relations, or direct negotiations. China was then too weak militarily to declare war, a course nobody would advocate except young students. Both Sun Fo and Eugene Chen suggested the breaking off of diplomatic relations with Japan, but this was opposed by Wang Ching-wei, Chen Ming-shu, and Chang Chi.[16]

While Hu Han-min seemed to be the first person to advocate direct negotiations, T. V. Soong was the first to try it. On the day following the Mukden Incident, Soong and Japanese Minister Shigemitsu met in a secret conference at Shanghai. Soong suggested that three senior members each be appointed by the Chinese and the Japanese governments to form a joint committee which would proceed to Mukden to prevent the aggravation of the incident, and to seek a method of resolving the Manchurian-Mongolian question on the spot. On that day, Shigemitsu twice telegraphed Shidehara recommending that the proposal be accepted. Shidehara's approval was received in a special telegram dated September 20. Nevertheless, public opinion in China had reached a boiling point; the Chinese government was apprehensive lest any diplomacy of compromise might cause the youth masses to be further influenced by the Communists. Thus, it was decided to stop direct negotiations.[17]

In mid-November, the Fourth Congress of the Kuomintang was held in Nanking. The Congress issued a statement declaring that "China is prepared to recover Manchuria by force." On November 20, the Congress adopted a resolution asking "Generalissimo Chiang to proceed north at once to defend Chinese territory and to recover lost lands." Another resolution was adopted on the ensuing day that "the National Government be empowered to take all necessary measures of self-defense." By that time, however, Chinchow had been bombarded (October 8); Henry Pu-yi had been kidnapped in Tientsin (November 12), and the League of Nations had decided to send a mission of enquiry to China for an investigation (November 21). Thus, there were drastic changes in the outlook for a settlement.

Early in December, the situation at Chinchow worsened. The Chinese government had approved Wellington Koo's formula for the setting up of a neutral zone in Chinchow and this was to be submitted to the League.[18] Nevertheless, at that time, the Canton government was using its pressure to bring about Generalissimo Chiang's resignation, with the result that the Central Government would be left without a head. It was then impossible either to talk peace or to go to war. This also rendered futile both the strategy of resistance at Chinchow, formulated by the Special Foreign Affairs Committee, and Wellington Koo's plan for the establishment of a neutral zone in Chinchow. Three years later when Chiang was recalling this episode, he said not without grief:

> Following the Mukden Incident, the authorities were hesitant, insisting on the principle that there could be no negotiations unless Japanese troops were withdrawn. This made it impossible for the moderate faction in Japan to rise; the military became more rampant and a settlement became more difficult. Even after the fall of Mukden and before the invasion of Shanhaikwan, it would still have been possible to stop the Japanese at Chinchow, making a change in the situation operative. It is regrettable that every opportunity was missed, thus creating an impossible situation. This cannot but be attributed to the lack of resolve and the irresponsibilty of the authorities.[19]

The predicament of indecision between war and peace at that moment can be seen clearly in this reference.

2. *Factors of the Dilemma*

The factors which led to this dilemma may be reviewed from three aspects: (A) The Student Movement; (B) the Chinese Communist party; (C) the Canton schismatic government.

(A) Student Movement

Ever since the May 4, 1919 Movement, student organizations had become objects of rivalry for influence between the Kuomintang and the Chinese Communist party. When the Kuomintang was reorganized in 1924, a Department of Youth was created by the Central Committee of the Party with Tsou Lu as Director. In this way, Kuomintang leadership was given to China's student movement. During the May 30, 1925 incident, the National Student Union was inaugurated in Shanghai. Yun Tai-ying of the Chinese Communist party then encouraged the students to join the worker and peasant movement, thereby enabling them to be absorbed into his own party. When two rival forces developed their respective political establishments in Nanking and Hankow during 1927, the Student Union also split into two antagonistic factions: one pro-Communist and the other anti-Communist. With the establishment of the National Government at Nanking in 1928, an order was issued prescribing the formulation by the Student Union of a "vertical" hierarchy. It was then thought by the Central Kuomintang Headquarters that the students, being naive and platonic, should not take part in political conflict. Thus, guidance of student movements was placed beyond mass movement training. The Student Union was changed into Student Self-Governing Association and, as a result, a period of tranquility was ushered in. In the wake of the Tsinan tragedy in May, 1928, students throughout China unleashed an anti-Japanese movement and their aim was entirely external. In the summer of 1929, Communist Youth leagues were uncovered in the foreign concessions in Shanghai. In the meantime, the concession authorities had ferreted out such organs, including also the Kiangsu Provincial Committee of the Chinese Communist party and its branches. Some fourteen schools were involved and ten students were arrested. In 1930, the so-called "Proletarian Literary Movement" became rampant, and the League of Left-wing Writers was founded in Shanghai. There was then considerable complaint against the Regulations for Screening Propaganda Literature, the Press Law and the Procedures of Registration enforced by the government. Because of this disaffection, it became possible for the League to infiltrate into student movements in order to make the latter a sort of camouflage for its work. The result was to further complicate the composition of China's student movement.[20]

Following the outbreak of the Mukden Incident, youth groups throughout China, fired by patriotism, vied with each other in taking part in the anti-Japanese national salvation movement. Notwithstanding their pure and noble motives, the movement, with the passage of time, was infiltrated by "professional students" of the Chinese Communist party and by members of the Nationalist Youth League. With a shifting of the goal of the student movement from foreign relations to domestic politics, demonstrations also changed from appeals for war with Japan, to agitation for subverting the Government.

Between September 20 and December 17, 1931, the student movements went through four phases. The tide of petition submission started at Shanghai universities. On the first day a National Anti-Japanese Association was inaugurated there, with some thirty schools participating. Fifty delegates out of the 100 or so participating were elected to submit petitions at Nanking, the capital.[21] On the following day, the Student Union demanded a declaration of war on Japan and student military training. An outline for the organization of volunteers was also adopted. In Peiping, the movement was started by Tsinghua and Yen Ching Universities.[22] On September 27, a mass anti-Japanese rally was sponsored by various organizations in Peiping; it was followed by demonstration and a parade. The students also decided to proceed southward in small groups and to demand that the government declare war on Japan. At Nanking, the movement was started at the Central University. On September 28, some 4,000 students assembled and went to the Central Kuomintang Headquarters to demand war on Japan. Under the tumult of mass hysteria, they wrecked the premises of the Foreign Office and assaulted Dr. C. T. Wang who was then the Minister. The Ministry of Education had previously (September 25) advised the students to refrain from strikes and illegal actions. Although this counsel was accepted by a segment of the middle school students, college students refused to heed. Generalissimo Chiang personally received the marchers. They dispersed after he had given some assurances and there were no further incidents.[23]

The second period produced a tide of petitioning. Futan University in Shanghai served as the center of the movement, in which some 4,000 students participated. Led by a Chou Hsiao-po, hundreds of delegates entrained for Nanking to petition for a declaration of war and for an economic boycott against Japan. Among the faculty and students of Futan were some Communists. When this became known to the authorities, four students were arrested for Communist affiliation.[24]

Yang Te-yao, who presided at the anti-Japanese rally of the Central University in Nanking, also was arrested as being a suspected Communist.[25] The students then became more violent. When the students from Shanghai arrived in Nanking, the Garrison Commander considered them politically oriented toward the Canton regime and the treatment they received was far from cordial. There were at Futan University posters with such slogans as: "The People of the Entire Nation Should Be Armed." [26] With the infiltration of the Chinese Communists into the student movement, one could not but be more vigilant from then on.

The third period was dominated by a tide of demonstrations, mainly by students from Peking University. At that time, it was common knowledge that the League of Nations was powerless to impose sanctions against Japan. Consequently, the students became more indignant, and their ranks were further reinforced. Yet the organization of the demonstration group of Peking University and their journey southward did not have the approval of the University's Student Union.[27] Though numbering only some 200, the group was so well disciplined that it became evident that it was trained by the so-called professional students.[28] But before its arrival in Nanking, the Student Union had telegraphed asking that status be denied to the group.[29] The Nanking police searched the delegates and confiscated sheaves of subversive propaganda. They were told to return to Peiping immediately. Instead, they went clandestinely to seek help from the students of the Central University. On December 6, the group went out to demonstrate in the streets of Nanking, displaying paper flags with Communist slogans and shouting, "Oppose the Selling Out of Manchuria by the Government," "Down with the Renegade Government," "Stand Up, the Proletariat of China," etc. The gendarmes and the Nanking police stopped the parade and escorted some 185 students to Hsiao-ling-wei for temporary detention. Clashes resulted also between the students of Central University and the police and gendarmes.[30]

In the fourth period a climax was reached. Chinchow was then in a critical state. The Chinese government was planning to make it a neutral zone, though direct negotiations with Japan were opposed by the students. The number of demonstrators had reached some 10,000. They demanded that China (1) quit the League of Nations, (2) declare war on Japan, (3) re-activate mass movements, and (4) bring about a peaceful unification of Nanking and Canton. On December 7, Generalissimo Chiang addressed the students for more than an hour at a public square in Nanking. He gave definite answers to their four-point demands. He also enjoined them not to allow themselves to be made use of by the Chinese Communist party.[31] Another appeal to the students was issued by the National Government. However, no sooner had this group of students dispersed than the students of Shanghai universities arrived. They held a mass demonstration on the afternoon of December 11, shouting such slogans as "Down with the Kuomintang" "Down with the National Government." They had shifted from anti-Japanese to anti-government stands. Gendarmes and police intervened and arrested Hsu Hsiu-tsen and Kiang Hsueh-ch'ien, both student leaders.[32]

When the news of this fracas reached Shanghai, some 5,000 students assembled. They surrounded the Shanghai Municipal Government and demanded that Mayor Chang Chun punish the Director of the Municipal Bureau of Public Safety, who had forbidden the students to parade. After the release of Hsu Hsiu-tsen and Kiang Hsueh-ch'ien, demonstration groups in Nanking held another parade on December 15. They carried red flags and red bands on their arms. Their first destination was the premises of the Foreign Office where they wrecked furniture and assaulted members of the staff. Another group of some 300 proceeded to the Central Koumintang Headquarters where they were received by Ts'ai Yuan-p'ei and Chen Ming-shu. Ts'ai was manhandled by students and suffered minor injuries but was rescued by police. The police and the gendarmes seized some of the flags on which "Long Live the Communist Party" was written.[33] A photograph of such flags and slogans was published in the *Central Daily News* the next day. The students, enraged by this exposure, marched to the premises of the newspaper and wrecked its printing press. It was then that the Garrison Commander of Nanking began to round up the rioting students, sixty-five of whom were arrested.[34]

The students themselves were divided in opinion. When those from Peiping went south to petition their respective student unions, precautions had already been taken against Communist elements.[35] Not only was the public wary of the action of the demonstration group of Peking University and those in Nanking on December 15 and 17, but most of the students also were disaffected. When the students from Tsinan expressed their desire to leave Nanking, they were deterred by the demonstration group from Peking University. Five hundred and twenty-eight students of the National Central University at Nanking published a mass protest denying that their institution had participated in the riots on those dates.[36] It was not until the gendarmes had escorted the Peking University group from the capital that the tide of demonstrations was stemmed. In *Tai Ch'uan-hsien Wen-ts'en* (Tai Ch'uan-hsien's Collected Writings) it was written:

> Most of the young students were, on the one hand, fired by their sense of patriotism and, on the other hand, utilized by those who wanted to fish in troubled water. As a result, they staged strikes and demonstrations, making themselves obnoxious at the Central Kuomintang Headquarters, the National Government and the Executive Yuan, where it not only became impossible for the employees to conduct routine business but also to move about.[37]

It was also said in *Chiang Tsung-t'ung Chi* (President Chiang's Collected Articles) that "the Chinese Communist party and fellow travelers were then smearing and denouncing the National Government under the cover of petitioning." [38] Otsuka Reizo, the Japanese authority on Chinese Communism, stated that the demonstrations were participated in by the Youth Leagues of the Communist party and a Nationalist faction, both being desirous of exploiting the patriotism of youth to harass the government.[39]

(B) The Chinese Communist Party

Even before the outbreak of the Mukden Incident, the Chinese Communist Red Army had already established a central Soviet regime at Chih-ping, in Jui-chin, Kiangsi. Chu Te and Mao Tse-tung were in charge respectively of military and political affairs, while Hsiang Ying headed the Central Political Bureau. This regime was then in partnership with Communist troops under (1) Peng Te-huai of the Kiangsi-Fukien border area, (2) Hsu Chi-shen (and later Chang Kuo-tao) of Hupeh-Honan-Anhwei border area, (3) Hsu Hsiang-chien and Chang Kuo-tao of Szechuan and Shensi border area, (4) Ho Lung and Chou I-chun of Hunan and West Hupeh area, (5) Li Ming-jui and Chang Yun-i of the Tso and Yu River area in Kwangsi, (6) Fang Chih-min of East Kiangsi area, (7) Tsai Cheng-i of the Hupeh-Honan border area, and (8) Tu Heng and Liu Tzu-tan of the Shensi-Kansu border area. Although the Chinese Communist armed forces claimed a strength of some 100,000 officers and men, the actual strength was considerably less. They were organized as regular Red troops and local units. Among the latter were also Red guards, young vanguards, auxiliary Red regiments, and others. They were short of fire arms, especially heavy artillery. Nonetheless, they were familiar with the topography of the area and adept at espionage and guerrilla tactics. The result was that though, in the year of 1930-31, the Nationalist Army had overwhelmed the Red Army with superior numbers and weaponry and had laid three sieges against the latter,[40] they were still unable to eradicate the Communist forces.

But the Nationalists had only themselves to blame. Ever since the establishment of their Government in Nanking, they were busy fighting among themselves thereby letting the Communists increase in strength. Within 30 months after the end of 1928, the Nationalists had engaged in armed conflict among themselves three times. First against the Kwang-si Clique (Li Tsung-Jen and Pai Chung-hsi) second, against Feng Yu-hsiang's faction and third, against Yen-Feng coalition Army.[41] In March, 1931, when Hu Han-min was held at Tang-shan, the Canton Group in the Kuomintang held an extraordinary Party Congress in Canton and established there a schismatic regime. Under these circumstances one can well imagine how seriously the

Nanking Government was impeded by internal strife in dealing with the Mukden Incident.

The Chinese Communist Party was then a branch of the Communist International and was subject to directions from the Soviet Union[42] from which it was getting a monthly subsidy of $70,000.[43] In the wake of the Mukden Incident, it was the consensus of public opinion in China that the Kuomintang and the Chinese Communist Party should immediately halt their strife and deal with the national crisis. The troops engaged in besieging the Red base in Kiangsi were then ordered to halt their advance; whereas, the Chinese Communist Party ordered its troops to take this opportunity to launch a counter attack (September 20).[44] On September 30, that Party further announced that "the Kuomintang is the permanent enemy of the Chinese Communist Party."[45] This was clearly a violation of the adage that brothers engaged in mutual recriminations should unite to fight an external foe. Yet, if one should analyze the very character of the Chinese Communist Party and the background of its struggle with the Kuomintang, it becomes clear that there could be no possibility of their joining in a common cause.

Views were divided in regard to the Mukden Incident. From the Chinese standpoint, it was Japan's aggression against China; from the standpoint of the Soviet Union, it was portentous of Japanese aggression against the USSR; in the views of the Chinese Communists, this incident would serve to facilitate solidarity between Nanking and Canton, and foreshadow their joint efforts against the Red Army. Thus, Stalin's reaction to the Mukden Incident was that *first* it was necessary to preserve the Soviet Union and second to preserve the Chinese Communist Party. Stalin's attitude could be gauged from such documents as, "Defend the Chinese Revolution and the Soviet Union," a statement issued by the Central Committees of the Communist Parties of Germany, France, Britain, the United States, Czechoslovakia and Poland;[46] the "Manifesto and the Defense of Chinese Revolution," issued by the Communist International's West European Bureau;[47] and the editorial of the official organ of the Communist International entitled, "The World Proletariat Unanimously Support the Chinese Revolution."[48] Moreover, the six-point manifesto adopted by the Twelfth Conference of the International Executive Council pointed out clearly and frankly that it was necessary to take advantage of the Japanese aggression to expand the Red Army and overthrow the Nationalist Government.[49]

Upon receipt of the Moscow directive, the Chinese Communist Party on September 22 adopted a resolution, in which it pointed out that Japanese aggression in Manchuria implied two things: (1) it was the signal for an imperialist attack on the Soviet Union, and (2) it would bring about the solidarity of the Kuomintang in joining forces to suppress the Communists. Consequently, the Party appealed to its comrades to defend their fatherland—the Soviet Union—and to overthrow Kuomintang rule.[50] Professor Wang Chien-min, an authority on the history of the Chinese Communist Party, said at that time Japan was attacking only China and not the Soviet Union. Moreover, there was no attempt on the part of the imperialists to attack the Soviet Union. Nonetheless, the Chinese Communist Party, in the wake of the Mukden Incident, seemed to be completely unconcerned with Japanese aggression against China. However, it was most solicitous about defending the Soviet Union. This shows that the Chinese Communist Party was more loyal to a foreign country than to its own. . . .[51] We cannot agree more fully with Professor Wang's appraisal.

Long before the Mukden Incident, the Chinese Communist Party had begun to regard the Soviet Union as its fatherland. There was then established in Moscow the Far Eastern Toilers' University (known briefly as the Far Eastern University) to train world Communist talent. At that time, such slogans as "Understand the Soviet Fatherland" and "Be Loyal to the Soviet Fatherland" were coined.[52] In the winter of 1929, the Chinese Northeastern troops were engaged in a battle with the Soviet troops of the Far Eastern region at Manchuli over a dispute concerning the Chinese Eastern Railway. It was then that the Central Committee of the Chinese Communist Party clamored for support of the Soviet Union. By then, Chen Tu-hsiu had been dismissed, though he still protested against this slogan, suggesting that one denouncing the "ineptitude of the Kuomintang" be used instead. Chu Ch'iu-pai, however, disagreed.[53]

At the time of the Mukden Incident, the so-called right opportunists under Chen Tu-hsiu, blind activists under Chu Ch'iu-pai, and the Li Li-san line had all been disgraced.[54] In the Central Committee of the Chinese Communist Party, such internationalists as Chen Shao-yu and Chin Pang-hsien were in power.[55] This faction was trained by Mif, who was the president of their university. It was then natural that Communists should be most subservient to directives from the Soviet Union and be oblivious to their own national crisis.

Following the purge on April 12, 1927 by the Kuomintang of the Chinese Communist Party, its members were persecuted and Party headquarters wiped out by gendarmes and police of the Nationalist Government. After the August 7, 1927 conference, the Chinese Communist Party went underground. To facilitate its operations, the Party Central Committee secretly moved into the Concession area in Shanghai. This was to seek the protection of foreign imperialists in order to subvert their own government. In order to cope with this situation, an investigation section was organized in the Central Kuomintang Party Headquarters with Hsu En-tseng as its chief, with a staff of some forty persons. A clandestine struggle was initiated between this section and the underground Communist workers. As a result of this section's operations, Chen Yen-nien, who was Chen Tu-hsiu's elder son and secretary of the Yangtze Bureau of the Chinese Communist Party, and his assistant Chen Shih-yen were arrested and executed in June, 1927. Also executed were Chen Chiao-nien, who was Chen Tu-hsiu's second son and a Central Committee member and Director of Organizations of the Chinese Communist Party; Hsu Pai-hao, Secretary of the Communist Youth League of Shanghai; and Peng Pai, an important figure in peasant movements and the leader of the riots in Hai-lu-feng. Hsiang Ying of the Central Political Bureau also was arrested but managed to escape. During 1931, many more Chinese Communist underground workers were apprehended. They included Ku Shun-chang, who was Chief of Secret Service in the Chinese Communist Party (for the Ku Shun-chang case, read *The Eastern Miscellany*, Vol. 29, No. 11, p. 107, Nov. 24, 1931), Hsiang Chung-fa (General Secretary of the Chinese Communist Party), Lo Chi-yuan and Yang Pao-an (both Central Committee members and important figures in the peasant movement), and Yang Tzu-chuang (army commissar in Kiangsu). They were all arrested and executed in that year. Also arrested were Yuan Hsiao-hsien, Pan Wen-yu and Liao Hua-ping, all Communist workers in Hopeh under the North China Bureau. A number of them either disappeared or surrendered. According to Hsu En-tseng's book entitled *The Invisible Conflict,* during the period of his incumbency, the Kuomintang organ had arrested three General Secretaries of the Chinese Communist Party (Chen Tu-hsiu, Hsiang Chung-fa and Chu Ch'iu-pai), 40 members of the Central Political Bureau, 829 members at the provincial committee level, 8,199 Communists on *hsien* (county) and village levels, and 155,250 Red Guards. Although this was the total number of Communists arrested during 1930-1949, it was obvious that there was a heavy debt of blood between the two antagonist parties which could hardly be obliterated by the national emergency.[56]

In 1930, the Central Committee of the Chinese Communist Party had planned to hold, on December 11, the day for commemorating the Canton uprising, the First National Congress of the Chinese Soviets. A preparatory committee was formed in Shanghai by the Central Committee of the Chinese Communist Party, the General Trade Union of China, the Mutual Aid Association, the Shanghai Trade Union, the Freedom League, the Anti-Imperialist League, the League of Social Scientists, and the League of Left-wing Writers. Each Red Army unit as well as all the various trade unions were asked to send delegates. Preparations were completed by the autumn of 1931, when the Mukden Incident erupted. On November 7, 1931, taking advantage of the temporary halt to the military siege by the Kuomintang, the Communist Central Committee convened the First National Congress of the Chinese Workers, Peasants and Soldiers Soviets at Yen p'ing in Jui-chin. This Congress proclaimed the inauguration of the Chinese Soviet Republic[57] and changed the name of Jui-chin into Jui-ching which was to be the capital of the new republic. Sixty-three Central Committee members were elected, with Mao Tse-tung as chairman and Hsiang Ying and Chang Kuo-tao as vice-chairmen.

At the Communist Congress held in Jui-chin, three documents were released;[58] "Statement to the Mass of Workers and Peasants in China." "Statement to China's Workers and Laboring Masses," and "Manifesto of the Provisional Government of the Chinese Soviet Republic to the World." In the first document, it was pointed out that, following the Mukden Incident, the imperialists would partition China and attack the Soviet Union. Since both the Nanking and the Canton governments were opposed to the anti-imperialist movement, it was only by overthrowing Kuomintang rule and setting up a Soviet government that China could be "liberated." In the second document it was stated that the Chinese Soviet Republic would collaborate with the proletariat of the world to support the Soviet fatherland. The third document announced that, while the Communists were opposed to international war as well as internal rebellions, it was, nonetheless, necessary to fight against the Nationalist Government to the very end.

All three documents put equal emphasis on anti-Japan and anti-Kuomintang themes. In other documents, however, the Chinese Communist Party was even more hostile to the Kuomintang than to Japan. Although Chang Kuo-tao's name had appeared as the second vice-chairman, he did not attend the Congress. On the very day when the Soviet Congress convened, he called the Second Soviet Congress in the Hupeh-Honan-Anhwei area, where his own Red troops were stationed, thereby indicating that he was by no means disposed to accept Mao Tse-tung's overlordship.[59] Although this was the Congress which established Mao Tse-tung's status as a political leader, it is nevertheless conceivable that had it not been for the Mukden Incident, the Nationalist troops could have wiped out the Red base in Kiangsi, thereby not only making the Jui-chin Congress abortive, but also putting an end to Jui-chin's career.

While the National Government was sending its troops northward, the Red Army moved from southern Kiangsi to attack Fukien. On December 10, Peng Te-huai's army attacked Kanchow when the situation in Chinchow was critical. When the Shanghai-Wusung hostilities were raging in January, 1932, the Red Army took Shang Hang and Wu-p'ing, and, in April,[60] captured Chang-chow. Thus, within a few months, the Chinese

Soviet area expanded to some 100,000 square miles.[61] When the Lytton Commission arrived in China in the autumn of 1932, it was convinced that, if there had been no Mukden Incident, the Kuomintang troops would have annihilated the Chinese Communist forces that year.[62] This then was how the Chinese Communist Party reacted to, and made use of, the Mukden Incident.

(C) The Canton Schismatic Government

There was the gravest rupture in the Kuomintang when the Mukden Incident occurred. Since the Northern expedition, there had been many such splits. Nevertheless, whereas most of them had occurred as a result of outside alienations and provocations, the 1931 break was caused mainly by intra-party strife, especially the house detention of Hu Han-min at Tangshan, Nanking, in March, 1931.[63] Although, by April, Hu had regained his nominal freedom and returned to his private residence at Nanking, the older Kuomintang leaders of the Canton faction held an emergency congress of the Party's Central Executive and Supervisory Committees, in Canton. They were further supported by Chen Chi-tang and, on May 28, formed a separate government to rival the Nanking Government. In June, Eugene Chen, Foreign Minister in the Canton regime, went to Tokyo and held three secret conversations with Japanese Foreign Minister Shidehara. He hoped that, by offering China's recognition of what rights Japan had already acquired in Manchuria, the latter would agree to the procurement of arms by Canton in Japan through T'ai-p'ing, a commercial firm.[64] Although it was true that prior to the Mukden Incident, the Cantonese troops were trying to attack Hunan and Kiangsi at a juncture when Nationalist troops were poised for a punitive expedition against Kwangtung, Generalissimo Chiang ordered his troops to halt their advance as soon as the Incident occurred. After his arrival in Nanking, Chiang immediately dispatched Chen Ming-shu, Ts'ai Yuan-p'ei and Chang Chi to Canton with his personal letter advising the comrades in Canton to dissolve their regime for the sake of unity, in order to cope with the external foe. His letter was couched in the most sincere language. It reads, in part:

> Recently Manchuria has been invaded; our armed forces have been beaten and our national territory has been encroached upon. We now face imminent peril. . . . As I watch the domestic situation, it seems that we are steeped in some emotional strife in which everyone is carried to extremes. It is most deplorable; our compatriots are saying tearfully that, unless there is solidarity, it will be impossible to prevent national oblivion. We are all sharing a revolutionary mission, and is there anything that cannot be sacrificed? I have been in power for the last three years and am conscious of my shortcomings, as well as my responsibility alone for what has happened in the past. It is hoped that our comrades will recognize the emergency of the Party and the country and be sincere toward each other so that outsiders will not say that the followers of Dr. Sun Yat-sen's Party are interested only in internal strife, notwithstanding the national emergency.[65]

Chiang's emissaries arrived in Hong Kong on September 28, and were met there by Wang Ching-wei, Sun Fo and Li Wen-fan on behalf of the Canton regime. They discussed matters far into the night and, as a result, drafted a statement of the basis for collaboration between Nanking and Canton as follows: (1) Chairman Chiang would assume the responsibility for the intra-party strife and issue a circular telegram announcing that he would resign as soon as a united government was formed; (2) the Canton regime also would admit mistakes and announce that it was necessary to save the country through unity, and that, therefore, the Canton Government would be dissolved; (3) the two telegrams were to be issued simultaneously, the first step being to stop mutual recriminations; (4) the garrison arrangements in Shanghai and Nanking were to be revamped so that the comrades from Canton could come to Nanking safely and hold meetings at the Sun Yat-sen Mausoleum to devise measures for a unified government.[66]

When the emissaries left Nanking, they conveyed to the Canton faction, at the request of Chiang, an expression of the following three principles: (1) if Canton feels that it is capable of coping with the national crisis, the entire group should come to Nanking to reorganize the Nationalist Government; (2) if they do not think that they can take this responsibility, then the comrades in Canton should come to Nanking to work together; (3) if the comrades in Canton aim at cooperation, they will be most welcome, and are asked to discuss, in person, the measures for participation in the government. Now it becomes obvious that despite the mildness of Chiang's attitude and his reasonable offers towards Canton, the Southern Kuomintang group was still insisting upon the retirement of Chiang as a first condition for reconciliation. It thus seemed almost hopeless to expect that the two parties could be brought together. For the sake of unity, the Nanking Government wished, however, to meet the Canton demand more than halfway by appointing General Chen Min-shu to garrison Nanking and Shanghai with his 19th Route Army whose loyalty to Canton was unquestionable. Furthermore, a fresh invitation was sent to Canton urging its envoys to come, at any rate, to Nanking for a conference.[67]

In response to this invitation, the Canton regime sent a five-man delegation (Wang Ching-wei, Sun Fo, Wu Chao-shu, Li Wen-fan and Eugene Chen) and announced that they would leave Canton for Nanking as soon as Hu Han-min had arrived in Shanghai, from Nanking.

On October 14, Hu Han-min arrived in Shanghai, and immediately telegraphed his comrades in Canton urging solidarity in the Party in order to cope with the external crisis.[68] The five delegates from Canton arrived in Shanghai on October 22. On the next day, Chiang came to Shanghai and met with Wang and Hu in Sun Fo's residence. Chiang told them how anxious he was to welcome them to Nanking, and he also modestly said that "he would highly respect the views of the elder statesmen." However, in deference to the wish of the comrades from Canton that a meeting be held in Shanghai first, five delegates (Li Shih-tseng, Chang Ching-chiang, Ts'ai Yuan-p'ei, Chang Chi and Chen Ming-shu) were sent by the Nanking government to meet with their counterparts in Shanghai, hence the Shanghai Unification Conference.

The Shanghai Unification Conference convened on October 27 and ended on November 4. There were six meetings which touched on two categories of agenda: political reform and Party affairs. Under political reform, the items discussed were military and political reorganization (such as the establishment of the National Defense Council and the non-stationing of troops in the hinterland provinces), financial reorganization (effectuation of a budgetary system and establishment of a financial committee) and local government reorganization (such as equalization of powers). However, the central point of discussion was to limit the qualification of the Chairman of the National Government (no military man to be appointed Chairman), deprive the Chairman of special powers (the Chairman to have no actual political power), abolish the office of Commander-in-Chief, and prevent military leaders from serving as Presidents of the five Yuan (Chairman Chiang was then serving concurrently as President of the Executive Yuan.).[69] This was not only contrary to the aim of solidarity, but also had nothing to do with national defense and resistance. Both Ts'ai and Chang thought that this was beyond what had been agreed upon in Hong Kong, and Chiang also deemed it improper.[70] Nevertheless, the Cantonese faction seemed to be more interested in personnel matters than in actual problems. In regard to personnel problems, besides Chiang, there was also Chang Hsueh-liang. Although Chiang was willing to retire, who was to replace him in such vital matters as armed resistance against Japan and suppression of Communist insurgency? No thought was given to this by Wang Ching-wei and Hu Han-min. Although Chang Hsueh-liang was culpable for his military failure and misconduct, there were then several hundred thousand Northeastern troops in Chinchow, Jehol and North China. Who could command them after Chang's dismissal? This also seemed to have escaped the attention of the Cantonese faction. When Eugene Chen, a Cantonese delegate, went to Tokyo in June, he intended to recognize Japan's existing rights and interests in Manchuria because he was interested in procuring Japanese armaments for Canton. Since the Mukden Incident, Chen had told Suma, who was then Japanese Consul General in Canton, that "Japan and the Canton regime had a community of interest in eliminating Chiang Kai-shek and Chang Hsueh-liang."[71] Shigemitsu, at that time, the Japanese Minister, telegraphed Foreign Minister Shidehara that the leaders of the Canton regime were interested in overthrowing Chiang Kai-shek. After Chiang's ouster, the Canton regime would take over the central government, thereby effecting rapprochement with Japan, in keeping with the pan-Asianism which Sun Yat-sen had championed in his speech at Kobe in 1925.[72] As a result of these developments, rumors were rampant in Nanking, Shanghai, and North China. Both Chen Tiao-yuan and Ho Ying-chin sent telegrams in support of Generalissimo Chiang.[73] Chang Hsueh-liang also secretly arrived in Nanking by the end of October to dissuade Chiang from retiring.[74] Although a political reform principle was agreed upon by the Shanghai Unification Conference on October 30, Chiang stated openly, at the weekly memorial service of the Nationalist Government on November 2, that "if posterity is disrespectful, the elders must take the blame." This was an oblique remark concerning the goings on at the Shanghai conference.[75]

At that time, the Japanese Army was pushing ahead steadily, thrusting against Kirin and Heilungkiang to the north and Chinchow and Jehol to the south. Apprehensive lest the conference break up, and thereby further aggravate the crisis, the Bankers' Association and Chamber of Commerce of Shanghai sent telegrams of appeal to both sides for national solidarity.[76] Mediators in both Nanking and Shanghai did their utmost to bring about a compromise; Nanking eventually made concessions on the political reform principle, and invited the prominent leaders of Canton to attend the Fourth Kuomintang Congress to be held in Nanking, on the ground that Chen Ming-shu's units were garrisoning the capital. This offered an ample guarantee for their personal safety.[77]

Yet, because of dissensions in the ranks of the Canton faction, both Wang Ching-wei and Sun Fo were influenced by their respective followers. The following compromise measures were then proposed: (1) the Central Party Headquarters of Nanking and Canton were to convene their own Fourth Congress; (2) each side was to elect twenty-four members of the Central Committee who would be mutually recognized; (3) the Central Committee members thus elected were to meet in Nanking to hold their first plenary meeting and to carry out the political reform suggestions. Though this was obviously a sort of make-shift arrangement, the measures were adopted at the sixth meeting in Shanghai on November 4, thus concluding the Unification Conference.

Following the adjournment of the Unification Conference, the Fourth National Congress of the Kuomintang was formally inaugurated in Nanking on November 14. At its fifth meeting on November 19, Generalissimo Chiang made two suggestions: (1) in electing the members of the Central Executive and Supervisory Committees, the list of the Canton faction should be accepted as far as possible; (2) he himself was resolved to proceed north to do his best to serve the Party and the country. His speech was warmly applauded, and the Congress immediately assigned him the responsibility of resisting the enemy. In Canton, however, the resolutions brought back by Sun Fo from Shanghai were vetoed by the Emergency Congress.[78] The Canton regime rejected also Wang Ching-wei's suggestion that all those who had been members of the First, Second, and Third Kuomintang Congresses be allowed to attend the Fourth Congress. As a result, the dispute between Nanking and Canton now developed into a fracas between Wang Ching-wei and the Canton faction. Since most of those who opposed Wang were aligned with Hu, the latter was consequently invited to Canton to mediate. Sun Fo was annoyed by these bickerings, and left for Hong Kong to show his displeasure.

Through Hu Han-min's mediation, the Fourth Congress of Canton was held on November 18. It accepted the Shanghai resolution by electing twenty-four Central Committee members. However, members of the Central Committee who were affiliated with Wang Ching-wei remained in Shanghai. Under Wang's auspices, they elected nine Central Committee members of their own at the "Great World" amusement center. Wang's men were supposed to compete with the members elected in Nanking and Canton. It was not until January, 1932 that these additional members were recognized by the First Plenary Meeting of the Central Committee, the condition being that Nanking was to elect five, and Canton four, additional members.

Commenting on the Shanghai Conference, Soong Ching-ling said: "The Kuomintang has already lost its status as a revolutionary party. After three months of bickering, all that the

Unification Conference did was to allocate the memberships of the Central Committee and to parcel out high offices. It showed no concern for the interests of the masses."[79] The *Ta Kung Pao* also censured the Party leaders for their concern over settling the score of old grievances, in total disregard of the national emergency.[80]

The Fourth Congress in Nanking was adjourned on November 23, and its Canton counterpart closed on December 7. Two days before the adjournment in Canton, Hu Han-min and others issued a circular telegram demanding Chiang Kai-shek's retirement. Chinchow was in its most critical phase when the Central Government reached the stage of a vacuum. Because of this lack of leadership, China's proposal at the League of Nations concerning the neutral zone of Chinchow had to be abandoned. The day on which Hu issued his circular telegram also witnessed the withdrawal of this Chinese proposal.[81] The British delegate told Alfred Sze that China would regret it,[82] and it proved so eventually.

On December 15, Generalissimo Chiang resigned and went back to his native village. At the First Plenary Meeting of the Central Committee, held in Nanking on December 21, Lin Sen was elected Chairman (of the Nationalist Government), Sun Fo to the Presidency of the Executive Yuan. Chiang Kai-shek, Wang Ching-wei and Hu Han-min were elected as standing members of the Central Committee to preside in rotation at that body. This arrangement was ironic because of the antipathy between Chiang and Hu and the recent fracas between Hu and Wang. As a result, Chiang remained at his own villa in Fenghua; Hu pretended illness in Canton; Wang was indisposed in Shanghai. The new government had been formed, but it lacked a center of gravity. Although Canton had agreed to return governmental powers to the Central Government, it established such quasi-independent organs as the Southwest Executive Headquarters, Southwest Political Council, and the Southwest Military Council, that it undermined true unification and perpetuated a separatist movement.

After Sun Fo had assumed the reins of government, in less than a month he felt mounting difficulties in foreign relations, military developments, and financial problems. He called on

Chiang Kai-Shek at Hangchow, and invited Wang Ching-wei to resume his post. Yu Yu-jen went to Hong Kong to visit Hu Han-min. On January 16, 1932, there was a meeting between Chiang and Wang in Hangchow, and it was then agreed that while Chiang was to assume the task of Communist suppression, Wang would head the Executive Yuan. On January 21, they arrived in Nanking. The government was thus reorganized with cooperation between Chiang and Wang, but Hu Han-min continued to be aloof. Chinchow had fallen 20 days earlier, and one week later, the Shanghai-Wusung hostilities between China and Japan broke out. This then was China's reaction in the wake of the Mukden Incident.

Chapter 6

The Causes of the Mukden Incident

Although the Mukden Incident stemmed from the Kwantung Army's plotting, this might not necessarily have been the sole cause. More than thirty years earlier, the seed of the Incident had been sown. Acts by the Kwantung Army served only to ignite the spark. The Japanese government was fully aware of what the Kwantung Army had done. Nonetheless, the government, in order to save Japan's face, had to cover up the flagrant insubordination in the armed forces. Accordingly, a number of pleas were coined in extenuation of the outrage, such as self-defense, Chinese provocations, infringements of Japanese rights, economic and population pressure, and so forth. In the march of history, facts came to light that stimulated speculation on the underlying causes of the sequence of events. It is generally said that the six causes [1] of the Mukden Incident advanced by Japanese diplomats, newspaper writers, and others between 1931 and 1934 are untenable while the three causes [2] of the Incident analysed by Japanese scholars, after the Sino-Japanese War, may be valid. It seems futile at this late date to review those causes which have been already judged as invalid but, in the light of some new findings in the Tokyo War Crime Trials, we may select one of them—the Nakamura Case—for further consideration.

The Nakamura Case

The Nakamura Case was the most serious issue during the Sino-Japanese controversy of 1931. According to the Chinese version, the case was as follows: On June 9, 1931, Captain Nakamura and his aides, four in all, posing as agricultural experts, with visas from the Japanese Consulate at Harbin to study agriculture in Manchuria, entered at I-li-ko-tu and proceeded towards Taonan. Early in August, the Japanese spread the rumor that Nakamura and his aides had been murdered by the soldiers of Kwan Yu-heng, Commander of the Third Regiment of the Reclamation Army. It was said that, after investigation, Nakamura and his aides had been detained by the soldiers because of their bogus status. During their detention, they tried to escape and were shot by Chinese soldiers. Maps were found on their bodies. It was suspected that they might be Japanese spies. On the day of the outbreak of the Mukden Incident, consultations for a solution were still being held.[3]

After the Tokyo Trial, it became known that Nakamura was not an agricultural expert but a military spy. He graduated in 1928 from the War College in Tokyo, and came to Manchuria in 1931 as captain in the Kwantung Army. On May 14th, he and Tsugi (another military officer) proceeded from Harbin to Tao-pei via Hu-lun-pei-erh—a place where no foreigner was allowed to go.[4] The details of the time and manner of Nakamura's murder are still obscure. The date of the murder, reported by the Lytton Commission as June 27, 1931, was fabricated by the Kwantung Army and the Japanese Consul General at Mukden.[5] On June 17, 1931, the Japanese Consul General at Harbin, after receiving rumors of the murder, was afraid that Nakamura's visa might fall into the hands of the Chinese authorities and be used as evidence to prove his spying on Chinese military installations.[6] The Consul General made a full report of the matter to the Japanese Foreign Office. Two weeks later, Ishihara, a staff officer of the Kwantung Army, and Major Hayana, an assistant in the Japanese Army Special Service Agency, asked Consul General Hayashi to demand that China pay an indemnity, apologize for the incident and guarantee that no such incident would recur. Hayashi, however, did not think that there was sufficient evidence, and he declined to make the demands. He telegraphed a report to Shidehara.[7] Later on, at the request of the Kwantung Army, Shidehara ordered Hayashi to negotiate with the Chinese authorities. Since he had no evidence to prove Nakamura's murder, it was then suggested that eye-witnesses be suborned. He said he would collaborate on this matter with Doihara and the Japanese consul at Heilungkiang.[8] In order to make a consistent story, the Kwantung Army fixed June 27 as the date of Nakamura's arrest, and July 1 as that of his murder. This was reported to Shidehara.[9] Actually no one knew whether Nakamura had been murdered, when he was murdered, who committed the murder, and how.

It is clear that Nakamura and his associates had disguised themselves as agricultural experts, and thus had entered Chinese territory under false pretences, which justified their conviction as spies. Moreover, their visas also specified that they were not to proceed to the area of Tao-so, where banditry was rampant.[10] The first report of their murder came from a Japanese woman at Angangchi on July 17.[11] Not until August 17, did the Japanese Consulate at Mukden ask the Chinese authorities to investigate. Toward the end of the month, the latter sent a team to conduct the investigation. The team returned empty-handed early in September. In mid-September, a later investigator reported that Nakamura and his companions were killed by gun fire when they tried to escape from their place of detention. It was also reported that the charge that they had been brutally murdered was untrue.[12] In the meantime, Kuan Yu-heng, the commander of the garrison, who was responsible for what happened, had been detained by Chinese authorities while awaiting trial in the military prison at Mukden. Inasmuch as the Chinese authorities had handled the incident with such promptness and impartiality, and in view of the Japanese falsification of visas and suborning of witnesses, it would seem unreasonable to say that China's handling of the Nakamura affair could have provoked the Mukden Incident. In June 1931, John Thorburn, a British subject was killed by a Colonel Huang in Soochow. Thorburn had been arrested by the Chinese authorities while traveling without a visa, and was killed while trying to force his way out of the detention house. The British Ambassador, Sir Miles Lampson, was satisfied when the errant Colonel Huang was tried and sentenced for his act.[13] What a world of difference in attitude between the British and the Japanese toward two parallel cases!

The Three Real Causes

In assessing the three probable causes of the Mukden Incident, this writer feels that while two of them, Japanese disregard for China's national unity, and conflict between

Chinese and Japanese nationalism, may be true the third cause, provocation offered to Japan by China's revolutionary diplomacy, is definitely questionable. If we could believe that the Mukden Incident had been provoked by diplomatic policy, the injured party would have to be China and not Japan. We know too well that Tanaka's "positive policy" of 1927-29, causing mass murder by Japanese troops in Tsinan of innocent Chinese people, was incomparably more provocative than any effect of C. T. Wang's "revolutionary diplomacy."

The present writer deems that the real causes of the Mukden Incident may be another three: (1) a subtle shift of naval strength in the Pacific; (2) fluctuations in Sino-Soviet relations; and (3) the hopelessness of the Manchurian-Mongolian separatist movement. The first gave Japan the erroneous idea that she could do as she pleased in the Far East; the second caused Japan to adjust the Manchurian-Mongolian problem to her own advantage, and the third precipitated Japan's resorting to force.

1. *The Subtle Shift in Naval Strength*

The distance between Yokohama and San Francisco is 4,536 miles. If there had been no sea or air communication, there could have been no cause for enmity between Japan and the United States. As it was, after the Spanish-American War (1898-99) and the Russo-Japanese War (1904-05), the two nations were brought very close to each other. The islands in the southwest Pacific had become the object of naval contention between the two countries.[14] Therefore, the idea that Japan and the United States were bound to go to war was, in itself, a consequence of war. Although the two nations confronted each other in the Pacific, their conflicts of interest were shaped in Manchuria. Japan's rights in Manchuria were derived from the Portsmouth Treaty which was signed by Japan and Russia on September 5, 1905, under the good offices of the United States. Nevertheless, shortly afterwards, Japan began to align herself with Russia to oppose the United States.[15] In March, 1906, Great Britain and the United States sent a joint communication to Japan asking her not to close off Manchuria as Russia had done.[16] This was the first Japanese-American confrontation in the Pacific. Following the failure of Harriman's plans to buy the South Manchuria Railway (1905) and to construct the Chinchow-Aigun line (1909), and Knox's plan to neutralize all foreign-owned railways in Manchuria (1909), Japanese-American relations became further strained.[17] Although Japan had a legitimate grievance in California's discriminatory legislation affecting Japanese school children, Japan's ill will was running high against the United States when such statesmen as Marshal Yamagata and Admiral Togo, in a memorial to the Emperor, listed the United States as well as Russia as potential enemies.[18] This memorial was stored in the vault of the General Staff for forty years. Had it not been for Japan's surrender in 1945, the document might not have come to light. Its contents, though revised from time to time, showed that, from the first, Japan had considered Russia her primary hypothetical enemy and the United States as the second. Between 1907 and 1936, this order of priority was twice revised. The first revision, in 1918, put the United States ahead of Russia, and China was added in third place. The second revision, in 1923, did not affect the relative place of the United States and Russia. Later on, Guam and the Philippines were listed as territories to be seized in case of war, and the Hiroshima infantry was trained for an invasion of the Philippines. This latest revision had been made following the signing of the Naval Treaty at the Washington Conference (1922).

At that Conference, Japan agreed, in a Nine-Power Treaty, to accept a ratio in capital ships of three-fifths of the aggregate tonnage, alloted to the United States and the United Kingdom. The Anglo-Japanese Alliance was replaced by a Four-Power Treaty, the other parties being the United States and France. In a Nine-Power Treaty regarding China, the other parties pledged themselves to courses of self-restraint in that country. This influenced the conclusion of a separate agreement between Japan and China, under which the latter recovered its rights in Shantung.

The fact that Japan gained freedom of action in Manchuria and Mongolia needs further explanation. During World War I, Japan, taking advantage of the Anglo-Japanese Alliance, had seized the German islands in the North Pacific, and had taken over German rights in Shantung. In 1915, as a result of her "Twenty-one Demands" she had usurped Chinese sovereignty in Mongolia and Manchuria. Various secret wartime agreements among Britain, France, and Russia, principally for postwar settlements, the Ishii-Lansing Agreement (1917) and the consideration that, until the war had been won, Japan's actions had to be tolerated, contributed to Japan's achieving a privileged position in the Far East. The Washington Conference may be compared to a common law court before which Japan had been arraigned to await a verdict. Japan was not unaware of this, and her delegates had been instructed to make concessions.[19]

Prior to the 20th century, Britain had been mistress of the seas, but by 1916, Britain's supremacy was superseded by that of the United States. A British naval base was constructed at Singapore. In 1914, under the Okuma Cabinet, a naval program, called the "8-8 plan" (eight battleships and eight cruisers) was planned, but, owing to a lack of funds, it had to be realized in stages. It was still uncompleted by the time of the Washington Conference.[20] A naval race had placed great financial burdens on all contestants. It was especially hard on Japan, a small nation with limited resources. In proportion to the national budget Japan's military expenses were much higher than those of Britain and the United States.[21] If the Washington Conference had not reached an agreement on naval curtailment, the race would have continued, and Japan's economy would have sustained a heavy blow. When Japan accepted the 5:5:3 ratio, Admiral Kato, the chief Japanese delegate, explained this to his colleagues in the following terms:

> Since the World War, a great change has taken place in the theory governing national defense. It is no longer the monopoly of the military, nor is the conduct of the war their exclusive responsibility. All future wars will be dependent upon general mobilization, for industrial and commercial expansion have become the bulwark of military strength. In the future, the financial resources for conducting a war will far exceed those of the Russo-Japanese War. In that war, Japan contracted loans in the United States. Should war break out between Japan and the United States, who can

> Japan ask for loans? Therefore, war between the two countries is out of the question.
>
> If a conference on naval reduction should fail, competition in naval construction will be further intensified. Our program for the 8-8 formula will not be completed until 1927, whereas the United States' second Three-Year Plan will be over in 1924. As time goes on, the difference between Japan and the United States in naval strength widens and the pressure on Japan will heighten. Although the proposed 5:5:3 ratio is not wholly satisfactory, it is better to accept it in view of what might happen should the conference fail.[22]

The admiral accepted the lower ratio in capital ships when an agreement was reached among Britain, Japan, and the United States that they would not strengthen the fortifications in their respective North Pacific island possessions, with certain reservations. In this way Japan was accorded an equality of security.

Thus, preponderance of sea power in the Western Pacific shifted to Japan. In those days, when neither supersonic airplanes nor radar had been developed, the effective range of naval war was 500 miles. Restricted by the agreement, the only naval bases which the United States could fortify in the Pacific were San Diego and Honolulu, which were at least 5,000 miles from Guam, and 6,000 miles from Manila. On the other hand, Japan's bases at Kure, Maizuru, and Yokosuka were within easy striking distance of Guam and Manila. Indeed, the entire China Sea came within Japan's sphere of naval influence. Japan was enabled to act freely in the Western Pacific area, thus whetting her ambitious designs in Manchuria and Mongolia. A letter dated February 23, 1932, addressed to Senator Borah by Secretary of State Stimson said, "The willingness of the American Government to surrender its then commanding lead in battleship construction and to leave its positions at Guam and in the Philippines without further fortifications was predicated upon, among other things, two self-denying covenants contained in the Nine-Power Treaty, which assured the nations of the world opportunity for their Eastern trade but also against the military aggrandizement of any other power at the expense of China.[23]

Unfortunately, Mr. Stimson's expectations of what these two self-denying measures would accomplish were not realized.

2. *Fluctuations in Sino-Soviet Relations*

After the Sino-Japanese War (1894) and the end of the Russo-Japanese War (1905), Japan's national defense policy was geared to preventing China and Russia from avenging their defeats. In December, 1921, soon after the Washington Naval Conference was convened, Maring, representing the Third International visited Dr. Sun Yat-sen in Kweilin.[24] Although there was no connection between these two events, in Japan's view, a virtual Anglo-American entente and Sino-Soviet collaboration were both serious blows. Anglo-American cooperation had already undermined Japan's dream of hegemony throughout East Asia; Sino-Soviet collaboration threatened a realization of avenging Japan's victories. Of the two, the second seemed a more frightening prospect. It is true that Russian strength had been sapped by the October, 1917 revolution, that she had become diplomatically isolated, that her economy had deteriorated, and that her people were on the verge of starvation. Yet, within a few years Russia was able, primarily through Lenin's machinations to restore her international prestige.

Four aspects of Lenin's chicanery were intimately related to the Far Eastern situation. (1) He founded the Third International, which normally constituted the bulwark of world revolution, but which actually served as Russia's Fifth Column abroad.[25] (2) He created the Far Eastern Republic at Chita in Transbaikal Province, which, though assuming the status of a newly independent nation, was under Soviet control.[26] (3) He proclaimed ostensibly that Russia would abandon Kamchatka, seemingly to expand trade with the United States, but actually to aggravate ill-will with Japan and the United States.[27] (4) He ordered the Chinese Communist Party to collaborate with the Kuomintang. Although it created the appearance that this was to help the Chinese Nationalist Revolution, his purpose was to strengthen the Soviet Union. While such maneuvers would normally take a few years to yield results, immediate favor of the Chinese people was gained, and fear in the Japanese government was aroused. This was strengthened by two proclamations, one by Chicherin and the other by Karakhan, renouncing the special interests that Czarist Russia had asserted in China.[28] The first Chinese persons to be chosen for collaboration by the Third International were warlords Wu pei-fu and Chen Chiung-min but not Sun Yat-sen, as had generally been expected.[29] It then was not too difficult to discern the real intent of the Russian Communists. However, since both Russia and China had been disappointed in the outcome of the Versailles Conference as having been slighted by the Western powers, China fell inadvertently into the trap of such slogans as anti-imperialism and the abolition of the unequal treaties. This was not only China's misfortune but also gave serious concern to Japan.

Among the Japanese, Baron Goto was the most concerned with Sino-Soviet collaboration. He was of the pro-Russian school and had been privy to several secret Russo-Japanese agreements. "When it was decided at the Washington Conference to replace the Anglo-Japanese Alliance by a Four-Power treaty," Goto advocated a Sino-Japanese-Russian alliance instead of Shidehara's proposed Anglo-American-Japanese entente. Goto's plan was to befriend Russia, which had been isolated by the other powers. Before the arrival in China of Joffe in 1922, there had been two Russo-Japanese conferences, one at Dairen and the other at Changchun. It was only when he learned that the talks had been unproductive that Joffe proceeded to China. When Goto learned that there was to be an agreement between Joffe and Sun Yat-sen, he sent his secretary, Yamaguchi, under an alias, to follow Joffe to Shanghai. Then Joffe, after signing a joint statement with Dr. Sun Yat-sen, returned to Tokyo with Liao Chung-kai, Sun Yat-sen's representative. From January to August, Joffe was reported as convalescing at Atami in Japan. Actually, he was conferring with Kawakami, Japanese Minister to Poland, on Soviet-Japanese relations and with Liao Chung-kai on the reorganization of the Kuomintang.[30] Joffe was an adept conspirator. While stationed in Berlin, he had sabotaged the German government by skillful use of diplomatic privileges. He was far more adroit than Kawakami or Liao.[31] Following Joffe's departure from Japan, Karakhan arrived in China. There he emulated Joffe's tactics in concluding a Sino-Soviet agreement with the Peking government and an agreement also with the Mukden regime. Concurrently he schemed to overthrow the Peking government through arrangements with the Nationalist Regime at Canton and warlord Feng Yu-hsiang's Kuominchun in North China.[32] An agreement re-establishing Soviet-Japanese relations was finally concluded in 1925. But by then, China, as well as most of the Western powers, had already concluded commercial treaties with the Soviet government. Goto's plan for forming an alliance between Japan, China and Russia was a failure

Military and financial aid was the basis for collaboration between the Russians and the Kuomintang. The latter's real intention was merely to obtain Russian military aid.[33] Political ideology played little part in bringing the two partners together. It was at the suggestion of the Third International that the Kuomintang admitted Chinese Communists to membership. Although collaboration with the Chinese Communists was not specified as a condition for China's Soviet orientation, it became necessary to pay due regard to the suggestions of the Third International. The foundations for alignment with Russia had already been laid in 1922 when Maring visited Sun Yat-sen, but the policy of collaborating with the Chinese Communists was not formally announced until July, 1924.[34]

The Chinese Communist Party had been independent. After May 1923, it joined the Third International and later became a branch of it. It received a monthly subsidy from Russia, and thus fell under the domination of Moscow.[35] In June, 1923, when the proposal for Communists joining the Kuomintang was brought to the Central Committee of the Chinese Communist Party, all five of its Standing Comimttee members, Chen Tu-hsiu, Li Ta-chao, Chang Kuo-tao, Kao Chun-yu, and Tsai Ho-sheng, opposed it.[36] They reconsidered their stand only after Maring had invoked the discipline of the Third International. Thus, coercion and bribery by the Third International were solely responsible for this result. More precisely, it was Stalin himself who acted in this matter because of his involvement in a conflict with Trotsky. Consequently, neither the collaboration nor the split between the Chinese Communist Party and Kuomintang was strictly an internal affair of China. Although it was Maring who carried out the Third

International's policy of pressing the Chinese Communist Party to join the Kuomintang, his successor, Voitinsky, had supervised the splitting of the Kuomintang into factions. In 1923, Voitinsky became the Third International's representative in China. He immediately instructed the Chinese to split the Kuomintang into right, left, and center factions. They were also expected to rally the left and center to attack the right.[37] Consequently, conflicts developed within the Kuomintang. From the outset Sun Yat-sen had consented to Chinese Communist Party members joining the Kuomintang but only as individuals, so that their action after joining, in maintaining a highly organized central committee, was a gross violation of the conditions originally agreed to. Sun frequently told Maring that he would not tolerate any violation of the Kuomintang's principles and discipline, and that if such violation occurred, he would not hesitate to dismiss Chen Tu-hsiu and oppose the Soviet Union.[38] So, had Sun lived in the period of international communists' conspiracy against the Kuomintang, he would probably have done what Chiang Kai-shek did in 1927-28.

The forces in China utilized by the Soviet Union were not limited to the Kuomintang. There were also the Second National Army under Hu Ching-yi,[39] the first National Army under Feng Yu-hsiang,[40] the North-eastern Army under Kuo Sung-lin,[41] and even those students who, on March 18, 1926, demonstrated before the Office of the Chief Executive of the Peking Government.[42] From secret documents obtained in a raid on the Soviet Embassy in Peking, and from books such as *World-wide Soviet Plot in China,* by Mitaravsky, *Revelations of a Soviet Diplomat,* by Grigori Besedovsky, and *Nationalism, Communism and Soviet Advisers, 1918-1927* by Wilbur and How, we learn that, in 1925-26, when Borodin and Kissanka were active in Canton, Karakhan also was playing an influential role among the National Armies in the North. Since Canton was in a British sphere of influence, London was alarmed by the collaboration between the Chinese Nationalists and the Communists. Sino-Soviet collaboration in North China, coveted by Japan, precipitated rash actions by the Japanese militarists. While Britain faced the situation with serenity and gave up her gunboat policy, Japan persisted in her mailed-fist policy, and thereby fell into the Soviet trap.

Karakhan's utilization of Feng Yu-hsiang and Kuo Sung-lin conflicted with Japan's support of Chang Tso-lin and Tuan Chi-jui. When the Kwantung Army halted Kuo Sung-lin's advance into Mukden, Ivanov, general manager of the Chinese Eastern Railway, retaliated by impeding the transporting of Chang's troops from Kirin and Heilungkiang.[43] When the Kwantung Army was pressing on Kuo Sung-lin, and Chang arrested Ivanov, Karakhan twice requested Moscow to send in troops. War between Russia and Japan seemed imminent. It was averted only because Russia realized her own military weaknesses.[44] The collaboration between Karakhan and Feng Yu-hsiang had begun after the death of General Hu Ching-yi on April 10, 1925. Theretofore, there had been an agreement between the Russians and Hu for the dispatch of a military training mission to China. Hu died shortly after the mission arrived. The Russians then turned to deal with Feng Yu-hsiang.[44] Although Feng was glad to receive Russian military aid, he was reluctant to permit the Communists to participate in political work in his army.

In March, 1926, Feng Yu-hsiang's army was defeated at Tientsin and was withdrawn into the Nankou pass. Feng left Kalgan for Ping-ti-chuan and Urga. During his subsequent sojourn in Russia he joined the Kuomintang and began the study of Communism.[45] As early as when initial military contracts had been made between Karakhan and Feng, there were rumors in Tokyo that Russia had agreed to make him a loan of three million rubles.[46] In the documents obtained from the raid on the Soviet Embassy, it was revealed that Feng had received six million rubles worth of arms from the Soviet Union. Included were 59,000 rifles, 320 machine guns, 150 cannons, 4 heavy cannons, 8 planes, and a number of tanks. There were 114 military instructors in his artillery, 240 in his cavalry, 180 in his machine gun corps, 40 in his engineering corps, and 60 in his signal corps. Russia's aid to Feng was not less than that to the Whampoa Military Academy.[47]

In March, 1926, Kissanka lost favor with Chiang Kai-shek and was expelled from Canton. In August of the same year,

Karakhan also was having trouble with Chang Tso-lin, and left Peking. Thus, Sino-Soviet relations reached a low ebb. Realizing that the Third International could not hoodwink the Kuomintang indefinitely, Stalin changed his tactics. He promoted Soviet trade with Japan from (U.S.) $600,000 in 1925 to (U.S.) $6,000,000 in 1931,[48] concluded a fishery agreement with Japan in 1928, and offered Tokyo a non-aggression pact three times but without success.[49] On the other hand, in 1926, he instigated the Nanking Incident against the Western Powers and Japan; in 1927, he engineered the Chientao riot against Japan,[50] and in early 1937, intensified the anti-Japanese movement in Liaoning and Kirin provinces.[51] Each of these was skillfully managed through Chinese Communists. The result was that the Soviet Union was saved; whereas, Sino-Japanese relations seriously deteriorated.

The Sino-Soviet conflict over the Chinese Eastern Railway in 1930 also encouraged Japan's aggression against China. During the conflict, all of the great powers, except the United States, seemed indifferent to the Chinese situation and even American good offices were ineffective.[52] This convinced the Japanese that they could act freely in Manchuria. It was then that Kwantung Army officers started making expeditions to North Manchuria in preparation for disposing of their problems in Mongolia and Manchuria by force. It is in this way that the fluctuations in Sino-Soviet relations had a bearing on the development of the Mukden Incident.

3. *Hopelessness of the Manchurian-Mongolian Separatist Movement.*

The movement to detach Manchuria and Mongolia from China constituted a prime factor in Japan's continental policy. It had lasted uninterruptedly from 1911 to 1931. In this movement, there were three outstanding episodes. The first was Kawashima Ronsoku's plan for the partitioning of Manchuria and Mongolia;[53] the second, the incident at Chao-yang-po perpetrated by Baputsapu,[54] and the third, the dispatch of troops to Shantung by the Tanaka Cabinet.[55] The Tanaka Cabinet was formed on April 20, 1927. Although its life was but a little more than two years, it sent three military expeditions to

China.[56] Historians generally hold this as being a clear demonstration of Tanaka's "positive policy," but we now know that it was formulated by Mori Kaku. Mori was a Seiyukai Party member. During the first year of the Republic of China, when Yuan Shih-k'ai was in power, he planned to offer Dr. Sun Yat-sen twenty million yen for his third revolution against Yuan in exchange for Sun's pledge that Japan was to obtain Manchuria and Mongolia.[57] The offer was never accepted. In 1926, when Chiang's Northern Expeditionary forces reached Wuhan, Mori, along with Yamamoto (Jotaro) and Matsuoka, was sent to Hankow as a representative of the Seiyukai Party. There he met Eugene Chen, Sun Fo and Borodin and also met Chiang Kai-shek at Kiukiang.[58] Upon his return, he reported that the Soviet Union was the prime mover behind the Chinese Revolution, and that the Nanking Incident was planned jointly by the Soviet Union and the Chinese Communists.[59] In the Tanaka Cabinet, Mori was merely a vice-foreign minister responsible for parliamentary affairs and by no means close to Tanaka.[60] But within the Seiyukai Party, he was virtually the boss, although Tanaka was nominally its president.[61]

In the autumn of 1927, two important Conferences concerning China's policy took place. One was the Second Eastern Conference presided by Tanaka and the other, the Dairen Conference headed by Mori.[62] Both were aimed at the seizure of Manchuria by force.[63] In the Eastern Conference, "the Eight Points Program" was adopted. Six of which were announced, and two, the seventh and the eighth, were concealed until Japanese surrender. Point seven stated that the political stability of Manchuria should be maintained by its inhabitants themselves, and that Japan would support any regime that respected Japan's special privileges there. Point eight was to the effect that, should chaos arise in Manchuria and Mongolia, thereby affecting Japan's special interests or endangering the lives and livelihood of the Japanese residents, Japan would take appropriate remedial action.[64] In the record of that Conference, two conflicting views about China appeared, one moderate, the other, radical. The moderates were Muto Noyuboshi and Yoshizawa Kenkichi and the radicals Muto, Komoto Daisaku, and Yoshida

Shigeru. The following dialogue between Muto and Prime Minister Tanaka is interesting.

Muto: If this program is carried out, it is bound to precipitate war between Japan and the United States. Are you prepared to risk a war with the United States or even a world war?

Tanaka: I am determined to cope with whatever consequences this policy may bring.

Muto: Are you sure that your determination will not falter?

Tanaka: I will not falter.

Muto: Since the government has the determination, we will obey orders and say nothing.[65]

This assurance apparenty silenced Muto, but as we shall see, Tanaka did change his mind later.

After the Eastern Conference, Yoshida Shigeru returned to Mukden, where he was Consul General. He saw Chinese authorities there on matters such as the construction of parallel railways, the establishment of a Japanese consulate at Maoerhshan, and the stopping of the riots at Chientao. His attitude was so arrogant that he provoked a boycott of Japanese goods. The civil and military authorities of the Kwantung Leased Territory expressed concern for Chang Tso-lin's political status, and tried to advise Tanaka not to be obdurate. Tanaka, however, took the view that if Chang were subjected to heavier pressure, he would need Japanese help all the more.[66] Tanaka, in fact, had conceived another secret plan, which was being communicated sub-rosa to Chang.

Before the convening of the Eastern Conference, Tanaka had secretly sent to Peking, Yamamoto, President of the South Manchuria Railway Company, and Machino, Chang Tso-lin's adviser and confidant. Their mission was to demand of Chang an exclusive right for Japan to construct five new railways in Manchuria and Mongolia.[67] These were: (1) Tun-tu line (Tunwa-Tumen River); (2) Chang-ta line (Changchun-Tali); (3) Ki-wu line (Ki-lin-Wu-chang); (4) Yen-hai line (Yen-chi-Hailin and (5) Tao-so line (Taonan-Solun). All of these railways would have military and economic value. For example, the

Tun-tu line would form the last section of the Ki-hui (Ki-lin to Huining) line. When completed the travel time from Changchun to Osaka via Dairen would be shortened by 35 hours, and since the route would be out of range of attack by enemy vessels, military transportation would be safe. This project had long been Japan's dream.[68] On October 8, 1927, a two days' negotiation between them and Chang Tso-lin at Peking yielded an arrangement under which Chang would consent to Japan's having the railway right, in exchange for a political and economic agreement, which would be signed. Japan would pay ten million yen for the land used, one half of which would be paid in advance. However, it was still to be decided whether the agreement would be sealed by an official diplomatic document or would be a private agreement between Tanaka and Chang.[69] About that time, the Dairen Conference, under Mori's initiative, had decided upon a drastic China policy. Yamamoto was afraid that his work would be ruined, so he returned immediately to Tokyo to report to Tanaka. There, he also invited Mori and others to his home to brief them on his mission. Only then did Mori learn about the railway negotiations. In November, Yamamoto went back to Peking. By February, 1928, the negotiations were completed. By then the Nanking government had already decided to proceed with the second stage of the Northern Expedition.

The Kuomintang Northern Expedition was approaching Tsinan so rapidly that it caught both Japan and the Peking Government unprepared. The Japanese military attachés (Sakai and Fujii) hurriedly requested that several thousand troops be sent to protect the 2,000 Japanese residents in Tsinan where they had peacefully lived. When the dispatch of troops was first proposed, the War Ministry had misgivings. Having evacuated his first expeditionary troops from Shantung in August, 1927 [70] and having talked with Chiang Kai-shek in November of the same year, Tanaka knew that the Kuomintang was anti-Communist, and that Japan's interests in China would not be jeopardized. Therefore, he was all the more reluctant to comply with the request, but because of Mori's insistence, 5,000 troops were again dispatched to Tsingtao. They were intended to demonstrate only, but their commander, Fukuda, instigated by Sakai, moved them to Tsinan [71] and challenged China with an ultimatum.[72] Sakai also shocked the Tokyo authorities by magnifying twenty-three fold the number of Japanese victims.[73] Consequently, for a third time, troops were dispatched to Shantung. On May 8, they launched a massive attack. Thus Sakai's role in the Tsinan incident was comparable to the role played by Kanda, Ishihara, and Itagaki in the Mukden Incident.

When, on May 4, Chinese and Japanese troops clashed at Tsinan at 9:37 A.M., this writer was there as manager of the Chinese American Bank of Commerce, which was located on Weishan Road next to the Yokohama Specie Bank, where Fukuda maintained his headquarters. According to Japanese sources, the clash had been caused by the intrusion of Chinese soldiers into the residence of Yoshida Ryohei, correspondent of the *Manchuria Daily News*.[74] According to more reliable Japanese sources now available, it was caused by Sakai's intrigues.[75] No Japanese information is available on the tragic death of Tsai Kung-shih, Commissioner for Foreign Affairs.

In his address on the first anniversary of the Tsinan incident, Chiang Kai-shek threw some light on what had occurred in Tsinan. He said:

> At 8 A.M. on May 3, the Japanese Consul, Nishida Koichi and a Japanese gendarme called on me, praising highly the discipline of the Revolutionary Army. About ten minutes after they had left, machine gun fire was suddenly heard. I instructed my aide to investigate and learned that Japanese troops were clashing with ours. I immediately ordered the commanders of our several divisions to restrain their soldiers and try to avoid clashes with the Japanese. At the same time, I also requested Fukuda to take corresponding measures. He sent a man to inform me that he would do so.
>
> At 5 P.M. Foreign Minister Huang Fu telephoned me that he was at the Japanese Army Headquarters, and asked me to send a car for him. I informed Fukuda that the Chinese forces would leave Tsinan before 5 P.M. and told him to restrain his soldiers from reckless shooting, which could only endanger innocent civilians. Fukuda requested that we send someone to attend a meeting. It

was then agreed that the meeting would be held in the office of the Commissioner for Foreign Affairs. I promptly sent Hsiung Shih-hui as our representative.

In the meantime, Foreign Minister Huang Fu had returned. I asked him why he went to the Japanese army headquarters. He replied that, as soon as machine gun fire was heard, the office of the Commissioner for Foreign Affairs was surrounded. He revealed his identity to a Japanese officer, who invited him to accompany the officer to the Japanese headquarters. Once there, Huang was ordered to wait in a small room and asked to sign a document admitting that the clash between Chinese and Japanese was caused by looting on the part of Chinese troops. Huang refused to sign. The Japanese officer then threatened him with a pistol, saying, 'if you want to live, you must sign.' Huang then reprimanded him for his insolence, after which the Japanese became more abusive. At that moment, the man (Chinese) who had been sent by Huang in the morning to investigate, returned with a Japanese soldier. The Japanese officer pointed to the Chinese who the officer said, had witnessed the killing of a Japanese soldier by a Chinese, and that therefore Huang should sign the report submitted by the Chinese to authenticate it. Huang replied that he could only write the word 'read' on the report. It was only after he had done so that he was allowed to leave.

At the meeting, the Japanese demanded that the Tsingtao-Tsinan Railway must not be used to transport troops, and that the Chinese forces must be withdrawn to a distance of 20 miles from Tsinan. Hsiung Shih-hui replied that all he could do was to report the demands, but he could not sign. I realized that Japan's purpose was to bring pressure to bear on our military progress so that China's unification could not be achieved. Accordingly, I ordered my troops to cross the river secretly that evening. On the following day, when the Japanese learned about it, they began a massive bombing of Tsinan.

The manner of Tsai Kung-shih's death was revealed by his aide, who had hidden behind a door while Tsai was being tried. It was said that, after he had been bound and taken to the Japanese headquarters, he was ordered to kneel but refused. In order to frighten him, the

> Japanese shot and killed on the spot a dozen or so Chinese. When Tsai remained firm, they broke his legs. Tsai collapsed but still was able to shout back at his captors. They first cut off his tongue and then shot him.[76]

As the Northern Expeditionary force approached Peking and Tientsin, Japan realized that Chang Tso-lin's regime in Manchuria was in imminent danger. The Japanese tried to take advantage of this situation to gain further concessions from the warlord. On May 12, Eto Toyozo, representing the South Manchuria Railway, pressed Chang to sign the agreement for the five railways. Chang Yin-huai, then Minister of Communications of the Peking Government, left for Tientsin, and Liu Ching-shan, Director of the Department of Railways, sent in his resignation. Both of them were adverse to serving as tools for the Japanese. Consequently, the Japanese had to apply direct pressure on Chang Tso-lin.[77] Chao Chen, Director of the Department of Navigation, was appointed acting Minister of Communications. On May 13, he stamped the Ministry's official seal on the agreement which granted the Japanese monopoly rights to the Tun-tu and Chang-ta lines.[78] On the day following, the Japanese found a number of flaws in the agreement. First, Chao Chen's appointment would not be effective until the 15th; second, though the agreement was signed on the 13th, which fell on Sunday, it was then agreed to have the date changed to May 15. It is not clear how many railways were included in the agreement because the pertinent document on this matter, according to Mukden officials, had been destroyed during the blasting of Chang Tso-lin's train by the Japanese at Huangkutun. According to Japanese sources, the agreement covered four railways, the Tun-tu, Chang-ta, Yen-hai, and Tao-so lines. Only the Ki-wu line required further negotiations after Chang Tso-lin's return to Mukden.[79]

Tanaka had intended not only to make Chang sign the railway agreement, but also to disarm Mukden troops inside Shanhaikwan, and to force Chang to retire. On May 18, three days after the signing of the railway agreement, the Tokyo government presented an aide memoire to both the Nanking and Peking governments and to the Western powers, stating that should the turmoil of war reach Manchuria and Mongolia, Japan would take effective measures to maintain peace and order in those areas.[80] On the eve of this communication, Minister Yoshizawa was instructed to supervise the withdrawal in Manchuria of Chang Tso-lin's army. In case his army was retreating in defeat, the Japanese troops would disarm it in the vicinity of Shanhaikwan.[81] On May 20, the General Staff at Tokyo prepared a secret mobilization, which consisted of the following five points: (1) Japanese units stationed in Manchuria were to move immediately toward Mukden; (2) a brigade, which had been withdrawn from Tsinan to Dairen would be re-routed to Mukden; (3) the main Japanese forces in Manchuria were to concentrate in Mukden; (4) crack units would be sent to Chinchow, Ichou, Shanhaikwan and Chao-yang-chen to watch over the Mukden troops; (5) Japanese troops to be assigned to maintain peace and security in Hsinmintun and Hsinchiatun.

The General Staff and the Kwantung Army had agreed in advance that an Imperial Order authorizing the mobilization would take effect on May 22.[82] Accordingly, on that day, Muraoka, Saito and Komoto met at the Kwantung Army headquarters to await the Imperial Order. At midnight they received word that the order had been postponed.[83] On the following day, Colonel Tashiro Kanichiro arrived from Tokyo and informed them that the Government had changed its original plan. It had been decided to let Chang Tso-lin retain his status. The Kwantung Army was disappointed and telegraphed the War Ministry for a quick decision.

The Tokyo Government's indecision had been caused by the attitude of the United States. When Japan's aide memoire reached Washington, the State Department told Matsumoto, the Japanese Ambassador, that the sovereignty of the three Northeastern Provinces belonged exclusively to China.[84] Mr. Borah, Chairman of the Senate Foreign Relations Committee, also told the press that the Japanese move was too unyielding. On the next day, the United States formally asked that Japan inform the United States before any positive actions were taken.[85] The Japanese Foreign Ministry immediately invited the War, Navy and other ministries concerned to discuss counter measures.

There were many suggestions but no decision was reached. Araki, then Chief of the Section of Operations, War Ministry, said heatedly, "You gentlemen should have made your decision on this matter at the Eastern Conference. Why did you wait until today?" Mori suggested that the original plan be adhered to. But the Navy opposed it.[86] Tanaka wavered. On May 25th, two higher officers, Arita Hachiro of the Foreign Office, and Abe Nobuyuki of the War Ministry called on Tanaka for a final decision. After long contemplation, Tanaka decided to halt Mori's plan.[87] When the news reached the Kwantung Army, gloom came over Komoto, Muraoka and Saito.

Assassination of Chang Tso-lin

On June 4, 1928 Chang Tso-lin[88] was killed by a bomb when his train was passing Huangkutun on the way to Mukden. Initially, the government in Tokyo suppressed news of the tragedy. Japanese news agencies abroad alleged that plain clothes assassins from the south (Kuomintang) had used hand grenades to carry out the plot. To confuse public opniion they reported the discovery of corpses of two Chinese and a letter written to "Junhsien" as evidence. Both the Chinese and the Japanese authorities in Mukden twice conducted joint investigations but without reaching any agreement.[89] The Lytton Commission stated that the responsibility for this outrage was enshrouded in clouds. At a conference of the Institute of Pacific Relations at Kyoto in 1932, China's delegate, David Yu, said that Japan should bear the responsibility for the incident. The entire Japanese delegation withdrew as a gesture of protest.[90] In July, 1946, at the Tokyo War Crimes Trial, Admiral Okada, Navy Minister in the Tanaka Cabinet and later Prime Minister, testified that Chang Tso-lin's assassination was the work of the Kwantung Army staff.[91] The secret of an international assassination was unveiled fifteen years after the act.

The relations between Chang Tso-lin and Japan were anomalous. During the Ching dynasty, he had been captured by the Japanese as a Russian spy but released when he promised to spy for the Japanese. In 1916, with Japanese aid, he succeeded in ousting his superior, Tuan Chih-kuei. However, at that time he was almost assassinated by the Japanese. In 1925, he suppressed the defection of Kuo Sung-lin, with indispensable help from the South Manchuria Railway. Yet, later he decided to build his own railway network to avoid the threat of the Japanese railway. At the time of the "Twenty-One Demands," Chang offered Yuan Shih-k'ai troops to resist Japan. However, during the May 4, 1919 movement, he prohibited boycotting Japanese goods in Manchuria. This shows that Chang's attitude toward Japan was inconsistent. The Japanese also regarded Chang with mixed feelings: sometimes with gratitude, other times with displeasure. Even shortly before his assassination, the Japanese had no wish to eliminate him, for he was to be retained in order to realize their plan for detaching Manchuria and Mongolia from China. Chang eventually became, however, a victim of the Kwantung Army. It seems that though he had been friendly to Japan, when Japan wanted him to betray China he could not but refuse. This was the commendable side of this famous warlord and also why Japan failed to detach Manchuria and Mongolia from China.

Circumstances of the Bombing

At 1:00 A.M. on June 3, Chang Tso-lin left his Peking residence and ten minutes later arrived at the east station at Chienmen. The train left 1:15 A.M. Accompanying him were Pan Fu, Mo Teh-hui, Liu Che, and Yu Kuo-han, all high officials. There were also two Japanese advisers: Col. Machino Takema and Major Soga Reiya. At Tientsin, Pan Fu and Machino disembarked, and Chang Yin-huai joined the entourage. The special train consisted of eighteen cars. When the train left Peking, Chang's car was the third. Wu Chun-sheng boarded the train at Shanhaikwan, and Chang shifted to the fourth car, which was adjacent to the blue express, and was, therefore, easily identified.[92] It was said that before the train left Peking, Chang's agents had given warning of a plot to assassinate him and that Chang sought Machino's advice. To reassure Chang, Machino offered to accompany him on the trip. Soga, however, did go all the way with Chang. As a result of the bombing, Wu Chunsheng died immediately. Chang Tso-lin was mortally wounded and died at 10:00 that morning. Soga had a slight leg wound.

In June, Alexander Ramsay of the Reuter Agency made an on-the-spot investigation. He reported that the incident had occurred under a suspension bridge of the South Manchuria Railway. The bridge had three sections, supported by thick concrete columns. An explosion was first heard, followed by the collapse of the bridge span, which fell squarely on Chang's car as well as on those on either side of it. Chang died from injuries sustained in the crash. The car ceilings were completely wrecked, though the car bodies were not severely damaged. The explosion apparently came from above, and the damage was not caused by ground mines or hand grenades. The force of the explosion indicated that it had been ignited by electric current. The timing of the bombing was so accurate that the explosion came only seconds after the train had entered the underpass. Such accuracy required a high degree of engineering technology and not less than six hours of preparation. Two hundred pounds of TNT must have been used.[93]

Details of the Assassination Plot

The assassination plot was initiated by Muraoka, Commander-in-Chief of the Kwantung Army. At first he had ordered Lieutenant Colonel Takeshita, a military attaché from Harbin to proceed to Peking to carry it out. Komoto suggested that Peking, being a great metropolis, might be a difficult place to commit the deed successfully. It was then decided that the assassination should be carried out while Chang Tso-lin was on the way to Mukden. The date was set for May 31 after the Kwantung Army had received orders to cancel its planned attack on Chinchow and Hsinmintun. Initially, a bridge over the Chuliu River had been picked for the deed, but later the Huangkutun underpass was chosen instead. This was because the other place was well guarded by Chinese soldiers and police, which made it impossible to survey the route to the bombing site. Teams and individual officers were assigned to various duties: surveying the bombing site, electrically detonating bombs, setting the electric current, organizing a bayonet corps to deal with military emergencies, studying Chang's up-to-the minute travel time table. Japanese agents were stationed all along the train route to report the train's movement. Komoto was in charge of all operations and also provided explosives and funds. The plot was so well planned that nothing could have gone wrong.[94] Arrangements had been made to exonerate the perpetrators. Adachi, a ronin, had bought the services of Liu Tai-minh, an unemployed veteran of the Chinese Army, to help find three Chinese beggars. At midnight on June 3, the beggars were brought to a Japanese bath-house in the railway zone to wash up and change clothes. They were then taken to the Huangkutun underpass to be stabbed to death. One of the beggars was more alert and escaped. Later on, he secretly reported what had happened to some of Chang Hsueh-liang's men. After Chang's assassination the Japanese said they had found two corpses, which of course were those of the hapless Chinese beggars.[95] The bath-house owner, out of curiosity, had also gone to take a look at the corpses. When he realized that these were those of his customers of the night before, he immediately reported the matter to the Japanese gendarmes in Mukden. It was his report that was the basis of the subsequent story circulated in Tokyo of the Kwantung Army's plot to assassinate Chang.[96]

Liu Tai-minh had served under General Meng En-yuan, who had been expelled from Kirin by Chang Tso-lin. Liu, in revenge, had collaborated with the Japanese. Adachi had promised him a record amount, but except for a down payment of one thousand yen, the promise for the balance was not kept. But when Premier Tanaka and other high officials heard of it, they were apprehensive lest Liu reveal to Chang Hsueh-liang Japan's sinister designs, and he was paid the balance, which provided him the capital to open an opium den in Dairen. Nothing further was heard of him.

Political Repercussions

The Kwantung Army's purpose in assassinating Chang Tso-lin was to create a situation more favorable for establishing an independent state in Manchuria and Mongolia. At the time of the assassination, the Chief of Staff of the Kwantung Army was holding in his hand the "plan of national salvation by invading China" [97] and advocating openly the formation of a puppet government in Manchuria and Mongolia. On the day of the bombing, Komoto had sent a company of Japanese soldiers to be stationed in the railway zone. Because he had not made contact with Saito about this adventure, the latter refused to let them in. On that day, the Kwantung Army had telephoned the Japanese Consulate several times, asking permission to send troops to maintain order outside the railway zone. These requests also were rejected by Consul Morishima. Also on that day, many ronin tried to create panic in the Japanese residential and business areas of Mukden by throwing home-made bombs. However, because of the calmness of the Chinese authorities in handling the situation, the ronin failed to create incidents.[98]

In Tokyo, it was Premier Tanaka who was the most disappointed by the assassination of Chang Tso-lin. This was because agreement on the constructing of the five new railways had just been signed and Chang Tso-lin had also accepted Japanese advice to return to Manchuria. Tanaka was then hopeful that he could coerce Chang to co-operate toward the realization of Japan's design of detaching Manchuria and Mongolia from China. He told General Ugaki and Admiral Okada to punish the Kwantung Army and the culprits in the assassination.[99] Prince Saionji also suggested that a tightening of the discipline in the army was needed.[100] The militarists in the General Staff and the Ministry, however, considered the Kwantung Army, rather than suffering punishment, would be commended for its loyalty. They insisted that if there was to be any punishment it should not go beyond administrative action. The Seiyukai also suggested that Tanaka deal with the matter leniently. After mulling over the issue for a year, Tanaka finally decided to report to the Emperor that the Kwantung Army "was innocent of any involvement in Chang Tso-lin's assassination." Emperor Hirohito felt that Tanaka was inconsistent in his report, which was tantamount to deception, and told his aide that he did not wish to see Tanaka again. Tanaka felt greatly humiliated and resigned. A few months later he died.[101]

By May 1937, when "Manchukuo" had been in existence five years, General Ueda, who was then concurrently Japanese

Ambassador and Commander-in-Chief of the Kwantung Army, held a Buddhist burial service for Chang Tso-lin, and his remains were removed for burial next to his mother's grave at Chinchow. There is no doubt that this Japanese gesture was calculated to win the good-will of the people of Manchuria.

Manchuria's Adherence to the Nanking Government

Although Chang Tso-lin's assassination did not alter Japan's basic goal of detaching Manchuria and Mongolia from China, arrangements had to be made for a successor. The Kwantung Army Staff proposed several candidates. General Matsui, who had been adviser to Chang Tso-lin, favored Yang Yu-ting; Hata, head of the Intelligence Agency at Mukden, recommended Chang Hsueh-liang and Komoto proposed Chang Ching-hui.[102] But all of them agreed with Tokyo that the Nanking government's influence must not be permitted to enter Manchuria. After the Huangkutun incident, the Chinese people and army forces in Manchuria became panicky. Japanese troops were everywhere, from Mukden to Chinchow. The news of Chang's death was not published until June 18, ten days after the Kwantung Army had the news. If at that time the Kwantung Army Commander had been Honjo instead of Muraoka and the War Minister, Araki instead of Shirakawa, "Manchukuo" might have been established before the Mukden Incident. At the time of Chang Tso-lin's assassination, his son, Chang Hsueh-liang was in Paoting, south of Peking. He postponed the announcement of his father's death and hurried under cover to Mukden via Chinwangtao. Two weeks later he was elected Governor of Fengtien by the Provincial Council.[103] He then became Commander-in-Chief of the Security Forces of the Three Northeastern Provinces and Chairman of the Committee for the Maintenance of Peace. At his inaugural ceremony, he issued a circular telegram advocating peace between Nanking and the Northern regime. The Japanese Consul General at Mukden was the first to congratulate him. On the surface there was mutual good-will, but in fact, Chang was under heavy pressure. Archives of the Japanese Foreign Office reveal that between June 15 and 16, Chief of Staff of the Kwantung Army and Military Attaché of the Japanese Embassy in Peiping, Tatekawa, had independently reported to the War Ministry that "the time to detach Manchuria from China proper has ripened." [104] Arita, Director of the Bureau of Asian Affairs of the Foreign Office, also had drafted a China policy. This consisted of a general course regarding China as a whole and special provisions on Manchuria. Part one called for, among other things, recognition of the Nationalist Government in concert with the other powers, and part two, the detachment of Manchuria from China proper "to prevent its Bolshevization." [105] On Japanese policy toward Manchuria there once were two schools of thought: the observance of treaties school and the domination by force school. The Foreign Office had up to then consistently been of the first school. Thus the new policy marked a chnge in Tanaka's attitude following the death of Chang Tso-lin.

Japan's pressure on Chang Hsueh-liang had two objectives: one, to prevent his aligning himself with Nanking; and two, to make him yield to Japan's demands for the expansion of her railway interests in Manchuria and Mongolia. To oppose Chang's alignment with Nanking was tantamount to blocking China's unification. This was censured by Britain and the United States, and even Japan's diplomats in China, including Minister Yoshizawa and Consuls General Hayashi and Yada, advised against it.[106] Tanaka, however, was determined to have his own way. On June 25 and again on June 26, he telegraphed Hayashi instructions to warn Chang Hsueh-liang not to compromise with the Nanking government. On July 18, Tanaka repeated his instructions. On June 29, and again on July 19, Hayashi called on Chang. On the latter occasion, Hayashi conveyed the message from his government that the Nanking government was Communistic; that its status had not yet been stabilized; that if Nanking used military force against Manchuria, Japan would do her best to assist the latter, and that if Manchuria should need financial aid, the Yokohama Specie Bank would extend ample assistance.[107]

Chang then asked Hayashi whether he might inform the Nanking government of Japan's unwillingness to see Chang pledge adherence to the Nanking government and thus assure a unified

China. Hayashi evaded the question. The next day Chang called on Muraoka and repeated his question. Muraoka gave no answer, though he later reported the meeting to Tanaka. On July 25, at a meeting of the National Security Forces held at the North-Eastern Commander-in-Chief's headquarters, it was unanimously decided that the three Northeast provinces should pledge allegiance to Nanking, but this should not be carried out immediately. Thus, Tanaka's first intervention was temporarily successful.

Before Japan's intervention, both Yen Hsi-shan and Li Lieh-chun had advised Chang to help consummate China's unification by political means.[108] By June and July, the Kuomintang flag flew throughout China proper except in Tsinan and the Chimo District in Shantung, which were under Japanese military occupation. Even remote Sinkiang Province had pledged allegiance to Nanking. China's diplomatic representatives abroad also had come over to the new government. This proved that the Kuomintang government at Nanking had popular support over all of China, including the three Northeastern provinces. Tanaka, however, insisted upon having his way. He sent a veteran diplomat, Hayashi Gonsuke, as a special envoy to attend Chang Tso-lin's funeral. At the same time, Hayashi was carrying with him a highly confidential document, which has been included in the files of the Tokyo War Crimes Trials. It read, in translation, as follows:

> From Japan's point of view, it is inimical for the three Northeastern provinces to come to terms with the Nanking government. Fortunately Chang Hsueh-liang has offered to stop further negotiations with the South. In this way, Manchuria will become the most advanced province in China. Had Marshal Chang Tso-lin lived, he would have been pleased to see this achievement. By following this course, Chang Hsueh-liang is fulfilling the wishes of his late father.
>
> If the enemy should invade Manchuria, Japan will endure any sacrifice to carry out her present policy and to maintain order in the three Northeastern provinces.[109]

Hayashi had had long experience in China and had just been appointed ambassador to France. He regarded Chang

Hsueh-liang as a teenager. Between August 4 and 12, the two had four secret talks. Hayashi's tone on the 9th was characteristically minatory.

The following is an excerpt from their dialogue:

> Hayashi: The Nanking Government is seething with internal dissension and also is communist-oriented. Japan's rights in Manchuria might be impaired. Therefore it would be best to take a wait-and-see attitude. Should you disregard Japan's warning we are resolved to exercise freedom of action. We hope you will therefore try to suppress undesirable elements. Japan will give you every help that you may need.
>
> Chang: Being Chinese, I must proceed from the Chinese viewpoint. The only reason for my desire to cooperate with the Nanking Government is that I want to see a unified China. Although I am willing to consider Japan's advice, nevertheless ultimately my course will depend upon the will of the people of Manchuria. I do not understand why Japan has time and again threatened me so severely.
>
> Hayashi: Japan has already decided that even if she has to interfere in China's affairs she will do so. I hope you will soon make your decision.
>
> Chang: My decision is that I must abide by the will of the people of Manchuria. I cannot disregard public opinion.

During the interview, Wang Chia-cheng and Major-General Sato were present. Sato suggested that this was not the time to discuss what was right and what was wrong. He intimated that if Chang acted contrary to Tanaka's wishes there would be serious trouble in Manchuria.[110]

From this dialogue we can see how arrogantly Japanese officials treated Chinese officials. Chang had not reached his thirtieth birthday. His resistance to such heavy pressure as that of the Kwantung Army and his defense of China's sovereignty was therefore especially commendable. He was, nonetheless, aware also that unless he made some concessions, there would be a second Tsinan incident. Accordingly, on the following day, he sent Liu Che to tell Hayashi that he would postpone for three months his declaration of allegiance to the National Government. In July, China and the United States signed a tariff agreement. At first, Japan wanted China to recognize the unsecured Nishihara loan as a condition for tariff autonomy. Japan asked Britain for her support in that stand but Britain declined.[111] China also refused Tanaka's demand that the settlement of outstanding issues in Manchuria be made a condition for the withdrawal of Japanese troops from Tsinan.[112] In June and July, there was a boycott of Japanese goods, which caused Japan a seventeen million yen loss in trade. Count Uchida's representations to the American Secretary of State were also fruitless.[113] In the meantime, the Nanking government did its best to comply with Chang Hsueh-liang's request. Jehol was transferred to be incorporated with the three Northeastern provinces to make four. The National government appointed Chang as a member of the State Council. The arrangement included also the training of Kuomintang members in the Northeast to enable the effecting of peaceful cooperation between it and the Central government, thus depriving Japan of any excuse for intervention. By the year's end, some twelve nations had recognized China's tariff autonomy. Japan was isolated. Taking advantage of the opportunity, Chang, on December 29, 1928, announced that the three provinces of Liaoning, Kirin, and Heilungkiang would adhere to the National Government as of from that day. Thus, the centripetal force of China's unification progress had overcome the centrifugal force of Japan's efforts toward detaching Manchuria and Mongolia from China.

Although Tanaka tried to conceal his disappointment by saying that this was not unexpected, he then began to press for the carrying-out of the next step in moving toward his goal. This step was to achieve confirmation of the railway rights agreement signed by Chang Tso-lin just prior to his departure from Peking to meet his death.

Although lease rights were mentioned in Japan's demands, the real aim was to put into effect the Yamamoto-Chang Tso-lin secret agreement. Chang Hsueh-liang denied that there had been any such agreement since there was no documentary evidence to confirm it. On July 17, when Hayashi called on Chang to congratulate him on his new appointment, Hayashi again mentioned the construction of the Tun-tu, Chang-ta, Yen-hai and Tao-so railways, Chang replied that it would be difficult to go ahead with them. Again in September, Hayashi, then accompanied by Saito, a new director of the South Manchuria Railway, asked Chang about the matter. Chang answered that the decision would have to be made by the Central Government. Two days after Chang's declaration of adherence to the National Government, Hayashi for a third time pressed Chang about the matter. Although the argument went on for two hours, Chang insisted that he could not do anything about it.[114] Originally, Hayashi had believed that it would have been more profitable for Japan to enlarge her railway claims without trying to interfere in Chang's adherence to the National Government. Hayashi now became more aggressive in his importuning. Chang rightfully insisted that "the Central government was in charge of all foreign relations." In November, 1927, it was announced to all the foreign powers that no agreements would be valid unless they were signed by the Central government. Consequently, the secret agreement between Yamamoto and Chang Tso-lin had no legal basis.

In January, 1929, Tanaka instructed Machino to negotiate with Chang, who replied as he had the other three times. Machino then called on Yang Yu-ting in the hope that the background facts relating to the agreement in controversy might be published, but that evening Yang Yu-ting and Chang Yin-huai were shot in Chang Hsueh-liang's residence by his men. There was considerable speculation regarding the reasons for doing away with Yang, and it is not certain whether this had anything to do with his negotiations with Machino. When Consul General Hayashi learned about the death, he contemplated issuing Chang Hsueh-liang an ultimatum.[115] Following Machino's failure, Tanaka on January 14 and again on February 1 instructed Hayashi to make serious representations to Chang on the Tun-tu railway projects. In his telegram of February 1, Tanaka said that if Chang would not negotiate, Japan would use military force to survey and construct those lines. On March 29, Hayashi and Saito conveyed Tanaka's message to Chang in person.

Chang still insisted that the matter had to be decided by the Central Government, and that, if Japanese military force were employed to survey the route for a new railway, there might be instituted a boycott on Japanese goods for which he would not be responsible.[116] Since the agreement for those lines stipulated that construction had to be completed within a year of the date of signing, the Kwantung Army decided to start surveying and constructing by force on April 4. At that juncture, the Tsinan incident had just been settled and, as a result of negotiations between the Japanese Minister, Yoshizawa and Dr. C. T. Wang, considerable progress had been made in such outstanding issues as the Nanking and Hankow incidents and the Treaty of Commerce between China and Japan. Japanese diplomats in China suggested that emphasis be placed on the larger issues and that high-handed measures on railway projects might cause international criticism and the loss of Japanese trade.[117] Tanaka was finally won over by those who subscribed to the treaty rights view. On April 18, the Japanese Foreign Office decided not to recognize the Chang Hsueh-liang regime. Thus, at that time the movement to detach Manchuria and Mongolia from China was suspended.[118]

Since it became hopeless otherwise to achieve their objectives, the militarists, ronin, and other rightist elements began plotting to seize Manchuria and Mongolia by force. In May, 1929, at an intelligence conference a study was made on an overall military course in Manchuria. In July it was decided to send there a staff officers' group on a strategy planning tour. There were also Ishihara's "Plan for Acquiring Manchuria and Mongolia," Kanji's "Formula for Disturbances in North Manchuria," Mujita's "Mongolian Independence Plan," and Amakasu's "Riots for Chientao." [119] There was a general demand among military circles for the annexation of Manchuria and Mongolia and for a "Showa Reformation." Among Japanese residents, the Manchuria Youth League demanded the establishment of a Manchurian-Mongolian state and opposed the abrogation of consular jurisdiction in China. These demands and protests were in direct contradiction to the attitude of the Chinese Communists, who agitated for the retrocession to China of Dairen and Port Arthur, the withdrawal of Japanese Railway Guard, the overthrow of the Mukden clique, and a halt to the "traitorous" diplomacy of the Nanking Government.

In January, 1929, Chang Hsueh-liang was appointed Commander-in-Chief of the Northeastern Border Defense Army and served concurrently as Chairman of the Northeast Political Council. He became also a member of the Kuomintang. Thus, Manchuria was brought closer into the orbit of the Central government. In November, 1930, the Fourth Plenum of the Second Central Committee decided to have Manchuria's foreign relations, communications, and finance placed directly under the National Government, and the Peking-Laoning, the Supingchin-Taonan, and the Changchun Railways centrally operated as national railways, while the Kitung, Kihai, Taoang and Huhai lines be designated as provincial railways to be supervised by the Central government. Another decision was that the Hulou Harbor project be pushed under a contract with the Netherlands Harbor Construction Company.[120] While all of these measures were Chinese domestic concerns, they were interpreted by Japan as designed to encircle the South Manchuria Railway and to antagonize Japan. The deep-seated conflicts between Japan and China thus provided an excellent opportunity for the Communist International to aggravate the tangle in Manchuria.

It was only after Tanaka's second dispatch of troops to Shantung in July, 1928, that the Communist International began to push its activities in Manchuria. In November, the Manchurian Committee, headed by Tang Hung-ching and Wang Likung, issued its first statement attacking both Japan and the Nanking Government. It also instigated the Korean Communists to launch anti-Japanese movements. In 1929, the Central Committee of the Chinese Communist Party expanded the guerrilla operations areas in Manchuria. On May 30, riots were staged in Chientao. In June and July, armed disturbances were created along the Kirin-Tunhwa railway. Established also were the Manchurian General Action Committee and military committees at *hsien* (county) and municipal levels. Party headquarters were also provided with arms. In 1931, when Kuomintang branches were set up widely, the lower echelon organs were all infiltrated by Communists. They used the slogan of nationalism to aggravate Sino-Japanese conflicts. As the pressure of the Kwantung Army on Manchuria increased, the Communist tactics of nationalism also became more effective. In 1931, efforts were made by Chang Hsueh-liang and Kimura, the new Director of the South Manchuria Railway, to adjust through-transportation on railways of the Northeast but, because of Communist agitation activities,[121] no headway was made. After 1929, Shidehara's policy had shifted from Tanaka's militarism to one of economic precedence.[122] The railway negotiations initiated by Shidehara were concerned mainly with the technical matters of competing lines and the adjustment of freight rates. This new approach was basically different from Tanaka's insistence on carrying out the Yamamoto-Chang Tso-lin secret agreement. According to Shidehara, among the five new railways demanded by Tanaka, the Tun-tu line only was necessary. All of the others could be abandoned or modified.[123] In spite of Shidehara's conciliatory policy, he failed to prevent the perpetration of the Mukden Incident. This demonstrates the unsurmountable antagonism that existed between the two countries. Some Japanese scholars maintained that Tanaka's "positive" China policy failed because he did not understand China's then-mounting nationalism. Because Shidehara did not grasp the new tide of Japanese nationalism, he was criticized for his weak policy toward China.[124] The history of Sino-Japanese relations from 1927 to 1931 might appropriately be summed up in this way.

Conclusion

From the events we have reviewed here, it is clear that the Mukden Incident was but a part of the grand conspiracy plotted by the young officer group of the Japanese Army. Their purpose was to supplant Japan's constitutional system with a fascist-type regime under a military dictatorship that would drive ruthlessly for internal regimentation and external expansion. Having failed in the "Cherry Revolution" of March, they perpetrated the Mukden Incident in September. Faced with undesirable developments flowing from the Mukden Incident, they followed it up with the Silk-banner Revolution in October. Encouraged by China's non-resistance policy, they committed further aggression at Shanhaikwan, in Jehol, and in North China. Consequently, China was forced to fight, the United States became involved, and Japan collapsed. The Grand Plan benefitted no nation except, perhaps, the Soviet Union.

In the course of its development, the Mukden Incident underwent several changes. In 1931, with the bombing of Chinchow, it was a conflict between local armies—the Kwantung Army and China's Northeast Army. In 1932, with the formation of the puppet regime of "Manchukou," it became a national conflict between Japan and China. In 1933, with the Geneva vote of 41 to 1, and Japan's withdrawal from the League of Nations, it became a conflict between Japan and an array of world powers except Nazi Germany and Fascist Italy. It is, therefore, fair to say that the spark ignited at Mukden spread until it kindled World War II.

Footnotes — Chapter 1

[1] In February 1912, Kawashima Naniwa submitted to the Japanese General Staff a plan for the partitioning of China (*Biographies of the Vigilant Martyrs in East Asia,* Vol. II, p. 324). It was suggested that the Manchu Prince Su and Mongol Prince Pa-lin cooperate in setting up a Manchurian-Mongolian kingdom to be financed and armed by Japan. The General Staff, therefore, sent Colonel Matsui, Tada, Kimura, and others to confer with Pa-lin. Premier Saionji called off the plot before it got out of control. In the course of its development, Japanese arms were captured at Kungchulin, Colonel Matsui was injured, and thirteen Japanese were killed. See the *Japanese Foreign Ministry's Annual Report and Other Important Documents 1840-1945,* Vol. I, p. 356, and *The Study of Japanese Foreign Relations* (Taisho), pp. 53-56.

[2] Under Japanese instigation, Babuchapu, a Mongolian cavalry commander, plotted with the Manchu Restoration Party to set up an independent state of Manchuria-Mongolia. The master-minding was done by Lieutenant-General Tanaka Giichi and Fukuda Masataro, the Chief of Staff of the Kwantung Army. Koiso Kuniaki (who later became Premier) also participated. At first it called for the overthrow of Yuan Shih-kai. In 1916, Yuan died, and Premier Hara ordered a halt to the plot. Both the Japanese ronin and Mongolian rebels agitated for a go ahead. Colonel Doi then planned to disguise himself as a Chinese to lead an army to occupy Mukden. The plot was blocked by Consul General Yada. Consequently, there was a clash between the Japanese and Chinese troops at Cheng-chia-tun and this event has thus come to be known as "the Cheng-chia-tun incident." For details, see Korihara Eiji's *The First and Second Movements for Mongolian Independence.* (*The Study of the History of Japanese Foreign Relations,* Summer Issue, 1958.)

[3] The affair was at first instigated by Premier Tanaka, but was stopped at the eleventh hour. See Chapter 6, C. (b). Assassination of Chang Tso-lin.

[4] *The Problem of Manchuria* by Chang Chi-yun (published by *The Central Daily,* Kweiyang, China, 1942).

[5] *The Memoirs of Imamura Hitoshi,* 1960, Tokyo, Vol. 2, p. 194.

[6] *Hanaya, Himerareta Showashi,* p. 44; Morishima, *Conspiracy, Assassination and Swords,* pp. 50-52; Yoshihashi Takahiko: *Conspiracy at Mukden,* p. 152, N. 4.

[7] *Japan and Her Destiny,* by Shigemitsu Mamoru, 1958, New York (E. P. Dutton Company), pp. 66-67.

[8] The Tokyo War Crimes Trial refers to The International Military Tribunal of the Far East (IMTFE). Itagaki Seishiro and Doihara Kenji were hanged as war criminals at Sugamo Prison (December 24, 1948).

[9] These are the records of IMTFE. They consist of the record of proceedings, exhibits, prosecution, and defense opinions, judgments, etc. The record of proceedings alone consists of 48,288 pages; the exhibits constitute 30,000 pages.

[10] The U. S. War Department micro-filmed the archives of the Japanese Foreign Ministry (1868-1945) which were sent to the Library of Congress. The materials are divided into: the Meiji, Taisho, and Showa Periods. There are also Special Studies and Unclassified Documents. The University of Michigan has a check-list available for reference.

[11] Credit Anstalt, established by the Rothschilds in 1855, was the most dependable private banking concern of Austria. In May 1931, when it faced imminent collapse, the Austrian Government spent one billion dollars of treasury notes for its rescue. For details, see *Survey of International Affairs,* 1931, p. 208.

[12] The Hoover Moratorium was approved by leaders of both Houses of the United States Congress during a time when the Congress was in recess. However, because of this, Hoover never received the sympathy of the Congress. For figures of financial losses suffered by the various countries, see *Survey of International Affairs,* 1931, p. 104.

[13] On July 15, Britain borrowed twenty million pounds from France to tide over her financial difficulties. See *Survey,* 1931, p. 28.

[14] For details on the Economic Depression, see *Survey,* 1931, pp. 1-136.

[15] On September 15, 1931, the British Admiralty announced that the sailors of H.M.S. Invergordon of the Atlantic Fleet were summoned back to England for trial on charges of their protest against pay reduction. See *Survey,* 1931, p. 110.

[16] The British "Chilean-Fleet" stationed at Coquimbo mutinied in protest against pay reduction and sent an ultimatum to the government in September. They surrendered when they were bombed by the air force. See *Survey,* 1931, p. 111.

[17] *The Road to the Pacific War,* Vol. I, p. 360 (Published by Asahi Shinbunsha, 1962, Tokyo).

[18] *The Japanese Foreign Ministry's Annual Report and Other Important Documents (1840-1945),* Vol. II, p. 102; *An Outline History of the Republic of China* by Chang Chi-yun, Vol. II, p. 177; also see Baba Akira's unpublished draft on "The First Military expedition in Shantung and Tanaka."

[19] *Major Events of the Republic of China* by Kao-Ying-tso, p. 278.

[20] *Documents of the Revolution* by Lo Chia-lun, Vol. 16, p. 117.

[21] In January 1927, Great Britain intended to resort to gunboat policy to thwart the Nationalist Northern Expedition, but it was opposed by Japan. At that time, the Japanese General Staff at Tokyo had reports from China reporting their observance of amity with the Nationalist Revolutionary Army. For the telegram, see *The Record of the Japanese Foreign Ministry* and *The Road to the Pacific War,* Vol. II, p. 196.

In March, 1927, the Nationalist troops under Cheng Chen and Lu Ti-ping entered Nanking. Lin Pai-chu and Li Fu-chun, both members of the Communist party, were in the army. There were rioters wearing army uniforms pillaging foreign premises. The United States and British warships in Hsiakwan shelled Nanking in retaliation but the Japanese gunboats refused to participate. See *The Road to the Pacific War,* Vol. II, pp. 198-199.

[22] The order issued on July 18, 1929. The Anti-Japanese Association was renamed as The Association for the Promotion of the Abolition of Unequal Treaties. See *The Road to the Pacific War,* p. 331.

[23] See *The Japanese Foreign Ministry's Annual Report and Other Important Documents,* Vol. II, p. 56.

[24] Saburi Sadao advocated Sino-Japanese co-operation on the ground that China was rich in economic resources while Japan was strong in political organization. (See *The Record of the Japanese Foreign Ministry,* microfilm No. 59, 1498-1499.) On November 20, 1929, he returned to Japan to report on his duties. He was murdered on November 29 at Hakone. The Japanese Government declared his death a suicide. However, a few years later, Saburi's brother revealed in a lengthy statement that his brother's case was not suicide but murder. (See *China Weekly Review,* February 4, 1933, p. 396, and Shidehara Memoirs, pp. 92-94.)

[25] Obata Torikichi was counselor of the Japanese Legation in Peking at the time when Japan presented the Twenty-one Demands to China. In December 1926, he was designated by Shidehara as Japanese Minister to China, but China considered him *persona-non-grata.* See *Yochihashi, Conspiracy at Mukden,* Yale University Press, 1963, p. 121.

[26] The organizations were: "Young Men's Association for Independence," "The Union for Freedom," "The Citizen's Party," "The Association for Young Comrades,' etc. See *The Road to the Pacific War,* Vol. I, p. 360.

[27] *Ibid.,* pp. 360, 368, and 394.

[28] *Ibid.,* pp. 395 and 397.

[29] On June 30, Endo Sakuro with the delegates from "The League of Youth' paid a visit to Inukai Tsuyoshi and expressed his concern over the weak foreign policy of Shidehara. *Ibid.,* p. 396. For further details, see *The History of the League for Manchurian Youth,* pp. 459-466.

[30] *The Economic Alliance with Japan,* pp. 559-561.

[31] See Consul Okada's telegram to the Japanese Foreign Ministry on June 20, 1930, *The Road to the Pacific War,* Vol. I, pp. 337, 339.

[32] *The Road to the Pacific War,* Vol. I, p. 37.

[33] For details, see "On Japan's Militarism," by Liu Ch'i-fu, in *Foreign Affairs Monthly,* No. 3; also, Yale C. Maxon's *Control of Japanese Policy* (1951), University of California Press, pp. 43-272.

Footnotes — Chapter 2

[1] *The Chinese White Paper,* No. 26, published by the Ministry of Foreign Affairs of the Republic of China, 1933, pp. 50-56.

[2] *Ta Kung Pao,* September 20, 1931.

[3] International Military Tribunal of the Far East (IMTFE) was organized in accordance with Article I of the Potsdam Proclamation for the purpose of trying war criminals. On September 2, 1945, when Japan signed the Declaration of Capitulation, she accepted the stipulation. General MacArthur, in January, 1946, announced the seventeen regulations of IMTFE. On February 15, the Allied nations (Australia, Canada, China, France, England, India, the Netherlands, New Zealand, the Philippines, the Soviet Union, and the United States) appointed eleven judges and a number of prosecutors and interpreters to handle the trial. The Tribunal began its work on December 8, 1945; it began the trials on May 3, 1946, and announced its judgments on November 4, 1948. There were 28 Class A criminals among whom were Tojo, Minami, Itagaki, Doihara, Hirota, etc. The seven who were sentenced to death were Doihara, Hirota, Itagaki, Kimura, Matsui, Muto, and Tojo. The rest were either sentenced to life imprisonment or to serve in prison for varying periods of time. For details, see Soliz Horwitz's *The Tokyo Trial,* No. 465, November 1950.

[4] IMTFE Proceedings, p. 19,246 and exhibit No, 2,403.

[5] IMTFE Proceedings, July 2-July 5, 1941, p. 1,792.

[6] *The Chinese White Paper,* No. 26 Koo's Memorandum, No. 1, p. 522.

[7] On October 9, 1932, Lord Lytton gave a speech at Chatham House. See *The Sino-Japanese Controversy and the League of Nations* by Westel W. Willoughby, John Hopkins Press, Baltimore, 1935, p. 27.

[8] See Yoshino's article in Japan's *Central Forum,* May 1932, and Nagano's preface in *On Mongolian and Manchurian National Independence* (1932).

[9] In 1933, Tanaka Ryukichi was a staff officer in the Kwantung Army. He was the one who instigated Prince Teh of Inner Mongolia to plot for Mongolian independence. After the War, he was persuaded by the U.S. Army to reveal all the secrets of the Japanese Army to the American prosecutors. He, therefore, became one of the star witnesses during the Tokyo Trial. For this testimony, see IMTFE Proceedings, p. 2,036.

[10] Miyake Mitsuharu was Chief of Staff of the Kwantung Army during the Incident. In 1945, he was captured by the Soviet Union. This testimony was given on February 26, 1946. For the testimony, see IMTFE Exhibit No. 699.

[11] Morishima Morito was Consul in Mukden and an assistant to Consul General Hayashi Hisajiro in 1931. After the War, he wrote *Conspiracies, Assassinations and Sword.* The quotation is taken from his book (1950 ed.), p. 38.

[12] See IMTFE Proceedings, No. 181, and I.P.S. (The International Prosecution Section) Doc. 2,984D.

[13] Ito Masanori: *The History of the Rise and Fall of Militarism,* Tokyo, 1958, Vol. II, p. 188.

[14] *The Road to the Pacific War,* Vol. I, p. 439.

[15] *The Chinese White Paper,* No. 64, Memorandum No. 3: "The Japanese propaganda agency issued a statement saying that the damage to the South Manchuria Railway was on one side of the tracks only. . . . According to passengers, the damage was so slight that the train shook only slightly when it passed over the spot."

[16] See the conversation of Hayashi Hisajiro, recorded in the Appendix of *The Road to the Pacific War,* Vol. I.

[17] On September 14, 1931, the office of the Commanding General of the Kwantung Army sent a secret letter to the Japanese Consulate General which stated that of late the South Manchuria Railway had been frequently harassed by bandits, and therefore the Commanding General had ordered that henceforth the Kwantung Army would not only attack the bandits within the Railway zone, but as well drive the intruders outside the Railway zone. On September 17, Consul General replied in correspondence No. 27 that if the Kwantung Army wished to punish intruders in areas outside the Railway zone, the Army must first consult with the Consulate. See *The Record of the Japanese Foreign Ministry,* micro-film S7, 66, No. 524; I.P.S. Doc. 2,984-B.

[18] *The Memoirs of Tsou Lu,* Vol. II, p. 698.

[19] *The Chinese White Paper,* No. 24, p. 109.

[20] *Ibid.,* pp. 110-111.

[21] *Ibid.,* p. 110.

[22] *Ibid.,* p. 111.

[23] *The Record of the Japanese Foreign Ministry,* micro-film S 42602.

[24] *The Chinese White Paper,* No. 26, pp. 50-51.

[25] *The Record of the Japanese Foreign Ministry,* micro-film S 42602, 279-281.

[26] *The Road to the Pacific War,* Vol. I, p. 434.

[27] *The Chinese White Paper* No. 26, p. 118.

[28] *Wai-chao Yuo-pao Monthly,* Vol. I, No. 4, pp. 22-26.

[29] *The Chinese White Paper,* Memorandum No. 3, Doc. B. Also, Koo's Memorandum to the Lytton Commission, Vol. I, p. 122.

[30] See Shidehara's reply to the Privy Council when the Japanese-Soviet Treaty was reviewed by it. Also see *The Road to the Pacific War,* Vol. 1, pp. 264-265.

[31] *The Chinese White Paper,* No. 26; "A Memorandum Concerning the South Manchuria Railway Patrols," pp. 122-123.

Footnotes — Chapter 3

[1] Yamaguchi Shegeji: *The Tragic General: Ishihara Kanji,* p. 96.

[2] Mugita Hirao was a reservist colonel. He was manager of the Japanese Aviation Company's branch office in Dairen. Doihara ordered the action because he wanted to use Yen Hsi-shan to oppose Chang Hsueh-liang. Both Saionji and Shidehara were greatly disaffected by the Kwantung Army's direct interference with the internal affairs of China bypassing the Foreign Office. See *The Road to the Pacific War,* Vol. I, p. 423.

[3] *The History of the Rise and Fall of Militarism,* Vol. II, p. 98.

[4] *On the Last World War,* by Ishihara Kanji, 1942, pp. 189-190.

[5] *The Tragic General: Ishihara Kanji,* p. 106.

[6] *The Road to the Pacific War,* Vol. I, pp. 366, 372, 379, 384.

[7] *Ibid.,* 391; on p. 388 it was stated that Hanaya, Hashimoto, and Nemoto had, in June 1931, decided to solve simultaneously government reorganization in Japan and the Manchurian-Mongolian problem. Document No. 1107 of I.P.S. contains "On Rectifying the Army," an article written by Muranaka and Isobe. The article has a detailed analysis of the relationship between the March and October plots and the Mukden Incident.

[8] IMTFE Exhibit No. 2177A: the testimony of Okawa Shumei.

[9] *The Diary of Saionji,* recorded by Harada Kumao (English translation), p. 104.

[10] IMTFE Exhibit No. 183; I.P.S. Document No. 12; Hata Ikuhiko's "The Interest of the Cherry Blossom Society," *Education on Japanese History,* Vol. VI, No. 4, pp. 81-88 (1958 ed.).

[11] The order prohibiting Japanese militarists to participate in political associations was found in the decree of Emperor Meiji issued on January 4, 1882, collected in the *Compendium on Modern Japan* (1933) pp. 224-227. Article 25 of the Penal Code of the Japanese Army and Navy stated that those militarists who organized parties and used their forces for political ends should be punished by death; those who instigated others to participate should be dismissed from service and be given prison sentences not exceeding five years and all others who participated sentences not exceeding three years.

[12] A list table of Japanese exports and imports from 1923 to 1931 is available on p. 402, *Survey of International Affairs,* 1931.

[13] Mori Shozo: *Gunkoku Taiheikite,* 1955, Vol. II, p. 70.

[14] Ugaki, under a secret order of the Hamaguchi Cabinet, instructed Nagata to draft a plan which would reduce the Japanese Army by several divisions but raise the combat strength of each division by increasing its air force, armed and mechanized units. See "Japan's

China Policy" by James Buckley Crowley (1958 dissertation, University of Michigan).

[15] The Saga Left Shoulder Party seemed to be the forerunner of the Japanese Army's Imperial Way Clique, because members of the Imperial Way Clique such as Muto Nobuyoshi, Muraoka Chotaro, Majaki Jinzaburo, Hata Masatsugu, Araki Sadao, Fukuda Masataro, Yamashita Hebun, and Yamaoka Shigeatsu were all members of that party. See *The Road to the Pacific War,* Vol. I, p. 364.

[16] *Gunkoku Taiheikite,* pp. 21-22.

[17] For details of the area inclusion of the Great East Asia Co-Prosperity Sphere, see IMTFE Exhibit No. 675A. The area was of two categories: (1) Japanese territories such as Hainan Island, Hong Kong, Southeast Asia, Sumatra, Borneo, Ceylon, and the Coast of India; (2) independent states under Japan's supervision in foreign affairs in matters of national defense: "Manchukuo," China (excluding North China and Fukien), Burma, Indochina, India, the Philippines, Afghanistan, Siam (Thailand), Java, etc. The economies of these states should be integrated with that of Japan to function as a single unit. See also I.P.S. Document No. 490: "The Road to Remake the World" by Hashimoto.

[18] *Gunkoku Taihekite,* pp. 24-26.

[19] *The History of Military Fascist Movement* (1962 ed.) by Hata Ikuhiko, p. 68.

[20] *Ibid.,* p. 74.

[21] The key officers of the General Staff and the Ministry of War deemed Emperor Meiji's edict could not proscribe the military in their discussing national defense. Thus, they formed a national defense forum. When Tatekawa was the director of the Intelligence Department of the General Staff, he went to lecture in that forum frequently. See "Japan's China Policy" (1958 dissertation, University of Michigan); *Gunkoku Taiheikite,* p. 70.

[22] IMTFE Proceedings, pp. 15, 582-15, 584; I.P.S. Document No. 12.

[23] In *The History of the Rise and Fall of Militarism,* p. 144, Ito Masanori says that Hashimoto, Cho Isamu, and others were radicals while Tanaka Hiyoshi belonged to the opposition group and the rest were neutral. In the beginning, opinions were evenly divided, but finally advocates for the plan became predominant.

[24] IMTFE Exhibit No. 157; IMTFE Proceedings, p. 1,402; Maruyama Masao, *Modern Japanese Political Movements* (1957 ed.) p. 28; Aoki Takuzo, *The History Leading to the Pacific War,* 1953, pp. 125-128.

[25] For details, see I.P.S. Document No. 12. The Society had seven objectives: (1) to establish a revolutionary Japan; (2) to fulfill the national aspirations of Japan; (3) to form a more national state organization; (4) to liberate the Japanese people; (5) to carry out just diplomacy; (6) to coordinate with the reform movements; (7) to foster militant spirit. For details on Yuzon-sha ("The Survival Society") see I.P.S. Document No. 12. Yuzon-sha had been very influential among

the militarists after the Mukden Incident. Okawa also became the leader of Gyoji-kai Jimmu-kai. For details, see *The History Leading to the Pacific War,* 1953, pp. 132-133; *The Secret Record on the Japanese Revolutionary Movements,* Tokyo Police Department; Chitoshi Yanaga, *Japan Since Perry,* 1966, pp. 492, 498, 499, and 504.

[26] IMTFE Proceedings, p. 15,560; IMTFE Exhibit No. 2,177A.

[27] During the trial in the IMTFE, Ugaki's lawyer submitted a letter sent by Okawa to Ugaki on March 6, 1931. In the letter, Okawa was still trying to persuade Ugaki to approve the plan for the coup. The lawyer thus pointed out that Ugaki did not approve of the plan at the time when Okawa met him.

[28] Richard Storry, *Double Patriot,* Houghton Mifflin, Boston, 1957, p. 58.

[29] On February 13, 1931, three days after the meeting between Ugaki and Okawa, the former had sent for Koiso, Matsuyama, the Vice Minister of War, and Ninonmiya Harushige, the Deputy Chief of the General Staff, to discuss Okawa's interview. This proved that he did not reject Okawa's proposal during the meeting. See Imamura Hitoshi's *When Did the War in Manchuria Begin?*

[30] IMTFE Proceedings, p. 1,966.

[31] "The Manchurian Crisis and the Kwantung Army," an unpublished master's thesis by Kobayashi Kiyotane of Columbia University (1956), p. 19, footnote 34.

[32] IMFTE Proceedings, pp. 1,404-1,411.

[33] Mori Shozoi: *Twenty Years of Whirlwind,* p. 68.

[34] IMTFE Proceedings, p. 31,409; Exhibit No. 3340.

[35] IMFTE Proceedings, pp. 1,463-1,464; Exhibit No. 160.

[36] I.P.S. Document No. 1,107, p. 2.

[37] Komoto Daisaku was also one of those who prepared the personnel for the conspiracy. In 1931, he arranged to transfer Amakasu Masahiko to Manchuria to serve under Itagaki and Ishihara. See *The Road to the Pacific War,* Vol. I, p. 378. For further details, see *Gunköhu Taiheikite,* pp. 120-122.

[38] IMTFE Proceedings, Exhibit No. 160: "The Testimony of Fujita Isamu."

[39] *The Road to the Pacific War,* Vol. I, p. 408.

[40] Ishihara was transferred to the Kwantung Army as Komoto Daisaku's successor. He knew about Komoto's plot to assassinate Chang Tsolin, and so he drew up a secret plan to attack Mukden in blitzkrieg tactics. For details, see Inaga Masao's *History of the Wars of Showa,* Chapter on "The Manchurian Crisis," *National Defense Magazine,* No. 6, 1962.

[41] "During the stage of pacification, all of China's political and economic systems in Manchuria should be destroyed. During the stage of domination, Koreans would be used to till the fields, Chinese would be assigned to operate small businesses and Japanese would be entrusted with the operation of big enterprises. During the stage of

national defense, revenues from Manchuria would be sufficient to meet Japan's expenses of occupation." *The Road to the Pacific War,* Vol. I, p. 377.

[42] This plan aimed at a prolonged war with the United States. In regard to China, a policy of moderate domination should be adopted so as to prevent her from allying with the United States against Japan. Unless it became absolutely necessary, Japan would not occupy Northern China. However, Japan might even wage a war with Britain. See *The Road to the Pacific War,* Vol. I, p. 383.

[43] *The Road to the Pacific War,* Vol. I, p. 383.

[44] *Imamura Memoirs,* Vol. 2, 1960, pp. 196-198.

[45] Hashimoto's view on priorities for domestic reorganization and Itagaki's view on priorities for external expansion were diametrically opposed. In June 1931, Hanaya returned to Tokyo to confer with Nemoto Hiroshi and Hashimoto. During the conference, they agreed that both internal reform and external expansion should be carried out simultaneously. See *The Secret History of the Showa Era,* p. 43. Nagata told Itagaki that the Kwantung Army's decision to use force must have the approval of the Army in Tokyo and sanctioned by national as well as international opinion. Refer to *The Road to the Pacific War,* Vol. I, p. 398.

[46] *Imamura Memoirs,* Vol. 2, p. 195. Towards the end of June, 1931, at a meeting of the section chiefs of the Navy's Department of Operations, Tatekawa told them that the Army intended to spend one year in preparations. See *The Road to the Pacific War,* Vol. I, p. 393.

[47] *Imamura Memoirs,* Vol. 2, pp. 193-194; *The Biography of Minami Jiro* by Mitarai Tatsuo, pp. 242-243.

[48] *The History of the Rise and Fall of Militarism,* Vol. II, p. 198.

[49] IMFTE Proceedings pp. 1,980-1,984.

[50] *The History of the League for Manchurian Youth,* pp. 11, 12, 467, 469, 459, and 466; *On the Pacific War,* p. 397: At the Congress of the Great Japan Productive Party, Uchida Ryohei, Tsukuda Toshio, and Katsura Yoshihisa advocated the punishment of China.

[51] *The Tokyo Asahi Shirnbun,* September 7, 1931.

[52] IMTFE Exhibit No. 3,016; IMTFE Proceedings, p. 1,192.

[53] Richard Storry: *The Double Patriots,* p. 70.

[54] IMTFE Exhibit No. 2,718B; IMTFE Proceedings, p. 15,597.

[55] IMTFE Exhibit No. 1,822: Okada said, "The Mukden Incident was no surprise to the Japanese Government because the latter had heard about it early in 1931."

[56] IMTFE Proceedings, p. 22,108: Ishihara testified, "At that time the Kwantung Army cancelled all leaves because it was aware that the Incident was about to break out."

[57] *The Diary of Saionji*: entered on August 31, 1931.

[58] IMTFE Exhibit No. 1,632; IMTFE Proceedings, p. 1,938.

[59] *The Memoirs of Koiso Kuniaki* (as recorded by Hanaya Tadashi).

[60] For Tanaka's speech, see IMTFE Proceedings, pp. 15,732-15,733.

[61] For Ozaki's interrogation, see IMTFE Exhibit No. 184; IMTFE Proceedings, pp. 2,193-2, 194.

[62] *The Biography of Minami Jiro.*

[63] *The Road to the Pacific War,* Vol. I, p. 357.

[64] *The Memoirs of Komoto Daisaku; The Road to the Pacific War,* Vol. I, p. 439.

[65] *Gunkoku Taiheikite,* p. 120; *The Road to the Pacific War,* Vol. I, p. 404.

[66] Shido Yasusuke: *The Life of General Nagata,* 1939, pp. 165-166.

[67] Ueda Shunkichi: *The Fluctuations and Freedom of Democracy During the Showa Era,* November 1961.

[68] IMTFE Proceedings, p. 22,206.

[69] *Conspiracies, Assassination and the Sword* (1950 ed.), p. 48; IMTFE Proceedings, p. 3,024.

[70] *The Double Patriots,* p. 78.

[71] IMTFE Proceedings, pp. 1,990-1, 1,992; p. 19,875.

[72] *The Road to the Pacific War,* Vol. I, p. 424. An interview among Mitani Kiyoshi, Kawashima Tadashi, and the representative of the Asahi Shinobunsha on November 20, 1962.

[73] *The Record of the Foreign Ministry,* Micro-film S 42602, 279-281.

[74] *The Road to the Pacific War,* Vol. I, Note 31, p. 429-30; *The Chinese White Paper,* No. 26, Memorandum No. 3, p. 70.

[75] *The Road to the Pacific War,* Vol. I, p. 416: "This information was given by Yoshimura Tsuyoshi of the Kwantung Special Intelligence Agency. He learned it from Hanaya. See the *Secret War Diary* of the Military Affairs Bureau of the Japanese General Staff."

[76] IMTFE Proceedings, p. 30,343.

[77] *The Road to the Pacific War,* Vol. I, p. 432, as told by Hayashi Hisajiro.

[78] *The Memoirs of Komoto Daisaku.*

[79] Marada Kumao: *Prince Saionji and the Political Development,* Vol. 2, pp. 50-52.

[80] *Ibid.,* p. 54

[81] At that time, Nakahara of the Japanese General Staff proposed that Japan should make use of the Nakamura's case to dispose of the Manchurian-Mongolian problem; some members of the Military Council favored it. But they retracted when they learned that the Emperor had cautioned against any incidents. See *The Tokyo Current Events,* September 17, 1931.

[82] For Doihara's report, see *The Road to the Pacific War,* Vol. I, pp. 414-415; for Shibayama's report, *Ibid.,* p. 420.

[83] *The Biography of Minami Jiro,* p. 255.

[84] *Imamura Memoirs,* Vol. I, p. 197.

[85] IMTFE Proceedings, pp. 2,006, 22,149, and 18,993 and IMTFE Exhibit No. 2,207, p. 33,629.

[86] *The Memoirs of Koiso Kuniaki.*

[87] *The Diary of Saionji,* September 23, 1931.

[88] *The Memoirs of Komoto Daisaku*

[89] *The History of the Rise and Fall of Militarism,* Vol. 2, p. 188-198.

[90] *The Road to the Pacific War,* Vol. I, p. 419; IMTFE Exhibit No. 245; p. 3,019: the testimony of Morishima.

[91] *The Memoirs of Mitani Kiyoshi* (as recorded by Hanaya); *The Road to the Pacific War,* Vol. I, p. 434.

[92] *The Tragic General: Ishihara Kanji,* pp. 112-113.

[93] *Ibid.,* pp. 112-113.

[94] *Ibid.,* pp. 113-114.

[95] *The History of the Rise and Fall of Militarism,* p. 186.

[96] *Conspiracies, Assassination and the Sword,* p. 49.

[97] C. R. Storry: "The Mukden Incident," *Far Eastern Affairs,* No. 1, (*St. Anthony's Paper,* No. 2), 1957.

[98] IMTFE Proceedings, p. 25,078, p. 2,012-2,013.

[99] *The Road to the Pacific War,* Vol. I, p. 439; Vol. II, p. 4; *Conspiracies, Assassination and the Sword,* p. 52.

[100] IMTFE Proceedings, pp. 18,890-92: the testimony of Katakura Tadashi; "The Manchurian Crisis and the Kwantung Army," an unpublished master's thesis, Columbia University (1956).

[101] IMTFE Proceedings, p. 22,898.

[102] IMTFE Proceedings, p. 22,129; *Double Patriot,* p. 80.

[103] Tsuda refused to send help to Mukden. See IMTFE Proceedings, p. 18,641; the testimony of Okamoto Toshi.

Footnotes — Chapter 4

[1] Morishima Morito, *Conspiracies, Assassination and the Sword,* Tokyo, 1950, p. 52; IMTFE Proceedings, p. 2,165, pp. 3,052-53, Exhibit No. 165.

[2] *The Japanese Foreign Ministry's Annual Report and Other Important Documents,* Tokyo, 1955, Vol. 2, p. 180; IMTFE Proceedings, p. 2,178.

[3] IMTFE Proceedings, pp. 22,126-22,127; Exhibit No. 182, Section II.

[4] I.P.S. Exhibit No. 2,943.

[5] IMTFE Exhibit No. 246, Minister Shegemitsu's telegram to Foreign Minister Shidehara, September 24, 1931.

[6] On September 22, at 8 p.m., Johnson, the American Minister to China, sent a telegram to Stimson, the Secretary of State, to report that the Japanese troops at Changchun, Niu-chuang, Kou Pang-tzu, and Halutoao had been mobilized simultaneously. This shows that there was a premeditated military plan, and that the dynamiting of railroad tracks was the sole cause of the incident is unbelievable. He also reported that ten days earlier he was secretly informed by J. C. Ferguson (a former adviser of the Nationalist Government) that Japan had planned to seize Manchuria within three months, but at that time he refused to believe it. He thought that according to the existing situation it seemed that Japan would not stop her aggression until she found a satisfactory solution for the Manchurian problem. See *U. S. Foreign Relations, Japan,* 1931-41, Vol. 1, pp. 3-4.

[7] *The Memoirs of Imamura Hitoshi,* Tokyo, 1960, Vol. 2, pp. 196-198.

[8] *The Road to the Pacific War,* 1962, Vol. 2, p. 12.

[9] *Ibid.*, p. 12.

[10] IMTFE Proceedings, pp. 1,554-1,558; p. 19,282, Exhibit No. 162.

[11] *The Road to the Pacific War,* Vol. 2, p. 35.

[12] *Ibid.*, p. 7.

[13] *Ibid.*, p. 8.

[14] *Ibid.*, p. 10.

[15] *Ibid.*, pp. 11-12. In 1900 when the Boxer Rebellion erupted in China, Japan did not send any troops into China until the Japanese Cabinet had appropriated the funds. Thus, in accordance with this precedent, the troops in Korea could not be sent out of Korean territory until the Japanese Cabinet had discussed the matter. It was not possible for Kanaya to petition the Emperor direct. Thus, Kanaya appealed to Premier Wakatsuki for help, but Wakatsuki at first refused. See IMTFE Exhibit No. 179H.

[16] On September 21, four telegrams from Yoshimura were received, reporting that at 1 p.m., the first fleet of cars had started; it would

cross the Yalu River at 1:20 p.m.; and at 5 p.m., it would be placed under the command of the Kwantung Army and would arrive safely at Antung.

[17] *The Road to the Pacific War,* Vol. 2, p. 12.

[18] The telegram Korean Staff No. 60 arrived Tokyo on September 21 at 3:22 p.m.

[19] *The Memoir of Imamura Itoshi,* Vol. 2, p. 202.

[20] *The Road to the Pacific War,* Vol. 2, p. 35, pp. 45-48.

[21] Imamura, *When Did the War in Manchuria Begin?* pp. 65-66; James Buckley Crowley, "Japan's China Policy," an unpublished 1959 University of Michigan doctoral dissertation.

[22] The General Staff's telegram No. 15 was read in translation as follows:

> Your resolute action of September 18 to uphold the prestige of the Imperial Army was most appropriate. From now on, this affair must be dealt with in accordance with the Cabinet's decision that it not be carried beyond the necessary limits.

The War Ministry telegram No. 104 was read in translation as follows:

> Although the hostility was caused by the Chinese Army's damaging the South Manchuria Railway for which China is to blame, the Imperial Government does not wish to aggravate the Incident. Please observe this injunction.

For original text, refer to *The Road to the Pacific War,* Vol. 2, p. 26.

[23] For the two telegrams of Honjo, see *The Road to the Pacific War,* Vol. 2, p. 28.

[24] For the texts of the telegrams of the General Staff and the Ministry of War, see *The Road to the Pacific War,* Vol. 2, pp. 31-32.

[25] *The Road to the Pacific War,* Vol. 2, pp. 29-30.

[26] *Ibid.,* pp. 29-30.

[27] *Ibid.,* p. 41; IMTFE Proceedings, p. 18,941.

[28] *Ishihara Kanji: The Tragic General,* p. 143.

[29] W. W. Willoughby: *The Sino-Japanese Controversy and the League of Nations,* p. 30.

[30] *U.S. Foreign Relations, Japan,* 1931-41, Vol. 1, p. 5.

[31] *The Minutes of the League of Nations' Council at Geneva,* December 1931.

[32] *The Road to the Pacific War,* Vol. 2, p. 320.

[33] *Ibid.*

[34] *Ibid.,* pp. 44-45; IMTFE Proceedings, p. 18,924.

[35] *Ibid.,* p. 48.

[36] I.P.C. Document 12; IMTFE Exhibit No. 183.

[37] *The Double Patriots,* p. 85; Harada Kumao: *Saionji and Political Developments,* Tokyo, 1950, October 2, 1931.

[38] IMTFE Exhibits Nos. 2,178A, 2,178B, 2,180A, 2,183 and 2,184; IMTFE Proceedings, p. 15,590.

[39] *A Secret Record of Japanese Reform Movements,* pp. 30-33, p. 37.

[40] *The Memoirs of Imamura Itoshi,* Volume 2, p. 218. Imamura recorded that a document of the October incident was found by Teiichu Yoshimoto, and it was read by Nagata, Tojo, and Yoshimoto. Minami ordered Koiso to have it burned.

[41] See Ai Hsiu-feng, "The Thinking of the Japanese Young Officers," *Kuo-wen Weekly*, Tientsin, Vol. 10.

[42] See Tsao Chung-san, "The Development of Nipponism in the Past Decade," *Foreign Affairs Monthly,* Nanking, Vol. 10, No. 27.

[43] In 1925, Shumei Okawa founded the magazine: *Japan.* In it he advocated: (1) construction of a new Japan, (2) establishment of national ideals, (3) practice of spiritual freedom, (4) realization of political equality, (5) realization of economic cooperation, (6) liberation of colored races, (7) unification of world morality. The organizations and Tinmu-kai developed their constitutions from these ideas.

[44] For details, see "A Summary of the May 15 Incident" issued jointly by the Ministries of War, Navy and Justice. The entire text was published by *Kuo-wen Weekly,* Tientsin, Vol. 10, No. 32.

[45] Kita's program for the reform of Japan was published in 1919 and became the bible of the rightists. His recommendations consisted of the following items: (1) the government should be responsible for the upbringing of orphans; (2) the government should take care of the needs of the poor and the aged; (3) the government should set the maximal limit for personal property and corporation wealth; (4) the abolition of nobility and the reformation of the Cabinet; the Treasury should grant 300,000 yen annually for the maintenance of the Imperial household; (5) the government should have the right to redistribute the wealth of the nation and the right to declare war; (6) the Reservists should serve as the promoters for the reform; they are to have the power to investigate and assess property. For details, see *Japan Since Perry,* p. 402.

[46] In his program for reform, Kita also advocated the abolition of social classes. He also said that every nation has the right to declare war, whether for self-defense or for selfish purposes; for Japan's survival, it is necessary to seize Siberia, Mongolia, Manchuria, Southeast Asia, the Philippines, and Australia; even though China should remain an independent nation, she should accept and follow the guidance of Japan. He also said that there is an urgency for reform in Japan and that this urgency far exceeds that which prompted the Meiji Reformation.

[47] *Japanese Chronicle Weekly*, March 19, 1936, p. 354.

[48] *A Secret Record of the Japanese Reform Movements,* p. 47.

[49] I.P.S. No. 12, p. 6.

[50] *The History of the Rise and Fall of Militarism*, Vol. 2, p. 202.

[51] Tanaka Hiyoshi wrote an article, "A Secret History of the Army—the Truth of the March and October Incidents," which was published in the *World Culture,* Tokyo, March 1946. An excerpt of this article was listed as IMTFE Exhibit No. 1,402B.

[52] *The Memoirs of Imamura,* Vol. 2, p. 311; Ito: *The History of the Rise and Fall of Militarism,* Vol. 2, p. 202.

[53] *A Secret Record of the Japanese Reform Movements,* p. 179, pp. 183-185.

[54] *Ibid.*, pp. 187-188; Royal Jules War, "The Young Officers' Movement in Japan (1925-1937)," an unpublished 1949 doctoral dissertation, University of California.

[55] *A Secret Record of the Japanese Reform Movements,* p. 173.

[56] *Ibid.*, pp. 183-185.

[57] *Saionji Diary,* Entry, October 11, 1931.

[58] IMTFE Proceedings, p. 30,733; Exhibit No. 3340.

[59] *Ibid.*, p. 31,330.

[60] *The Memoirs of Imamura,* Vol. 2, p. 219.

[61] Yamaguchi Shigeji: *The Tragic General,* 1952, p. 160; *The Imamura Memoirs,* Vol. 2, pp. 221-225.

[62] IMTFE Proceedings, p. 2,017-2,018.

[63] *The Imamura Diary,* Vol. 2, pp. 220-227.

[64] I.P.S. Document No. 1.019, Minami's report (November 4, 1931).

[65] On October 30, Koiso, in his capacity as Director of the Bureau of Military Affairs of the War Ministry, telegraphed Honjo cautioning him against sending troops to northern Manchuria so as not to provoke the Soviet Union. He also asked Honjo how much money would be needed to bribe Ma Chan-shan. The Kwantung Army replied that a minimum of three million yen would be needed. *The Road to the Pacific War,* Vol. 2, pp. 53-54

[66] Katakura Tadashi: *A Top Secret Political Diary.*

[67] *The Road to the Pacific War,* Vol. 2, p. 33.

[68] *The Chinese White Paper,* Memorandum 26, No. 3, p. 78; *The Road to the Pacific War,* Vol. 2. p. 49.

[69] *The Chinese White Paper,* Memorandum 26, No. 3.

[70] On October 29, Ohashi paid a visit to the Soviet Consulate in Harbin. The Soviet Consul denied that the Soviet Union was giving aid to Ma Chan-shan. He also indicated that the Soviet Union had no intention of interfering with the Kwantung Army's plan to repair the bridge over Nonni River. See *A Top Secret Political Diary.*

[71] The October 30 telegram was sent to Miyake by Ninomiya, the deputy chief of the General Staff. The telegram was numbered 105. See *The Road to the Pacific War,* Vol. 2, pp. 52-53.

[72] The November 2 telegram was sent to Honjo by Kanaya, chief of the General Staff. The telegram was numbered 108. It reads: "After the bridge has been repaired, the troops should be withdrawn as soon as possible. In view of the current national and international situation, it is absolutely impermissible for the troops to cross the river northward." The tone of the telegram was very firm, because at the League of Nations, Japan was reprimanded by delegates of other nations. On October 24, the Council of the League passed by a majority of 13 to 1 a resolution that the Japanese troops should be withdrawn

no later than November 16. Because of this, Japan felt isolated and was uncertain what the League would do to her when the Council reconvened on November 16. Thus, Kanaya was concerned about "the national and international situation." See Prentiss Gilbert's (U.S. Consul in Geneva) telegram to Stimson, Secretary of State, United States, *Foreign Relations, Japan,* 1931-41, Vol. 1, p. 33.

[73] Katakura Tadashi: *A Top Secret Political Diary.*

[74] See Kwantung Army's telegram No. 15 to General Staff, Tokyo.

[75] *The Road to the Pacific War,* Vol. 2, p. 61.

[76] *Ibid.*, pp. 62-64.

[77] When Uchida Yasuya, President of the Board of Directors of the Southern Manchuria Railway Company, returned to Tokyo, he made a moving speech before the Privy Council pleading the cause of the Kwantung Army. Originally, Uchida had been recommended by Shidehara to the position for the specific purpose of checkmating the views of the Kwantung Army. He now took the view of the Kwantung Army. Hayashi telegraphed Shidehara and expressed the idea that though he opposed the actions of the Kwantung Army in principle, in view of the then current situation, he had no choice but to give tacit approval to the Kwantung Army's military actions. Because of the sudden change of heart on the part of Uchida and Hayashi, Shidehara's attitude was weakened. This explained the apparent modification of policy as indicated by the third Provisional Imperial Mandate order. See *The Road to the Pacific War,* Vol. 2, pp. 59-70.

[78] *The Road to the Pacific War,* Vol. 2, p. 74.

[79] *Ibid.*

[80] Ma Chan-shan retreated to Hai-lun on November 18, and the Kwantung Army entered the capital of Heilungkiang in the morning of November 19. (See *The Chinese White Paper,* No. 24, p. 118.)

[81] At first the Kwantung Army feared that the Soviet Union might send troops southward under the pretext of protecting the rights of the Chinese Eastern Railway but on November 19, Itagaki telegraphed from Harbin that in northern Manchuria there were no anti-Japanese movements, and the Soviet Union also showed no signs of military maneuvers. He also said that it seems as if northern Manchuria might be taken over by political means in the future. Honjo was overjoyed, and he wanted to keep his troops in Heilungkiang to step up pressure on Ma Chan-shan. See *A Top Secret Political Diary.*

[82] *The Road to the Pacific War,* Vol. 2, p. 82.

[83] *The Tragic General: Ishihara Kanji.*

[84] Commander Tamon told the members of the Lytton Commission that the Kwantung Army had dispatched only 3,000 men to take Heilungkiang; when it withdrew the main force from Heilungkiang, only one battalion of infantry and one company of artillery were left behind, but this remaining force was never withdrawn as it should have been two weeks after the withdrawal of the main force. See *The Chinese White Paper,* No. 24, p. 118.

[85] The General Staff endorsed Honjo's report repudiating the Chang Hsueh-liang regime. See telegram sent by the American Embassy at Tokyo to Secretary Stimson on October 8, 1931, *U.S. Foreign Relations, Japan,* 1931-41, Vol. 1, p. 18.

[86] Shidehara, the Japanese Foreign Minister, said that the General Staff had no right to speak on behalf of the Tokyo Government. See the telegram sent by the American Embassy at Tokyo to Secretary Stimson on October 10, 1931. *U. S. Foreign Relations, Japan,* 1931-41, Vol. 1, p. 18.

[87] Chinchow was bombed at the time when Major General Hashimoto was in Mukden. He asked Ishihara why he had not been informed of the matter beforehand. Ishihara replied that because the matter was within the prerogatives of the Army, it was not necessary to inform or consult anybody. Hashimoto expressed his indignation to Tanaka Ryukichi and Morishima about the house detention in which the Kwantung Army had placed him. See *The Tragic General: Ishihara Kanji; Conspiracies, Assassinations and the Sword,* Vol. 2, p. 88.

[88] See the General Staff's telegram to the Commander of the Japanese Garrison in Tientsin on November 12, 1931. A copy of the telegram is contained in *The Road to the Pacific War,* Vol. 2, p. 90.

[89] *The Road to the Pacific War,* Vol. 2, p. 93.

[90] *Ibid.,* pp. 94-96.

[91] The plan of neutralization of Chinchow was first proposed by the Chinese delegate at the Council of the League of Nations. Under the supervision of the League, neutral nations would send troops to establish the neutralized zone. China intended to withdraw the Northeast Border Defense Army within Shankaikwan but Japan would not permit it until China had fulfilled the conditions which Japan had imposed on her. See *The Chinese White Paper,* No. 26, Memorandum No. 3, and No. 24, p. 123.

[92] See IMTFE Exhibit Nos. 187A and 192A; IMTFE Proceedings, pp. 2,220-2,223.

Footnotes — Chapter 5

[1] On July 12, Generalissimo Chiang telegraphed Chang Hsueh-liang that this is not the time to go to war with Japan. See archives of the Japanese Foreign Office on secret telegrams and intelligence relations. Yu Yu-jen also telegraphed Chang Hsueh-liang on July 13: "The Central Government regards it as its first duty to quash internal rebellion. Comrades of the Northeast must understand this policy." See *The Road to the Pacific War,* Vol. 2, p. 268.

[2] Chang Hsueh-liang's telegram to Jung Chen: "We will be beaten if we should start war with Japan, and as a result Japan would ask for reparations in land and money and the Northeast would become an abyss. It is necessary to avoid clashes and to resort to negotiations." Telegram from Kwantung Bureau to the Vice Minister of the Japanese Ministry of Foreign Affairs, dated July 15.

[3] Wang Jung-pao (Chinese Minister to Japan) had resigned and was in Peiping. He told T. F. Tsiang (Chiang Ting-fu) that Shidehara had said: "You should take advantage of my incumbency to improve Sino-Japanese relations so that the situation would not become impossible later on." Wang reported it to the government but no attention was paid to it. See *Tu Li Weekly*, No. 15 (September 4, 1932).

[4] Commenting on the responsibility for the Mukden Incident, T. F. Tsiang wrote: "The Kuomintang people are conceited and complacent. They fail to assess the urgency of the matter, but resort to the slogan of revolutionary diplomacy to intoxicate themselves." See *Tu Li Weekly,* No. 18, (September 18, 1933).

Dr. Hu Shih said: "The September 18 affair was not a planned nonresistance, but was a collapse like the sudden destruction of something decaying and dying." See *Tu Li Weekly,* No. 41, p. 2.

[5] Chang Hsueh-liang's telegram of September 19, 1931 may be found in *Compendium on Materials of Sino-Japanese Diplomatic Relations,* Ministry of Foreign Affairs, Taipei, Vol. 2, p. 21 (1965).

[6] *Kuo-wen Weekly,* Vol. i, No. 37.

[7] "Chow Fo-hai Works," *Spring and Autumn Magazine,* Hongkong, No. 218, p. 8.

[8] *President Chiang's Collected Articles,* National War College, Taipei, Taiwan, 1960, Vol. 1, p. 280.

[9] *Kuo-wen Weekly,* Vol. 8, No. 37.

[10] *Kuo-wen Weekly,* Vol. 8, No. 38.

[11] *Ibid.*

[12] *President Chiang's Collected Articles,* p. 572.

[13] *Tai Chi-t'ao's (Tai Ch'uan-hsien's) Collected Articles,* p. 380.

[14] According to *Tai Chi-t'ao's Collected Articles,* there were then three confidential documents in his custody, namely: (A) Report of the Special Foreign Relations Committee to the Central Political Council; (B) The Resolution of the Fourth National Congress; (C) Generalissimo Chiang's personal directive on foreign policy toward Japan. Both (B) and (C) had been published before; only document (A) may be considered classified material.

[15] *Tai Chi-t'ao's Collected Articles,* pp. 373-375.

[16] *Kuo-wen Weekly,* Vol. 9, No. 5.

[17] IMTFE Exhibit No. 246; Shidehara, *Fifty Years of Diplomacy.*

[18] W. W. Willoughby: *The Sino-Japanese Controversy,* P. 163. It said: "Chinese representative appealed to the League on November 25, 1931. China, for the sake of peace, could and would, if requested by the Council in the interest of peace withdraw her force within the Great Wall." *Foreign Affairs, Japan,* 1931-41, Vol. I, pp. 58, 62-64.

[19] *President Chiang's Collected Articles,* Vol. 2, p. 2,106.

[20] Huang Tsung: "Chinese Student Movements Siince May 4," in *Sociology World,* January 1932, Pao Tsun-p'eng: *The History of Modern Youth Movement in China* (1953 ed.).

[21] *Central Daily News,* September 21, 1931.

[22] *P'ing-hsi Pao,* September 25, 1931.

[23] Warren Israel: *The Chinese Student Movement,* Harvard University doctoral dissertation, 1963.

[24] *P'ing-hsi Pao,* October 20, 1931; also Israel, *op. cit.,* p. 84.

[25] *P'ing-hsi Pao,* October 20, 1931.

[26] *China Times,* November 10.

[27] Wang Chien-min: *The History of Kunchantang,* Vol. 3, Chapter 22, p. 5.

[28] *Peiping Morning Post,* November 27, 1931.

[29] The Student Union of Peking University telegraphed the Kuomintang Central Headquarters and the Nationalist Government in Nanking that they would not be responsible for the action of a few students who went south to demonstrate without its approval. See *The History of Kunchantang,* Vol. 3, p. 5.

[30] *Ibid.*

[31] *Ibid.*, Vol. 3, p. 6.

[32] *The Report of Peking University,* p. 223.

[33] FR, 1931, pp. 684-686.

[34] Israel, *op. cit.*, p. 134.

[35] Israel, *op. cit.*, p. 136.

[36] *Central Daily News,* (December 18, 1931).

[37] *Tai Chi-t'ao's Collected Articles,* p. 381.

[38] *President Chiang's Collected Articles,* p. 280.

[39] Otsuka Reizo: *The History of the Chinese Communist Party,* Vol. 1, p. 9.

[40] The three Nationalist sieges of Chinese Communist forces: The first began December 9, 1930 and ended January 3, 1931 involving

some 40,000 Nationalist and 42,000 Communist troops. The Nationalists were defeated, with division commander Chang Hui-chan captured and brutally murdered, while T'an Tao-yuan's division also suffered heavy losses. The second began April 1, 1931 and ended May 31, with some 110,000 Nationalist troops against 60,000 Communists. It also resulted in Nationalist defeat; division commander Hu Tsu-yu was killed in battle and heavy losses were suffered by Mao Ping-wen's division. The third began July 10, 1931 and ended September 20 (two days after the Mukden Incident). Some 130,000 Nationalist troops were pitched against 60,000 Communist troops. Though Nationalists suffered some reverses, they captured Ning-tu and Li-ch'uan. The suppression campaign was suspended because of the Mukden Incident. See Wang Chien-min: The *History of Kunchantang,* 1965, Taipei, Taiwan, Chapter 20; *The History of Bandit Supression Wars,* by the History Bureau of the Ministry of National Defense; also, *Mao Tse-tung's Selected Works* (Lawrence and Wishart, London, 1954), Vol. Two, pp. 267-281.

[41] See Lei Hsiao-ts'en: *Thirty Years of Tumultuous China,* Vol. 1, Chapter 5, 6, 7 (1955, Hongkong).

[42] The first article of the Constitution of the Chinese Communist Party states: "The CCP is a part of the Communist International; named as the Chinese Communist Party, it is a branch of the Communist International." See Wang Chien-min, *The History of Kunchantang,* Chapter 22, p. 26; Chapter 24, p. 28.

[43] Wang Chien-min, *op. cit.*, Chapter 13, p. 151.

[44] Otsuka Reizo: *The History of the Chinese Communist Party,* Vol. 1, p. 630: "On September 20, 1931, the Central Committee of the CCP telegraphed its comrades in Shanghai that Chiang Kai-shek's plan of encircling the Soviet area for the third time has been smashed. It behooves our party to observe the Central Directive in strengthening class struggle in the Soviet region and in pursuing the retreating enemy troops so that they would be deprived of the strength to stage another attack."

[45] Charles B. Maclane: *Soviet Policy and the Chinese Communism* 1931, p. 267.

[46] *Shanghai Red Flag Weekly*, N. 34.

[47] *Ibid.*

[48] *Kiangsi Struggle,* No. 4.

[49] The 6-point statement is the Kremlin's directive to the CCP: expansion of the Red Army is found in point 2; overthrow of the Nationalist Government is found in point 3. Text is found in Wang Chien-min, *op. cit.*, Chapter 22, p. 11.

[50] *The Compass of Antiimperialist Struggle and Defending the Soviet Union,* a pamphlet of the Propaganda Department of the Central Bureau of the CCP Soviet Regime in Kiangsi.

[51] Wang Chien-min, *op. cit.,* Chapter 27, p. 18.

[52] *Ibid.*, Chapter 13, p. 82.

[53] *Ibid.*, Chapter 13, p. 104.

[54] The Chen Tu-hsiu faction was liquidated on August 7, 1927; the Chu Ch'iu-pai faction was liquidated in July 1928, and the Li Li-san line was liquidated in January 1931.

[55] The Internationalists, headed by Chen Shao-yu and Chin Pang-hsien, have 28 leading cadres, known as the 28 stars. The name list may be found in Wang Chien-min's *History of Kunchantang*, Chapter 13, p. 100; also, *Red Documents* and "The Present Status of the Chinese Communist Party," *Kuo-wen Weekly*, Vol. 8, No. 29.

[56] *The Invisible Conflict* by Hsu En-tseng (English edition published in Hongkong 1958). The number of Communists killed appears on pp. 120-121; also, Wang Chien-min, *History of Kunchantang*, Chapter 13, p. 148-149.

[57] *Red Flag Weekly*, No. 22.

[58] *Red Flag Weekly*, No. 23, 24; *General Conditions of the Kiangsi Soviet Region*, compiled by Kuomintang Central Headquarters, December 1932.

[59] *Red Flag Weekly*, No. 25.

[60] *Red Chung Hwa*, Nos. 12 and 18.

[61] *President Chiang's Collected Articles*, p. 280.

[62] FR. 1932 (4), p. 150; telegram of U.S. Ambassador in Japan to the State Department, July 1932.

[63] Hu Han-min's episode, see Hu's own story on the Tang-shan episode; also, Lei Hsiao-ts'en, *op. cit.*, Vol. 1, pp. 181-198.

[64] *The Japanese Foreign Ministry's Annual Report and Other Important Documents*, Vol. 2, pp. 172-180.

[65] *Kuo-wen Weekly*, Vol. 8, No. 44.

[66] *Ibid.*, (telegram "yen" September 29 of Chen, Ts'ai and Chang to Generalissimo Chiang).

[67] *Ibid.*, (Chiang's telegram dated 2 and 5 October).

[68] Lei Hsiao-ts'en, *op. cit.*, Vol. 1, pp. 207-208.

[69] *Kuo-wen Weekly*, Vol. 8, No. 44.

[70] Chiang's telegram "yen" (October 29) to Representatives Ts'ai, Chen and Chang.

[71] *Archives of Japanese Foreign Office* (on Chinese civil war). Cf. Chapter VI, Note. 14.

[72] *Ibid.*

[73] *Kuo-wen Weekly*, Vol. 8, No. 42.

[74] *The Road to the Pacific War*, Vol. 2, p. 277.

[75] *Kuo-wen Weekly*, Vol. 8, No. 44.

[76] *The Road to the Pacific War*, Vol. 2, p. 278.

[77] *Kuo-wen Weekly*, Vol. 8, No. 44: telegram from Yu Yu-jen and Chang Chi to Wang Ching-wei and Sun Fo in Shanghai.

[78] *Kuo-wen Weekly*, Vol. 8, No. 47.

[79] Shanghai Japanese Consul General's telegram to Foreign Minister Shidehara: see *Archives* of Japanese Foreign Office (on Chinese civil war); *Kuo-wen Weekly*, Vol. 9, No. 2.

[80] *Ta Kung Pao* editorial, No. 8, 1931.

[81] *U. S. Foreign Relations, Japan,* 1931-41, Vol. 1, p. 62, and *President's Chiang's Collected Works,* Vol. 2, p. 2,106.

[82] The warning of Lord Cecil, see *Foreign Relations,* 1931 (3), pp. 621-622.

Footnotes — Chapter 6

[1] The six alleged causes are: (a) the Wanpaoshan Case, (b) the Nakamura case, (c) the 53 outstanding cases (d) the boycott on Japanese goods, (e) the infringement of Japanese vested rights in Manchuria (f) the charge that China is not a modern State. (See Koo's Memoranda to the Lytton Commission, Vol. 1-3, Chinese Culture Society, New York, 1932.)

[2] The three causes are: (a) disregard for China's national consciousness of unification, (b) conflict between Chinese and Japanese nationalism, (c) provocations by China's revolutionary diplomatic policy. (See author's *The September 18th Crisis,* Chinese edition, 1965, Hongkong.)

[3] *The Chinese White Paper,* Published by Waichiaopu, 1933, No. 26, Memorandum 11, p. 203.

[4] See IMTFE, I.P.S. No. 298, and Toriya Masakazu, *The Manchurian Crisis.* It was stated in the book that on May 31, 1931, Toyohara, the Japanese Consul General at Manchuli, sent a confidential telegram (No. 198) to Shidehara, the Japanese Foreign Minister, stating that Chinese authorities were keeping a close watch over the activities of the officers sent by the General Staff and the Ministry of War to Mongolia; Captain Nakamura had gone to Hu-lun-pei-erh as an agricultural expert and was accompanied by Major Niiguma.

[5] On September 9, 1931, Hayashi Hirajiro reported to Shidehara by telegram (No. 576) that the Kwantung Army has consulted him regarding the setting of June 27 and July 1 as respective dates for Nakamura's arrest and murder so that they would tally with other events. Hayashi requested that these dates be used when statements on the incident were issued.

[6] On July 29, Japanese Consul General at Harbin, Ohashi Tadakazu, sent a confidential telegram (No. 182) to Shidehara, reporting that Captain Nakamura had been murdered at Tao-nan; Nakamura's visa had been issued on May 14, by the Japanese Consulate at Harbin upon the request of the Japanese Special Intelligence Agency; since of late Japanese officials had frequently used false visas to get into the interior of China, if Nakamura's false documents were discovered by Chinese military authorities, he might be punished for spying. He asked whether such passports should be issued in the future. He requested Shidehara to pay special attention to the incident in order to prevent China from using it as a propaganda against Japan.

[7] See Hayashi Hisajiro's telegram to Shidehara on August 2 (No. 290).

[8] Hayashi Hisajiro sent two telegrams to Shidehara on September 6 and 8. He said: (1) It is doubtful whether China is willing to assume

responsibility for the Nakamura incident. If it is necessary, he would bribe witnesses and he has already talked with Doihara Kenji and the Consul at Heilungkiang. (2) Up to now all evidences about Nakamura's murder were from hearsay and he was thinking of getting substantial evidences by bribery.

[9] *Cf. supra,* 48.

[10] *Conspiracies, Assassinations and the Sword,* Vol. 2, p. 34; *The World Magazine,* Tokyo, No. 46, p. 37, June 1959.

[11] *Ibid.,* p. 36.

[12] *Ibid.,* p. 36. According to Morishima Morito, it was Yung Chen, the Chief of Staff, who told Morioka Shohei, the Japanese Consul.

[13] *Survey of International Affairs* (1931).

[14] Shimanuki Takeharu, *The National Defense of Japan* (1961 ed.).

[15] Before the Russo-Japanese War (1904-1905), the United States agreed to help Japan by remaining neutral. President Theodore Roosevelt informed France and Germany that the United States would go to the aid of Japan if they helped Russia. President Taft made an agreement with Japan specifying that if Japan would leave the Philippines alone, the United States would recognize Japan's suzerainty over Korea. For the agreement, see David J. Dallin, *The Rise of Russia in Asia* (1949 ed.), pp. 83-86. For the first Russo-Japanese secret agreement in 1907, see Yanaga, *Japan Since Perry,* p. 337.

[16] *The Japanese Foreign Ministry's Annual Report and Other Important Documents,* Vol. 1, pp. 258-259.

[17] Tang Er-ho, *The Diplomacy of the Manchurian Railway.* Peking, 1928.

[18] California's segregation law was passed in 1905. See *The Road to the Pacific War,* Vol. 1, p. 12. For Japan's policy on national defense, see Hayashi Saburo, *The Imperial Army* (1959 ed.), p. 2, footnote 5, and p. 64.

[19] See *The Road to the Pacific War,* Vol. 1, p. 23.

[20] Japan's original plan called for the gradual increase in the building of battleships, from 8-4 to 8-6, and then finally to 8-8. See Ito Masanori, *Kato Takaaki,* Vol. 2, p. 286.

[21] In 1921, at the opening of the 42nd Japanese Diet, the Constitutional Party pointed out that the budget for Japan's expenses had been set at 105,600,000 yen. The military expenses of the Army and Navy alone reached 60,000,000 yen, exceeding 48% of the entire budget.

The following is a table showing the percentage of military expenses of Britain, the United States, and Japan in their respective annual national expenditures and income (1919-1922):

	% of Military Expenses in Annual Outlays	*% of Military Expenses in National Income*
Britain	22.6%	3.3%
United States	23%	2.26%
Japan	43.54%	7.72%

(The table is taken from *The Road to the Pacific War,* Vol. 1, p. 18.)

[22] Arai: *The Naval Record.*

[23] Henry L. Stimson, *Far Eastern Crisis,* p. 171; *Survey,* 1932, p. 550.

[24] On December 23, 1921, Maring accompanied by Chang T'ai-lei visited Sun Yat-sen in Kweilin. See *A Chronological Biography of Sun Yat-sen,* p. 518; *President Chiang's Collected Articles,* p. 267.

[25] The Third International was established in March 1919. It was convened by Lenin at Moscow. This took place almost at the same time as the Versailles Conference. Refer to George F. Kennan, *Russia and the West Under Lenin and Stalin,* p. 159.

[26] In 1920, Japan occupied part of Siberia. Fearing that Japan might also occupy Chita, Omsk and Irkusk which Russia was unable to defend, Lenin decided to form a Far Eastern Republic at Chita with these regions and Vladivostok which had already been under Japanese occupation. The Republic was headed by Tobelas, an expatriate of Russia who had become a naturalized American citizen. This Republic retained private ownership system and prohibited Sovietization. It also adopted a consitutional system and allowed free elections thus giving the appearance of a genuine democracy. The Republic was established on April 6, and it was officially recognized by the Soviet Union on May 14. Russia also sent a diplomatic mission there. Taking advantage of the Republic's weakness, Japan wanted to have direct negotiations with it. She demanded that the military base at Vladivostok be demolished. The Washington Conference opened in November of the following year, and the Far Eastern Republic sent three delegates to the United States. American Public opinion was deeply moved by their propaganda. The New York Foreign Policy Association and C. H. Smith, a self-styled liberal, testified that the Republic had a strong desire for independence and democracy and should be supported. The State Department too exerted pressure on the Japanese delegation. Consequently, Japan was forced to inform the United States State Department the date on which she intended to withdraw her troops from Siberia. In the meantime, Japan continued her negotiations with the representatives of the Far Eastern Republic at Changchun and Dairen. Knowing the support of the United States for the Republic, the Chita delegates refused to make any concessions to Japan. Japan was thus obligated to withdraw her troops from Vladivostok in October, 1922 as had been scheduled, and the Chita Army entered Vladivostok. In less than a month, the Chita Government called for a popular election which approved the dissolution of the Republic, the merging with the Soviet Union, and the adoption of the Soviet system. Later, it was known that the whole affair came about as a result of Lenin's order issued on August 13, 1920. Lenin created the democratic republic in order to induce the support of the United States in forcing the withdrawal of Japanese troops from Siberia. See *The Rise of Russia in Asia,* pp. 168-176.

[27] Lenin announced that Russia would lease the 400,000 square miles of land in the Kamtchatka Peninsula to the United States for sixty years.

A certain Baker Vandership went to Russia for the deal. He claimed that he was an intimate of President Harding. Lenin received him in person. Lenin did this in order to pressure Japan to make concessions to Russia. See *The Rise of Russia in Asia,* pp. 164-166.

[28] The G. V. Chicherin statement was issued in July 1919. The Karakhan statement was made in September 1920. Goto Shimpei, a former Japanese Foreign Minister, said that he was greatly shaken by the Karakhan statement. See *The Road to the Pacific War,* Vol. 1, pp. 226-260.

[29] *Documents on Communism, Nationalism and Soviet Advisers,* pp. 139-140; Isaac, *Tragedy of the Chinese Revolution,* p. 9.

[30] *The Road to the Pacific War,* Vol. 1, p. 227.

[31] For Joffe's deportation from Germany, see George F. Kennan, *Russia and the West,* **pp. 151-152.**

[32] After Joffe's departure, Karakhan was sent to China. The Soviet Embassy became the center of Communist struggle in North China and developed close relations with Hu Ching-i, Feng Yu-hsiang, and Kuo Sung-lin.

[33] Russia's aid to the Whampoa Military Academy was about three million rubles. *Cf. The Rise of Russia in Asia,* p. 212.

[34] In 1922, when Maring, a delegate from the Third International proposed collaboration between the Kuomintang and the Chinese Communist party to Sun Yat-sen, Sun rejected it, but agreed to let individual members of the Chinese Communist party join the Kuomintang. *Documents on Communism, Nationalism and Soviet Advisers,* p. 83.

[35] George F. Kennan, *Russia and the West,* p. 267.

[36] *Documents on Communism, Nationalism and Soviet Advisers,* p. 84.

[37] *Ibid.,* 89.

[38] See *The Endeavor* (a weekly magazine) and *Documents on Communism, Nationalism and Soviet Advisers,* p. 63.

[39] See Jen Te-chiang's confidential report to the Red Army contained in *Documents on Soviet Russia's Intrigues,* pp. 19-23. Also see *World-wide Soviet Plot,* pp. 19-20 and *Documents on Communism, Nationalism and Soviet Advisers,* p. 341, Document 37.

[40] Jen Te-chiang's report stated that Russia's motive for collaboraiton with Feng Yu-hsiang was the desire to have Feng join the Chinese National Revolution so that it would in turn aid the world revolution envisioned by Russia. The report emphasized the importance of military aid.

[41] Kuo Sung-lin's defection from Chang Tso-lin's Northeast group was instigated by Karakhan. See *The Rise of Russia in Asia,* p. 252 Feng Yu-hsiang's Soviet adviser remarked that on November 12, 1925, ten days before Kuo Sung-lin telegraphed Chang Tso-lin of his intended defection, Feng Yu-hsiang had already informed him about the event.

[42] On December 5, 1925, Shirakawa Yoshinori, Commander-in-Chief of the Kwantung Army, notified both Chang Tso-lin and Kuo Sung-lin that their troops would not be allowed to fight in an area within 25

miles of the South Manchuria Railway. This was to prevent Kuo's forces from attacking Mukden, as Chang Tso-lin was withdrawing his troops into Mukden. In the following year, Chang personally went to Dairen to thank the Kwantung Army for its help. See Kao Yin-tsu, *Important Events of the Republic of China,* p. 195 and p. 217. When Kuo's army was at the height of its strength, the cavalries of Kirin and Heilungkiang were ordered by Chang Tso-lin to go south to reinforce his forces, but Ivanov, General Manager of the Chinese Eastern Railway, demanded immediate cash payment for transporting the troops. See Dallin, *The Rise of Russia in Asia,* p. 253.

[43] On January 24, 1925, Ivanov was arrested. Karakhan twice appealed to Russia for help. See Dallin, *The Rise of Russia in Asia,* pp. 253-254.

[44] A group of 29 military advisers led by Jen Te-chiang arrived in Peking in the middle of April 1925. Hu Ching-i had died a few days before and was succeeded by Yueh Wei-chun who had no connection with the Soviet Union. Consequently, Karakhan had to negotiate with Feng Yu-hsiang. Their first meeting took place on April 21. Borodin, Jen Te-chiang, a certain member of the Kuomintang's Central Committee and A. I. Gecher, a military attaché of the Soviet Embassy, were also present. See Jen Te-chiang's report to the Soviet Army, dated May 22, 1925. *Documents on Soviet Russia's Intrigues,* Vol. 3, p. 30.

[45] When Feng Yu-hsiang retreated from Ping-ti-chuan to Urga, Borodin, accompanied by a group of thirty persons, also arrived there. On April 7, Feng started for Russia accompanied by Hsu Ch'ien. On April 30, he arrived at Moscow. The Russians urged him to join the Kuomintang (at the time, the Russians were still collaborating with the Kuomintang), but he did not become a member until May 10. According to Wilbur and How, the reason for Feng Yu-hsiang's change of mind was Wu Pei-fu's refusal to cooperate with him. In March of that year, a delegate from the National Army started negotiations with Tien Wei-ch'in, a representative from the Chih-li clique. On April 9, Lu Chung-lin forced Tuan Chi-jui to resign and released Tsao K'un in preparation for Wu's assumption of power. Wu seemed to despise Feng because of his frequent double dealings. Feng was thus left without supporters and decided to join the Kuomintang. See *Documents on Communism, Nationalism and Soviet Advisers,* p. 333.

[46] *The Road to the Pacific War,* Vol. 1, pp. 275-276. Shidehara had ordered Adachi Kenzo to investigate the matter, and it was reported back in January 1926 that there were no evidences of a secret agreement but it was true that there had been purchase of arms.

[47] *Documents on Soviet Russia's Intrigues,* Vol. 3, pp. 1-16, Doc. 38.

[48] According to the Year Book of the United States' Department of Commerce, in 1925, Russia's imports from Japan were a mere $600,000 in value but in 1931, the figure ran to $12,000,000.

[49] Besedovsky, *The Revelations of a Soviet Diplomat,* p. 18. The author states that between 1926 and 1927, Stalin was so afraid of the

Japanese that he thrice ordered Besedovsky to negotiate a treaty of non-aggression with Japan.

[50] In July 1927, after the Eastern Conference, Mori Kaku's aggressive policy towards China was carried out, and Yoshida Shigeru was returned to his former post at Mukden as Consul General. He used high-handed methods in exacting additional privileges in Manchuria and Mongolia. On September 4, the Communist elements in various parts of Manchuria gathered together a group of 20,000 Chinese to demonstrate against the Japanese. See *The Record of the Japanese Foreign Ministry,* PVM 23 (459) and *The Road to the Pacific War,* Vol. 1, p. 293.

[51] In early 1931, the problems of transportation over the Manchurian Railway were discussed by the Chinese and Japanese authorities. The Foreign Policy Association of Liaoning advocated a strong attitude. In May, it further suggested that the rights of stationing Railway Guards in Antung, Mukden, Dairen, and Port Arthur and the postal rights be handed back to China. The Japanese Chamber of Commerce and industrial associations in Manchuria also held conferences to discuss the problems. They were opposed to China's demand for the abolition of consular jurisdiction. The young officers of the Japanese Army even clamored for the solution by force of Manchurian-Mongolian problems. See *The Road to the Pacific War,* Vol. 1, pp. 346-352.

[52] After the outbreak of the incident over the Chinese Eastern Railway, Russia started military maneuvers. The State Department of the United States twice invited delegates from England, France, Germany, Japan, and Italy to mediate. England, France, and Italy consented. Germany was reticent but Japan was opposed because it was the established policy of the Japanese Cabinet not to allow a third power to extend its influences into Manchuria and Mongolia. Consequently, Russia started a pro-Japanese and anti-American propaganda campaign. It was probably because of this that after the outbreak of the Mukden Incident, Japan insisted on direct negotiations with China. This event also showed the impotence of the United States to intervene in the Far Eastern crises.

[53] Kawashiwa Ransoku's plan for the annexation of Manchuria and Mongolia had the approval of Terauchi Masaki, the Governor General of Korea, and the secret support of the Japanese Ministry of War. It called for the establishment of a Manchurian-Mongolian state by supporting Prince Pa-lin of Mongolia. Among those Japanese officers who participated in this plan were Lieutenants Takayama, Kimimichi, and Matsui Kiyosuke, Captain Taga Soshi and others. *Cf. Supra* Chapter I, Section I, footnote 1.

[54] This was one of the great plots of 1915-1916 to overthrow Yuan Shih-k'ai and to annex Manchuria. The participants of this event came from various quarters, including Kato, Foreign Minister, Koike, a department head of the Foreign Ministry, Fukuda Masataro, Chief of the General Staff, Tanaka, deputy chief of the General Staff, Major Koiso Kuniaki, and Consul General Yada. There were also Okura Kihachiro, a financier and ronin, such as Goki Katsutoshi, Kizawa, Irie, and others.

However, they all had their own plans, and there was no unified strategy. The General Staff and the Foreign Ministry advocated collaboration with Prince Shu and Babuchapu who was the Mongolian cavalry commander. Consequently, they brought about the Cheng-chia-tun incident. Ishuin and Yada advocated cooperation with Chang Tso-lin to overthrow Tuan Chih-kuei, but this plan was dropped on account of the death of Yuan Shih-kai, Goto Shimpei, "The Movement of Japanese Troops in Manchuria and Mongolia;" Akana Kifu, *The Horse Bandit in Manchuria.*

[55] Henry L. Stimson, *On Active Service in Peace and War* (1947 ed.).

[56] On May 18, 1927, when Japanese troops were sent to Shantung for the first time, 2,000 soldiers from Himeji's 10th Division were mobilized; on April 19, 1928, the 6th Division was sent; on May 4, 1928, the 28th Division was sent. See Takakura Toichi, *The Life of Tanaka Giichi,* pp. 667, 675, and 673.

[57] Yamaura Kamichi, *Mori Kaku: A Japanese Politician* (1949 ed.), pp. 600-601; Abe Isoo, *A Secret Record of the War in East Asia,* p. 26; Abe Isoo, *Three Years' History of the Showa Era,* p. 115.

[58] Yoshihashi, *Conspiracy at Mukden,* p.18.

[59] "An Observation on China in Turmoil," *Mori Kaku: A Japanese Politician,* p. 537.

[60] Tanaka told Idebuchi, who was the Vice Minister, that he could make his own decisions in the Foreign Office without consulting Mori Kaku. Shigemitsu also expressed the view that Tanaka's opinion on the solution of the Tsinan incident was very different from Mori Kaku's instruction. See *The Life of Tanaka Giichi,* pp. 643-644; *The Memoirs of Shigemitsu,* pp. 65-66.

[61] After the death of Yokota, the President of the Seiyukai, Tanaka was elected to succeed him. Mori Kaku immediately told Tanaka that while Tanaka acted as the titular head, he himself would take over the actual control of the party. Tanaka listened to Mori Kaku without making any comment. Mori Kaku also told Matsuoka about what he had said to Tanaka. See *Mori Kaku: A Japanese Politician,* p. 494.

[62] *Conspiracy at Mukden,* p. 20; *The Diary of Ugaki Kazushige,* p. 316.

[63] Mori Kaku made four suggestions: (1) in order to protect Japanese in China, the Tanaka Cabinet should send troops no matter whether in China Proper or in Manchuria and Mongolia; (2) because Manchuria and Inner Mongolia formed the lines of national defense, it was imperative for Japan to maintain order and security there; (3) if the local administration of Manchuria could protect Japan's special interests, Japan should support it; (4) if the National Government of China should change the political setup in the Northeast, Japan should not hesitate to detach Manchuria and Mongolia from China and establish a puppet government. See *Mori Kaku: A Japanese Politician,* pp. 636-637.

[64] *The Japanese Foreign Ministry's Annual Report and Other Important Documents,* Vol. 2, p. 102.

[65] Yoshihashi, *Conspiracy at Mukden,* p. 26.

[66] *The Records of the Japanese Foreign Ministry* (micro-films), PVM 23, 411, 417, 444, 452, 502-506.

[67] Yoshihashi, *Conspiracy at Mukden,* pp. 15-16.

[68] Chen Shao-hsien, *A Study of the Sino-Japanese Problems,* the Commercial Press (1935 ed.).

[69] *The Records of the Japanese Foreign Ministry* (micro-films), PAM 24/2379; *The Road to the Pacific War,* Col. 1, pp. 294-296; the *Ta Kung Pao* did mention briefly about the Yamamoto-Chang Tso-lin Agreement. See Kao Yin-tsu, *Important Events of the Republic of China,* p. 273.

[70] Generalissimo Chiang Kai-shek and Chang Chun met Premier Tanaka on October 13, 1927. The meeting was recorded in *The Japanese Foreign Ministry's Annual Report and Other Important Documents,* Vol. 2, pp. 102-106. Most Japanese writers on the subject said that Japan had secured China's understanding regarding her special interests in Manchuria, but there was no such indication in the record. See *Mori Kaku: A Japanese Politician,* pp. 614-615; *Japan and Her Destiny,* pp. 34-35; *Secret History of the Showa Era,* pp. 24-25.

[71] *The China Incident in the Third Year of the Showa Era* (document of the Japanese General Staff), p. 86. *The Road to the Pacific War,* Vol. 1, p. 300.

[72] Takeuchi, *War and Diplomacy in the Japanese Empire,* p. 253; *The Road to the Pacific War,* Vol. 1, p. 301.

[73] During the Tsinan incident, only thirteen Japanese were killed, but Sakai Takashu exaggerated the casualty list twenty-three fold. The Foreign Ministry reprimanded him for the exaggeration, but the war Ministry protected Sakai. See *The China Incident in the Third Year of the Showa Era,* pp. 90-91.

[74] William F. Morton, *The Tsinan Incident* (an unpublished Master's thesis of Columbia University).

[75] Sakai ordered men of the special Japanese Intelligence Agency in Tsinan to open fire during the confrontation between the Japanese and the Chinese troops, thus causing the fighting.

[76] *President Chiang's Collected Articles,* Vol. 1, pp. 543-547.

[77] The Japanese threatened Chiang Tso-lin that if he should refuse to grant the Japanese the right to complete the Ki-hui Railway, they would not allow him to travel on the South Manchuria Railway. See the *Chinese White Paper,* No. 26, Memorandum 6, p. 115.

[78] *The Kuo-wen Weekly,* Vol. 5, No. 20.

[79] *The Biography of Yamamoto Jotaro,* pp. 604-612.

[80] *The Annual Report and Other Important Documents of the Japanese Foreign Ministry,* Vol. 2, p. 116, IMTFE, p. 1771.

[81] Yoshizawa Kenkichi, *Sixty Years of Diplomacy,* pp. 89-90; *Secret History of the Showa Era,* p. 29.

[82] *The Political Secrets of the Showa Era,* pp. 61-63.

[83] *The Road to the Pacific War,* Vol. 1, p. 306.

[84] *Foreign Relations,* 1928, Vol. 2, pp. 229-231.

[85] *Documents of the Department of State of the United States,* 793/941-1171; 793/23 Manchuria, 23.

[86] Usui Katsumi, "Tanaka's Foreign Policy and the Assassination of Chang Tso-lin," *Education on Japanese History,* Vol. 8, No. 2; IMTFE, pp. 1,818-1,820—The Testimony of Okada Keisuke; Okada Keisuke: *The Memoirs of Okada Keisuke,* pp. 34-35.

[87] *The Political Secrets of the Showa Era,* pp. 61-63; *The Road to the Pacific War,* Vol. 1, p. 308.

[88] Chang Tso-lin was born in 1875. His ancestors came from Ho-chien, Chihli. At 16, he joined the I (Fortitude) Army of the Manchu Government forces as a private. He fought in the Sino-Japanese War (1895). Later, he took part in freebooting and banditry. At 24, he married a girl from the Chao family. In 1901, his son, Hsueh-liang, was born. During the Russo-Japanese War, the Japanese arrested him on the ground that he was a Russian spy, but he was soon released. He then became a Japanese spy on the Russian Army, and thus made the acquaintance of Tanaka Giichi. To pacify Chang Tso-lin, Chang Hsi-luan, then the Taotai of Tung-p'ien, made him the commander of a cavalry unit stationed at Hsin-min. When Chao Erh-sheng became the governor of Fengtien, he promoted Chang to commander of the five route armies. After the establishment of the Chinese Republic, he rose from his post as Commander of the 27th Division to Military and Civil Governor of Fengtien and the High-Inspecting Commissioner of the Three Eastern Provinces. In 1924, the Mukden clique had expanded its influence into the provinces of Kiangsu, Anhwei, and Shantung. This was Chang Tso-lin's heyday of power. In 1927, he proclaimed himself Commander-in-Chief of the An-kao-Chun to reign over North China. See *The Kuo-wen Weekly*, June 24, 1928.

[89] See *The Kuo-wen Weekly,* August 11, 1928.

[90] *Eastern Miscellany*, Vol. 28, No. 15, pp. 10-15.

[91] IMTFE Proceedings, pp. 1,818-1,820.

[92] "A New Play on the State of Railway Politics," *The Kuo-wen Weekly,* Vol. 5, No. 21.

[93] References on Chang Tso-lin's assassination may be found in the following works:

(1) *China Weekly Review,* August 12, 1928.
(2) Kung Te-pai, *The Japanese Murdered Chang Tso-lin* (1929 edition).
(3) "A Certain Important Event in Manchuria," *Harada Kamao Papers.*
(4) The Testimony of Okada Keisuke, in the records of the IMTFE, July 2, 1946.
(5) Tanaka Ryukichi's Testimony, the IMTFE Proceedings, pp. 1,945-1,955.
(6) *The Memoirs of Okada Keisuke* (1950 edition).
(7) Morishima Morito, "The Assassination of Chang Tso-lin and Yang Yu-ting" from *The World Magazine*, Japan, Vol. 45.

(8) Paul S. Dull, "The Assassination of Chang Tso-lin," *Far Eastern Quarterly*, Vol. 4, 1952.
(9) Komoto Daisaku, "I Killed Chang Tso-lin," *The Bungei Shunju,* December 1954, p. 194.
(10) Ito Masanori, *The History, Rise and Fall of Militarism* (1958 edition).
(11) "Tanaka's Foreign Policy and the Assassination of Chang Tao-lin," Vol. 8, No. 2, February 1960, *Education on Japanese History*.
(12) Shinei Dayu, *The Assassination of Chang Tso-lin: The Political Secrets of the Showa Era,* March 1961.
(13) *The Road to the Pacific War,* edited by the Asahi Shinbum, Vol. 1, (1963 edition).
(14) Takehiko Yoshihashi, *Conspiracy at Mukden,* Yale University Press, 1963.

[94] *The Records of Komoto Daisaku, A History of the Political Assassinations of the Showa Era,* pp. 61-115; Marishima Morito, *The Huangkutun Incident; Yoshihashi, Conspiracy at Mukden,* pp. 41-43.

[95] According to Morishima Morito, Liu Che had discussed privately with Morioka Shokei, the Japanese Consul, about Wang's report. See *The Democratic Tide,* Vol. 3, No. 18.

[96] *Ibid.*

[97] See *The Records of Komoto Daisaku;* Usui Katsumi, *The Foreign Policy of Tanaka.* The plan for China's salvation consisted of the following three points: (1) the Peking Government should appeal to Japan for help in administrating Manchuria and Mongolia; (2) a Manchurian-Mongolian administration, headed by a Chinese should be established; (3) based on China's petition, Japan would proclaim to the powers her policy towards China. See Usui Katsumi, "The Foreign Policy of Tanaka," *Education on Japanese History,* Vol. 8, No. 2, February 1960.

[98] On the day of Chang Tso-lin's death, there were four explosions both inside and outside of the city of Mukden, but the Chinese military police handled the situation calmly without causing any incident. See *The Records of Komoto Daisaku; The Political Secrets of the Showa Era.*

[99] *The Diary of Ugaki Kazushige;* IMTFE Proceedings, pp. 1,818, 1,820.

[100] Y. C. Maxon, *The Control of Japanese Foreign Policy,* pp. 74-75.

[101] Harada: *Saionji Diary,* Appendix, p. 1-11.

[102] Komoto Daisaku, "I Killed Chang Tso-lin," *Bungei Shunju,* December 1954, p. 194-201.

[103] In 1962, Mr. Chu Kuang-mo, then on the staff of Chang Hsueh-liang, told this author than Chang returned to Mukden from Chinwangtao in one of the troop trains.

[104] Saito Wataru on July 7 and July 16 and Tatekawa Yoshitsuga on June 25 and July 16 sent telegrams addressed to Hata Shunroku. They

may be found in Professor Akita's article, "Chang Hsueh-liang and Japan," *Asian Studies,* Vol. 20, p. 33, 1960.

[105] *The Road to the Pacific War,* Vol. 1, p. 311.

[106] *Records of the Japanese Foreign Ministry,* PVM 53.

[107] *Ibid.,* PVM 63; Nomura Koichi, *The Manchurian Question Before the Manchurian Crisis: A Study of the Japanese Foreign Policy* (The Showa Era).

[108] For Yen Hsi-shan's telegram, see *Important Events of the Republic of China,* p. 296; for Li Lieh-chun's telegram, see *The Kuo-wen Weekly,* July 8, 1928.

[109] IMTFE Evidence No. 173; IMTFE Proceedings, pp. 1,775-1,776.

[110] *The Kuo-wen Weekly,* Vol. 42, No. 5

[111] Usui Katsumi, *The Foreign Policy of Tanaka; A Study of the Japanese Foreign Policy* (The Showa Era).

[112] *The Road to the Pacific War,* Vol. 1, p. 316.

[113] Upon instructions from Tanaka, Uchida Kasu visited Europe and America. He tried to convince London and Washington that China's unilateral abrogation of treaties was an irresponsible act. Kellogg, the Secretary of State of the United States, told him that support for the Chinese National Government meant security and peace in the Far East, and it would be thus beneficial to Japan. See Usui Katsumi, *The Foreign Policy of Tanaka.*

[114] *Records of the Japanese Foreign Ministry,* PVM, S. 101, 10-20, 2-5.

[115] *The Road to the Pacific War,* Vol. 1, p. 318.

[116] *The Foreign Policy of Tanaka: A Study of Japanese Foreign Policy* (The Showa Era).

[117] *Ibid.*

[118] *The Records of the Japanese Foreign Ministry,* PVM 23, 897-907.

[119] *Cf. supra,* Chapter III, Section 1 and Section 2.

[120] *The Road to the Pacific War,* Vol. 1, p. 343; Vol. 2, p. 238.

[121] When Kimura Eiichi came to Mukden to discuss with Chang Hsueh-liang competitive transportation lines, the Northeast Foreign Relations Association voiced its opposition vehemently. See *The Road to the Pacific War,* Vol. 1, p. 346.

[122] Shidehara wanted to use Japanese technology to aid China's economic development. He also had a plan to train Chinese technicians. See *Records of the Japanese Foreign Ministry,* S.P. 304, 258-298.

[123] *The Japanese Foreign Ministry Annual Report and Other Important Documents,* Vol. 2, pp. 168-171.

[124] Kanda Hikomatsu, *A Revised Japanese Foreign Policy* (1960), p. 249.

Glossary

Adachi	安達
Amakasu Masakiko	甘粕正彦
Amano	森連
Ando Rikichi	安藤利吉
Angangchi	昂昂溪
Anshan	鞍山
Antung	安東
Arai	新井
Araki Sadao	荒木貞夫
Asahi Shimbun	朝日新聞
Atami	熱海
Ayuzawa	鮎澤
Baputsapu	巴布扎布
Borodin	鮑羅廷
Chang Chi	張繼
Chang Ching-hui	張景惠
Chang Chun	張羣
Chang Hai-peng	張海鵬
Chang Hsueh-liang	張學良
Chang Kuo-tao	張國燾
Chang ta Line (Chang Chun-talai)	長大線
Chang Tso-hsiang	張作相
Chang Yin-huai	常蔭槐
Chao Chen	趙鎮
Chao Hsin-po	趙欣伯
Chao-yang-po	朝陽坡
Chen Chi-tang	陳濟棠
Chen Chiao-nein	陳喬年
Chen Chiung-min	陳炯明
Chen, Eugene	陳友仁
Chen Li-fu	陳立夫
Chen Ming-shu	陳銘樞
Chen Shao-yu	陳紹禹
Chen Shih-yen	陳士炎
Chen Tiao-yuan	陳調元
Chen Tu-hsiu	陳獨秀
Chen Yen-nien	陳延年
Cheng-chia-tun	鄭家屯
Chiang Kai-shek	蔣介石
Chiang Pai-li	蔣百里
Chiao-liu River	巨流河
Chiba	千葉
Chichibu, Prince	秩父宮親王
Chientao	間島
Chih-ping	赤坪
Chinhuangtao	秦皇島
Chin Pang-hsien	秦邦憲
Chinchow	錦州
Cho Isamu	長勇
Cho Shu	長州
Chou Hsiao-po	周孝伯
Chou I-chun	周逸羣
Chou-yang-chen	朝陽鎮
Chu Chao-hsin	朱兆莘
Chu Cheng	居正
Chu Ch'iu-pai	瞿秋白
Chu Te	朱德

Dobashi 土 僑
Doihara Kenji 土肥原賢二

Erh-tai-tzu 二 台 子

Fang Chih-ming 方 志 敏
Feng-hua 奉 化
Feng Yu-hsiang 馮 玉 祥
Fenghuangcheng 鳳 凰 城
Fengtien 奉 天
Fu Tan University 復旦大學
Fujii Hitoshi 藤 井 齊
Fujimi-ken 富 士 見 軒
Fujita Isamu 藤 田 勇
Fukuda Masataro 福田雅太郎
Fukui 福 井
Fushun 撫 順

Gondo 權 藤
Goto, Baron 後 藤

Hai-lu-feng 海 陸 豐
Hailin 海 林
Hanaya Tadashi 花 谷 正
Harada Kumao 原 田 熊 雄
Hashimoto Kingoro 橋本欣五郎
Hayashi Gunsuke 林 權 助
Hayashi Hisajiro 林 銑 十 郎
Hayashi Senjuro 林 久 治 郡
Hei-ho 海 河
Heilungkiang 黑 龍 江
Hibiya 日 比 谷
Higashikuni 菱 刈 隆

Higuchi Kisaburo 桶口喜三郎
Hirata Yukihiro 平 田 幸 弘
Hirohito, Emperor 昭 和 天 皇
Hiroshima 廣 島
Hirota 廣 田
Hishikari Takashi 東 久 邇
Ho Lung 賀 龍
Ho Ying-chin 何 應 欽
Honjo Shigeru 本 莊 繁
Hsi Ch'ia 熙 洽
Hsia Kwan 下 關
Hsiang Chung-fa 向 忠 發
Hsiang Yin 項 英
Hsiao-lin-wei 孝 陵 衛
Hsin-i-chou 新 義 州
Hsing-an Mountains 興 安 嶺
Hsinmintun 新 民 屯
Hsiung Shih-hui 熊 式 輝
Hsu Chi-shen 許 繼 慎
Hsu En-tseng 徐 恩 曾
Hsu Hsiang-chien 徐 向 前
Hsu Hsiu-tsen 徐 秀 岑
Hsu Pai-hao 許 白 昊
Hu Ching-i 胡 景 翼
Hu-hai Line 呼 海 線
Hu Han-min 胡 漢 民
Hu-kou 湖 口
Hu Shih 胡 適
Huang Hsing 黄 興
Huang Hu 黄 郛
Huangkutun 皇 姑 屯
Huloutao 葫 蘆 港
Hu-lun-pei-erh 呼 倫 貝 爾

Hunchun 琿春

Ichow 義州
Ida 飯田
Ikeda Samiyisa 池田純久
I-li-ko-tu 宜力克都
IMTFE (International Military Tribunal for the Far East) 遠東軍事裁判法庭
Imada Shintaro 今田新太郎
Imamura Hitoshi 今村均
Inoue Junnosuke 井上準之助
Inukai Isuyoshi 犬養毅
Ishida Itaro 石射猪太郎
Ishihara Kanji 石原莞爾
Isugi 井杉
Itagaki Seishiro 坂垣征四郎
Ito Masanori 伊藤正德

Jui-chin 瑞金
Jun-hsien 潤軒

Kagesa Sadaaki 影佐禎昭
Kalgan 張家口
Kanaya Hanzo 金谷範三
Kanazawa 金澤
Kan Chow 贛州
Kanda Masatane 神田正種
Kanin Nomiya 閑院宮親王
Kansei 關西
Kao Chun-yu 高君宇
Kashii 香椎
Katakura Tadashi 片倉忠
Kataoka 片岡
Kato 川上精一
Kawakami Seiichi 河本末守
Kawamoto Suemori 川島浪速
Kawashima Ronsoku 川島正
Kawashima Tadashi 萱野良知
Kayano Chochi 加藤
Kiang Hsueh-chien 江學乾
Kiangsi 江西
Kido Koichi 木戸幸一
Ki-hui Line 吉會線
Kimura 木村
Kirin 吉林
Kissanka 季山嘉
Kita Ikki 北一輝
Kita Tenjiro 北輝次郎
Kiukiang 九江
Kiwagishi 川岸
Ki-wu Line 吉五線
Koiso Kuniski 小磯國昭
Kojima Masanori 兒島正範
Komoto Daisaku 河本大作
Kono Masanao 河野正直
Koo, V. K. Wellington 顧維鈞
Ku Shun-chang 顧順章
Kuan-cheng-tzu 寬城子
Kuan Yu-heng 關玉衡
Kumamoto 熊本
Kung-chu-ling 公主嶺
Kung, H. H. 孔祥熙
Kuo Sung-lin 郭松齡
Kuomingchun 國民軍
Kure 吳港

Kwan-ti-miao 關帝廟
Kweilin 桂林

Li Li-san 李立三
Li Lieh-chun 李烈鈞
Li Ming-jui 李明瑞
Li Ta-chao 李大釗
Li Wen-fan 李文範
Liao Chung-kai 廖仲凱
Liao Hua-ping 廖划平
Liaoyang 遼陽
Liaoning 遼寧
Lin Sen 林森
Liu Che 劉哲
Liu Ching-chan 劉景山
Liu Hou-sheng 劉厚生
Liu Tai-minh 劉戴明
Liutiaokou 柳條溝
Liu Tse-tan 劉子丹
Lo Chi-yuan 羅綺園
Lung-ching Tsun 龍井村
Lung-kou 龍口

Ma Chan-shan 馬占山
Mabashi 前橋
Machino Takema 町野武馬
Maizuru 舞鶴
Makino 牧野
Manchuli 滿州里
Mao Tse-tung 毛澤東
Maoerhshan 帽兒山
Matsumuto 松本
Matsuoka 松岡

Meiji, Emperor 明治天皇
Minami Jiro 南次郎
Miraoka 村岡
Mitani Kiyoshi 三谷清
Mitsukawa Kamentaro 松川龜太郎
Miura 三浦
Miyake Mitsuharu 三宅光治
Mo Teh-hui 莫德惠
Momotake Harukichi 百武晴吉
Mori Kaku 森恪
Morishima Morito 森島守人
Mugita Hirao 麥田平雄
Mukden 瀋陽
Muto Akina 武藤章
Muto Nobuyoshi 武藤信義

Nagata Tetsuzan 永田鐵山
Nakajima Shinichi 中島信一
Nakamura 中村
Nakano 中野
Nakaya Shoichi 中谷政一
Nemoto Hiroshi 根本博
Ninomiya Harushige 二宮治重
Nishida Koichi 西田畊一
Nishida Zei 西田税
Nishihara Loan 西原借款
Noda 野田

Obata Torikichi 小幡酉吉
Ohara 小原
Ohashi Chuichi 大橋忠一
Okamura Neiji 間島
Okawa Shumei 大川周明

Ono Masao 小野正雄
Osako Michisada 大迫通貞
Ozaki Shiro 尾崎行雄

Pai-chi-pao 白旗堡
Panchihu 本溪湖
Pan Fu 潘復
Pan Wen-yu 潘聞友
Peng Pai 澎湃
Peng Te-huai 彭德懷
Pin-ti-chuan 平地泉
Pu-yi, Henry 溥儀

Rosokai 老壯會

Saburi Sadao 佐分利
Saga 佐賀
Saionji Kinmochi 西園寺公望
Sakanishi Rihachiro 阪西利八郎
Sakata Yoshiro 阪田義郎
Samoto 佐本
Sato 佐藤
Seiyukai 政友會
Shakee 沙基
Shankaikwan 山海關
Shang Hang 上杭
Shibayama Kunshiro 柴山謙四郎
Shidehara Kijuro 幣原喜重郎
Shigemitsu Mamoru 重光葵
Shigeto Chiaki 重藤千秋
Shih Yu-san 石友三
Shimamoto Masaichi 島本正一
Shimizu Konosuke 清水幸之助
Shirakawa Yoshimori 白川義則
So Lun 索倫
Soga Reizo 儀我誠也
Soong Ching-ling 宋慶齡
Soong, T. V. 宋子文
Suda 須田
Sugimoto 杉本
Sugiyama 杉山
Sun Fo 孫科
Sun Yat-sen 孫逸仙
Supingchieh 四平街
Suzuki Soroku 鈴木莊六

Ta-hsing 大興
Ta-hu-shan 打虎山
Ta-ling-ho 大凌河
Ta-pa-tai 大巴代
Tachibana Kosaburo 橘孝三郎
Tai Ch'uan-hsien 戴傳賢
Takeshita Yoshiharu 竹下義晴
Talai 大賚
Tamon Jiro 多門二郎
Tanaka Giichi 田中義一
Tanaka Hiyoshi 田中清
Tanaka Ryukichi 田中隆吉
Tang-chih 湯池
Tang Erh-ho 湯爾和
Tang Hung-ching 唐宏景
Tang Yu-lin 湯玉麟
Tangku 塘沽
Tang-shan 湯山
Tao-nan 洮南
Tao-nan-Angangchi 洮昂

Tao-pei 洮北
Tao-so Line 洮索線
Tashiro Kanichiro 田代皖一郎
Tatekawa Yoshitsugu 建川美次
Ting Wen-fen 丁惟汾
Togo 東鄉
Tokugawa 德川
Toumen 圖們江
Toyama 外山
Tsai Cheng-i 蔡承逸
Tsai Ho-sheng 蔡和森
Tsai Kung-shih 蔡公時
Ts'ai Yuan-p'ei 蔡元培
Tsiang, T. F. 蔣廷黻
Tsou Lu 鄒魯
Tsuda 津田
Tsugi 井杉
Tsukamoto Seiji 塚本清治
Tu Heng 杜衡
Tuan Chi-jui 段祺瑞
Tuan Chih-kuei 段芝貴
Tun-tu Line 敦圖線
Tung-hwa 敦化
Tung-liao Line 通遼線
Tung-pien-tao 東邊道

Ueda Shunkichi 植田俊吉
Uemara 上原
Ugaki Kazunari 宇垣一成
Utsuomiya Taro 宇都宮太郎

Voitinsky 胡定康

Wachi Takaji 和知鷹二
Wada Isoyoshi 和田勁
Wakatsuki Reijiro 若槻禮次郎
Wan Fu-lin 萬福麟
Wang Chia-cheng 王家楨
Wang Chien-min 王健民
Wang I-che 王以哲
Wang Jung-pao 汪榮寶
Wang Li-kung 王立功
Wanpaoshan 萬寶山
Watanabe Jotaro 渡邊錠太郎
Wei Cheng 魏徵
Wen-hsien 萬縣
Wenkuantu 文官屯
Wu Chang 五常
Wu Chun-sheng 吳俊陞
Wu Ken-hsiang 吳根香
Wu Ping 武平

Yalu River 鴨綠江
Yamagata 山縣
Yamaguchi 山口
Yamamoto Jotaro 山本條太郎
Yamazono Shigeatsu 山園重厚
Yang Pao-an 楊匏安
Yang Te-yao 楊德堯
Yang Tzu-chuang 楊子莊
Yang-Yu-ting 楊宇霆
Yano 矢野
Yasuoka Masaatsu 安岡正篤
Yazaki 矢崎
Yen-chi 延吉
Yen Ching University 燕京大學
Yen-hai Line 延海線
Yen Hsi-shan 閻錫山

Yen, W. W.	顏	惠	慶	Yu, David	余	日	章
Yinkow	營		口	Yu Chih-shan	于	芷	山
Yokosuka	橫	須	賀	Yu Kuo-han	于	國	翰
Yoshida Ryohei	吉	清	良平	Yu Ling	榆		林
Yoshida Shigeru	吉	田	茂	Yu Yu-jen	于	右	任
Yoshimura Sokichi	吉村	宗	吉	Yuan Hsiao-hsien	阮	嘯	仙
Yoshino	吉		野	Yuan Shih-kai	袁	世	凱
Yoshizawa Kenkichi	芳澤	謙	吉	Yun Tai-ying	惲	代	英

Selected Bibliography

1. *In English*

CROWLEY, JAMES B.
Japan's Foreign Ministry, Correspondences, Institutions, Communiques, etc., June 1929-May 1931, Reel, S112.

CROWLEY, JAMES B.
Japanese Army Factionalism in the 1930's, Journal of Asian Studies, V. 21, 1962, pp. 309-26.

DALLIN, DAVID JULIEVICH
The Rise of Russia in Asia. New Haven, Yale University Press, 1949.

DALLIN, DAVID JULIEVICH
Soviet Russia and the Far East. New Haven, Yale University Press, 1948.

DULL, PAUL S.
The Assassination of Chang Tso-Lin, Far Eastern Quarterly, November 1952, pp. 453-63.

FERRELL, ROBERT HUGH
Mukden Incident, Journal of Modern History, March 1955, pp. 66-72.

GREAT BRITAIN, FOREIGN OFFICE
Documents on British Foreign Policy, 1919-39. Second Series.

GREW, JOSEPH C.
Ten Years in Japan. New York, Simon & Schuster, 1944.

HSU, EN-TSENG
The Invisible Conflict. Hongkong, 1958.

INTERNATIONAL MILITARY TRIBUNAL FOR THE FAR EAST
Exhibits, Proceedings, and Judgement. Tokyo, 1948.

ISREAL, WARREN
The Chinese Student Movement. Boston, Harvard University Press, 1965.

KASE, TOSHIKAZU
Journey to the Missouri. New Haven, Yale University Press, 1950.

KENNEN, GEORGE FROST
Russia and the West Under Lenin and Stalin. Boston, Little, Brown, 1961.

KOBAYASHI, KIYOTANE
The Manchurian Crisis and the Kwantung Army. Unpublished M.A. Thesis, Columbia University.

MAKI, JOHN McGILVREY
Japan Militarism, Its Cause and Cure. New York, Knopf, 1945.

MAXON, YALE CANDEE
Control of Japanese Foreign Policy. Berkeley, University of California Press, 1957.

SCALAPINO, ROBERT A.
Democracy and the Party Movement in Prewar Japan. Berkeley, University of California Press, 1958.

SHIGEMITSU, MAMORU
Japan and Her Destiny. New York, E. P. Dutton, 1953.

SMITH, SARA RECTOR
The Manchurian Crisis, 1931-32. New York, Columbia University Press, 1948.

STIMSON, HENRY LEWIS
The Far Eastern Crisis. New York, Harper, 1936.

STIMSON, HENRY LEWIS
On Active Service in Peace and War. New York, Harper, 1948.

STORRY, RICHARD
The Double Patriots. Boston, Houghton Mifflin, 1957.

SURVEY OF INTERNATIONAL AFFAIRS, 1931 and 1932, London, Oxford University Press.

TAKEUCHI, TATSUJI
War and Diplomacy in the Japanese Empire. New York, Doubleday, 1935.

U. S. FOREIGN RELATIONS
Japan, 1931-41. Washington, D.C., Government Printing Office, 1943.

VESPA, AMLETO
Secret Agent of Japan. Boston, Little, Brown, 1938.

WALD, ROYAL L.
The Young Officer's Movement in Japan. Doctorial Dissertation, University of California, Berkeley, 1949.

WALTER, YOUNG C.
Japanese Special Position in Manchuria. Baltimore, Johns Hopkins Press, 1931.

WILBER, C. MARTIN
Documents on Communism, Nationalism and Soviet Advisers in China, 1918-27, New York, Columbia University Press, 1956.

WILLOUGHBY, WESTEL WOODBURY
The Sino-Japanese Controversy and the League of Nations. Baltimore, Johns Hopkins Press, 1935.

YANAGA, CHITOSHI
Japan Since Perry. New York, McGraw-Hill, 1949.

YOSHIHASHI, TAKEHIKO
Conspiracy at Mukden. New Haven, Yale University Press, 1963.

YOUNG, JOHN, COMP.
Check-List of Microfilm Reproduction of Selected Archives of the Japanese Army, Navy and Other Government Agencies, 1868-1945. Washington, D.C., Georgetown University Press, 1955.

2. *In Chinese* 中 文

外交部白皮書	南京外交部編
鄉會回憶錄	民國卅四年重慶獨立出版社印
外交月報	外交月報社發行
外交評論	外交評論社發行
國聞週報	天津國聞週報社發行
澄廬文集	鄉 會著
六十年之中國與日本	王芸生著
日本甲午挑戰史	陸奧宗光著 王仲廉譯
中華民國史綱	張其昀著
革命文獻	羅家倫編
戴季陶先生年譜	陳天錫著（民國四十年臺北中華日報社）
獨立評論	獨立評論社發行
蔣總統集	國防研究院印行
勦匪戰史	包遵彭著
中日外交史料叢編	陶希聖等編
中國革命戰爭的戰略問題	毛澤東
紅旗週報	紅旗週報社（上海印）

反帝鬪爭與保護蘇聯問題	中共蘇區中央局宣傳部
蘇聯陰謀文證彙編	民國十六年北京印行
開羅會議與中國	梁敬錞著 1963香港亞洲出版社 印行

3. *In Japanese* 日 文

陰謀暗殺與軍刀	森島守人著
軍閥興亡史	伊藤正德著
太平洋戰爭之道	朝日新聞社編
悲劇將軍石原莞爾	山口重次著
滿州事變情報（關東軍）	日本檔案膠捲
西園公與政局	原田熊雄
旋風二十年	森正藏著
太平洋戰爭前史	青木得三著
滿州事變何時發生	今村均著
革新運動祕密記錄	東京內務省公安課
今村均回憶錄	今村均著
昭和政治祕史	新名大夫著
小磯國昭回想錄	小磯國昭著
河木回顧錄	河木大作著
永田鐵山中將	志道保亮著
機密政略日誌	片倉衷著

外交五十年	幣原重喜郎著
日本軍閥闘爭之秘密	田中隆吉著
宇垣一成日記	宇垣一成著
中國共產黨史	大塚令三著
滿州事變外交史	榛原茂樹　柏正彦同著
田中義一傳	河谷往雄著
森恪—日本政治家	三浦貫一著
田中外交之覺書	臼井勝美著（日本教育史研究）
陸軍法西斯運動史	秦郁彦著
南次郎傳	御手洗辰男著
機密作戰日誌	日本參謀部作戰課編
支那共產黨史	波多野乾著
世界最終戰論	石原莞爾著
現代史資料	みちぢ書房編

Index

DATE DUE

6/20			
AP 22 '84			

GAYLORD PRINTED IN U.S.A.